A Fieldworker's Guide to the Golden Eagle

A FIELDWORKER'S GUIDE TO THE GOLDEN EAGLE

DAVE WALKER

Whittles Publishing

Published by
Whittles Publishing Ltd.,
Dunbeath,
Caithness, KW6 6EG,
Scotland, UK
www.whittlespublishing.com

ISBN 978-184995-224-8

By the same author

Call of the Eagle

Production Managed by Jellyfish Solutions Ltd.

CONTENTS

PREFACE

The golden eagle is a fascinating species and I have been extraordinarily lucky, not only to have worked with it for nearly forty years but to have been employed to do so in detail, in the long term, throughout the year and in a variety of areas and locations, from the Western Isles to central Perthshire, from Cumbria to Inverness-shire, at coastal sites, in deer forest and on sheep-walk, where plantation forest intrudes and where grouse management dominates the hills. As a result I have undertaken year-round studies of golden eagle behaviour and activity across entire territories and within population groups regardless of breeding performance; I have followed sites occupied by a succession of different eagles, territories that have fallen in and out of use and locations in which eagles have had only a temporary presence, where there is stability and where there has been change, both as a 'natural' progression reflecting habitat quality and where windfarms and plantation forest have changed the landscape.

As my very first experiences with the golden eagle, in 1979, led me to doubt the quality, or at least the depth and extent of the information available, I have always approached fieldwork with an inquisitive mind and never with the unjustified certainty that is so apparent throughout the literature. Given, I am glad to say, that I do not combine fieldwork with being a bird ringer, a photographer or a professional scientist, my main interest has always been the field ecology of golden eagles. There are gaps in my personal experience, of course, but the acknowledgement of limitations is an important theme in this work; there is no such thing as an expert, nor a definitive monograph of the golden eagle.

I have been at least partly employed to work with golden eagles in all but five of my 37 years in fieldwork and I am extremely grateful to Natural Research (Projects) and the RSPB for the opportunities that they have provided. A number of individuals have also been invaluable, notably Mike Madders (with whom I worked in Argyll from 1997 until his death in 2009) and Geoff Horne (with whom I first visited the Argyll eagles in 1985). Thanks are also due to the many landowners and managers (including United Utilities and Scottish Power), shepherds, stalkers and gamekeepers on whose ground I have had free access since the first day. Above all others, though, my wife, Wendy, deserves the greatest thanks for accepting and even encouraging my determination to study this species.

INTRODUCTION

The golden eagle is one of the most iconic of British birds and has all the attributes likely to engender fascination, dedication and obsession in birdwatchers: it is large in size, rare in status, peerless in flight, occupies remote locations, and is controversial, secretive and seen to be a top predator.

The species has long attracted dedicated watchers with at least 12 authors, from MacPherson (1909) to Watson (2010), producing books based specifically on their experiences with golden eagles in the UK, while others, including members of the Scottish Raptor Study Groups (SRSG), simply go about the business of watching, recording and protecting eagles for their own enjoyment and for the future of the species. There have also been many scientific studies published in peer-reviewed journals, along with commissioned reports, articles, commentaries and behavioural notes. All in all there would appear to be a wealth of information, knowledge and experience available to anyone wishing to learn more about the species, take advice on its ecology, management and conservation and aid the everyday understanding of what is seen. Not surprisingly, the golden eagle is widely considered to be an intensively studied and well-known species.

The collected information forms the received wisdom around the species and represents the standard of knowledge used in species and conservation management. This received wisdom is also what is known about golden eagles in an everyday sense; it is the knowledge against which observers compare and contrast their observations and the basis on which they reach conclusions. They might not know something from experience but they can make an acceptable interpretation on the basis of what has been seen elsewhere.

Because of the period of time over which the received wisdom has been compiled and the number of people involved during that period, it is generally considered to be highly reliable, if not exhaustive. There is a high degree of certainty in the knowledge and it seems that any query about conservation or day-to-day matters can be answered with confidence, even by those who lack a detailed personal experience of the species. Unfortunately for eagle conservation, this is a popular rather than a realistic image and one that is becoming increasingly difficult to counter.

It is not surprising that people want to be associated with the eagle and an unquestioned received wisdom allows this to happen without a person having any real involvement in the species; if there is broad agreement about a species' ecology, it is easy to appear knowledgeable. Unfortunately this also means that there is little disagreement about what is thought to be known and so, in effect, the extent of our knowledge has not only stagnated but has stagnated at a level that is much lower than most people seem willing to believe. The golden eagle is not a well-known species; it is only thought to be well-known because that allows people to appear knowledgeable. This should not be the case in the higher echelons of conservation, but over-confidence is as easily seen there as it is in fieldworkers.

This is not a popular opinion to offer, even though in his acclaimed monograph *The Golden Eagle* (1997 and 2010) Jeff Watson wrote that 'little is known about golden eagle behaviour outside the breeding season'. In fact, a review of that work finds words such as 'meagre', 'poor', 'circumstantial' and 'unquantified' being used in relation to most aspects of golden eagle ecology. People tend not to see these comments because they believe that they do not apply to them or to their knowledge and experience.

It is the failure to recognise these limitations that acts against competent species management, leads to decisions being based on assumptions rather than on evidence and allows unreliable guidance to be published and enacted. It is also what encourages fieldworkers to misinterpret their observations.

The received wisdom has been compiled via three basic approaches: site monitoring, investigative fieldwork and scientific research, each of which has its own equally important limitations.

Site monitoring can help with and identify problems relating to population size, distribution and productivity but it does not offer an explanation for change or stability, nor provide more than a basic insight into events at the site being visited. Although it is quite commonly attempted, it is also not possible, simply by monitoring breeding performance and recording what is found at successful nests, to reach competent conclusions about territory quality, food supply and related issues, or really even breeding performance itself.

There seems to be little investigative fieldwork undertaken apart from within professionally organised research. This may be due to a lack of opportunity or because it can be time-consuming and frustratingly unproductive, and probably also because it reaps little reward. A system that relies on uniformity of opinion does not encourage observers to look more closely. This is unfortunate because there is still valuable information to be collected, in part- or spare-time study, which could help to expand and improve our knowledge.

While scientific research should provide the most reliable of sources it suffers from three main problems; an almost inevitably too small a sample size, the extrapolation of limited results across a broad field and the mistaken belief that the use of statistical analysis is proof of correctness. Unfortunately, because of the perceived need to present 'scientific' evidence these come together in some aspects of species management. Also, because science, in effect, has to be professional it is perceived to be by definition more reliable but its standards are being judged by the terms it imposes on itself, and so it has pre-eminence in any debate regardless of its quality. As an associated aside, the peer-review process can be shown to be less than robust and it is not always evidence of completeness or reliability.

There is, in fact, only a very fine line separating supposedly robust scientific evidence from the seemingly worthless observational evidence. The latter has, for example, long been dismissed as anecdotal and therefore probably unreliable unless it can be used to support a contention, but applying the results of even the most robust scientific research to an area in which those data were not collected makes that anecdotal as well. It is not proof that the same factors are equally applicable in different locations unless it has been tested in other locations before it is used in a practical situation. Unfortunately it is used without being tested.

This is not to dismiss the value of scientific research, only to note that its limitations should be recognised for what they are, and in the same way as the limitations of observational evidence are recognised. It is also not to claim or suggest that the direct results of fieldwork are always more reliable. In fact, the obsession with nests means that most fieldwork has been conducted in a very old-fashioned manner and is of limited value to management.

It is the controlling aspect of professional conservation that is probably of greatest concern, because it means that even sound contradictory field evidence is too easily dismissed or classed as unrepresentative. While it is important to recognise that there is now a greater imperative for solid evidence to support species management, site-specific evidence is being passed over in favour of a more generic approach. For example, a computer-generated territory model provides a prediction, not an assessment of use or area, but such models are commonly used as evidence and as a means of reducing the need for site-specific investigation.

Because of its controlling influence, professional ornithology is also much slower than fieldwork to adopt new or alternative viewpoints or recognise its weaknesses. Control also allows controversial issues to be passed as sound management, regardless of what they actually mean. The Irish Golden Eagle Reintroduction Project provides an example of this because, while it appears to have conservation value, in Scotland it is actually a golden eagle removal project and acts against species conservation.

The limitations of the received wisdom are perhaps best illustrated by another controversial issue. The question, 'If we build a windfarm on that hill, how will it affect the nearest pair of eagles?' cannot be truthfully answered without saying, 'We don't know', but people seldom make that statement about this species. Windfarms are perceived as being intrusive, disruptive and potentially damaging to golden eagles but their effects are not known and cannot be reliably predicted. Believing that this issue is easily understood and addressed, or can be approached in a generic manner, will almost certainly be detrimental to golden eagles.

Uncertainty is something that rarely seems to bother golden eagle ornithology at any level and yet it is clear that we do not know as much about eagle ecology as is believed, that what is known is largely superficial and that expectations form a major part of decision making at all levels. What is not being recognised is the subjectivity of much of the available information and the limitations of the available evidence. This is probably because over-confidence means that potential ambiguities and their possible impacts are not recognised. A simple example of this is that two eagles with a visible size difference are not always a male and a female, a pair, or a pair that is resident in that location, and a failure to realise this can influence estimates of population size, the results of national surveys, occupancy data and the interpretation of behaviour.

These problems can only be addressed and our knowledge improved by questioning the quality of the received wisdom in a constructive manner, by collecting data without preconceived ideas or expectations, with proof or the recognition of uncertainty.

This has to begin at a very fundamental level. Contrary to popular belief, the golden eagle is not a predator, but a hunter-gatherer; it kills some of the food it eats but it also feeds extensively on animals that have died beforehand and, on some occasions, on animals that have been killed by other species To call the golden eagle a predator and using the word 'prey' instead of 'food' is to misrepresent its nature and ecology before any other decision has been made or conclusion reached.

The golden eagle is also a generalist species, which means that it does not lend itself to generalisations. No two eagle territories will be the same in any way; no two pairs of eagles will behave in the same way or use their territories in the same way; no two single eagles will spend their immature years in the same way; no two observers will have the same experiences; and no repeat scientific research projects will produce the same results.

It is with these points in mind that this work is presented as a field guide to the golden eagle. By examining behaviour and its interpretation, it considers most aspects of golden eagle ecology as they are encountered in the field. In this way it also highlights the limitations of the received wisdom, the difficulty of reaching sound conclusions and the ways in which improvements might be made. Most of all, though, it serves to show that investigative fieldwork still has a role to play in ornithology, provided that the limitations of the available evidence are recognised and that observers record what they see , rather than what they think they are seeing.

GOLDEN EAGLE FIELDWORK

The golden eagle is generally believed to be a well-known species for which there is an extensive library of information in the form of books, reports and peer-reviewed papers, available to be accessed and used with confidence when seeking advice and in matters of conservation management. Its popularity means that there is also a relatively large number of people with first-hand knowledge and experience of the species. It is therefore easy to believe that there would be few uncertainties, discrepancies or conflicting opinions about eagle ecology and management and this is exactly how golden eagle ornithology is both presented and applied. The phrase, 'I don't know' is rarely heard, and even people with little or no field experience provide guidance and advice because the information they are able to access is believed to be highly reliable. As a result, the golden eagle is believed to be an easily understood species and one with which it is easy to work.

However, the received wisdom is the full extent of most people's knowledge of the golden eagle and it is largely accepted and repeated without question or detailed consideration. Expert opinion is also seldom challenged because there is little on which to base a challenge. This also means that fresh evidence has become largely irrelevant to conservation management because it is, by definition, not supported by the available evidence.

In reality, the received wisdom is of dubious value and, in parts, hopelessly misleading. Perhaps what is most widely overlooked is that most of the available information and the bulk of personal experience are not the result of intensive studies, but originate with observers targeting nesting areas and having fairly casual encounters with largely unfamiliar eagles while monitoring breeding attempts. Most fieldwork is not truly investigative and too many conclusions have been reached about eagle ecology from monitoring breeding performance. It has to be said that the problem has long been exacerbated by the sheer lack of interest in what happens away from the active nest. In fact, most fieldwork does not even continue to the end of the breeding season, with the presence of a large nestling, rather than a fledged juvenile, being used as proof of breeding success (Hardey *et al* 2009) and an end to that year's effort.

The greater part of the year is actually spent without an active nest and the greater portion of the population do not produce young in any given year. In other words, most of the received wisdom (and therefore the knowledge used in conservation management) is based on a minority part of the population. While that may appear to be the most important part of the population, breeding success does not tell us why other pairs fail or fail to make breeding attempts; that cannot be determined by looking at successful nests.

The strength of belief in the received wisdom also encourages the use of assumptions and expectations and the influence of these factors on our overall knowledge cannot be over-emphasised. A simple example of this is the idea that when two eagles with a visible size difference are seen together in a known nesting area, they must be a pair that is resident in that location: a visible size difference is not proof of gender or status, and noting a pair rather than two birds influences the interpretation of everything seen in that location. The simplistic interpretation not only means that observers tend not to see intruders or visiting eagles: they commonly fail to realise just how common intrusions are and how many different eagles can be seen in the same location, even if it is part of an occupied territory.

Another problem which raises concerns about the received wisdom results from the way in which professional and scientific conservation has come to dominate and control golden eagle ornithology. Contrary to the impression commonly given, statistical significance is neither proof of correctness nor proof of reliability; it is a theoretical assessment of reliability with confidence limits that are usually ignored or undervalued. The problem is that, as an individualistic generalist species that exists under a wide variety of ecological conditions, the golden eagle does not lend itself to simplistic, generic or mean values. Although professional conservation is widely considered to be highly reliable, with the use of technology thought to improve our knowledge, it has in effect become more contrived, with less acceptance of the importance of variables, as golden eagle ornithology has passed from the realm of the field naturalist into that of the scientist.

As study and research has become more professionally controlled it has also become more insular and less open to broader and critical consultation, as can be seen in commissioned reports and peer-reviewed papers. These should be the best and most reliable sources of information and yet many can be seen to be influenced by preconceived ideas and/or requirements. Examples of this can be seen in commissioned guidance notes, such as Haworth and Fielding (2013), and even in what are ostensibly conservation documents, such as Fielding and Haworth (2014). Both of these documents use the word 'prey' instead of 'food', even though they are not synonyms, thereby diminishing the apparent value of carrion in a way that, in one, will help to ease the commercial afforestation of eagle territories and, in the other, will over-value areas currently not occupied by golden eagles in advance of 'positive intervention' (i.e. a 'recovery' project). Raptor workers are expected to accept such works without critical comment or constructive input simply because they have been professionally produced, but neither has positive value as a conservation document.

The predominant problem with fieldworkers is over-confidence in their ability to interpret their observations correctly: what they see is commonly reported in a way that confirms what they expected to see and what has been reported from elsewhere. There is almost certainly an element of needing to be in agreement, because any uncertainty about golden eagles is likely to be seen as a lack of knowledge rather than as evidence of a careful observer.

In all cases the overriding problem is the failure to recognise the limitations of the available evidence, be that what is seen in the field, the true extent of a person's experience or the influence of selective sampling on research projects.

FIELDWORK

The golden eagle is a specially protected species listed on Schedule 1 of the Wildlife and Countryside Act 1981 and amendments. The *Raptor Monitoring Manual* (Hardey *et al* 2009 and updates) details the full extent of the species' legal protection to date and should be read and referred to by everyone with an interest in birds of prey. Because most people are only interested in seeing or watching golden eagles, and those who wish to harm eagles will do so regardless of the law or the niceties of responsible behaviour, the topic of legality can be confined in this work to the question of disturbance.

It should be noted at the outset that there is no need to visit or go close to an active eagle nest unless it is required by a legitimate study, and even then most nest visits are of dubious value and justification. For example, and contrary to popular belief, there is little point in ringing golden eagles and ringing does not denote a greater knowledge of the species.

Raptor workers are often accused of elitism but secrecy over the location of breeding sites for a species that continues to be persecuted and subjected to other limiting constraints is understandable and justifiable. The accusation of elitism has also sprung from the fact that many eagle workers are issued with what are known as Schedule 1 licences (also known as disturbance or nest examination licences) which provide derogation under the 1981 Act. Responsible eagle watchers and researchers do not actually need to be licensed but most tend to be, as it provides tacit evidence of their accreditation. Being 'licensed' is also often a goal of the inexperienced because the established methodology encourages people to believe that you have to visit nests to be involved with eagles; Watson (2010) even wrongly claims that frequent nest visits are essential. However - and perhaps quite a few licence holders need to be reminded of this point - the licence is not an excuse to visit nests; a licence holder still has to have a legitimate reason to visit a nest and can cause damaging disturbance and commit the offence of reckless disturbance even if they are holding their licence in their hand at the time of the incident.

DISTURBANCE

Not surprisingly, the concept of disturbance can be difficult to grasp because it has not been clearly defined and its effects are not always immediate or immediately obvious. As a result, disturbance is generally not considered to be particularly harmful or inappropriate and it is clear that many people do not understand the potential harm or even what constitutes disturbance. During many years of protecting golden eagles in the English Lake District, hardly a week seemed to go by during the breeding season without the RSPB wardens removing birdwatchers 'wanting a closer look', and a common encounter involved people relating tales of their adventures in Scotland. On one memorable occasion, a visitor spoke at length about watching eagles on North Uist and ended the tale by saying that they knew they were not too close to the nest because both the adult eagles were circling above the site. Circling in this way is, of course, the classic golden eagle response to human intrusion.

Most sources of information fail to note that, unless the bird is suddenly taken by surprise, a disturbance event will have begun long before the eagles are seen to circle by the nest site. It should be recognised by all that by the time the eagles are circling in this way the disturbance event has probably already reached the point at which the survival of the adults outweighs the survival of whatever is in the nest. If that were not the case, the birds would not be reacting in that way.

The first response to human intrusion is for the eagle to become alert. Whether on the nest or on a perch, the bird tenses its body, tightening its plumage and craning its neck to gain a better view. If the intrusion moves closer, a perched bird will begin flying but an incubating or close-brooding bird will usually flatten itself into the nest and may rest its beak on the nest rim. If the intrusion continues, the sitting bird then becomes alert again, raising its body out of the sitting position and eventually stepping to the front of the nest. It might not immediately fly and may even appear to be quite relaxed, stroking its beak through its scapular feathers or nibbling those on its breast (a type of displacement behaviour), but it will eventually fly if the disturbance continues and only then will it perform the circling flights.

Because the sitting responses tend not to be recognised as disturbance behaviour, and because the human might stop moving when they see the eagle standing on the front of the nest, the disturbance event might actually be prolonged because the bird does not fly. This can be especially true if only one bird is in the nesting area at the time. If the person is aware of the classic response to disturbance they might only expect to see circling flights, and because the bird did not leave the nest they might conclude that no disturbance had occurred. However, because the eagle is no longer sitting and providing warmth, it is possible for eggs and small chicks to be harmed without a human intruder even being aware of their responsibility.

It must also be remembered that disturbance can involve eagles which are foraging, are not on the nest or which do not have an active nest. It must also be noted that disturbance behaviour is different to disturbance displays and can involve simple perch-to-perch flights. This is discussed in more detail in a later section.

A major problem is that as there are no hard and fast rules about disturbance distances, it cannot be said that it is safe to approach to within a set number of metres or that an action can safely take place beyond a certain distance from the nest. Clearly it is easier to approach more closely from behind a nest than it is to approach from the front without causing disturbance. Some eagles also react differently from others; while some appear to be very nervous of human presence, others will breed successfully in full view of a public road or relatively close to well-used footpaths. Similarly, the type of nest site can influence how the birds react: the more inaccessible or obscure the nest, the less prone the birds will be to disturbance. Making the correct judgement in the field about these situations is not always easy and so observers should always be willing to settle for a decent view rather than a close one.

In respect of the approach, it can only be safely said that, during breeding attempts, nest sites should only be approached from the front, and that if the birds are relaxed, the observer is at a safe distance and should watch from there. It is good to remember that the behaviour of disturbed eagles is of no interest or relevance to an understanding of their ecology.

There are other causes of disturbance, and one about which there needs to be greater awareness is that which can be termed industrial actions, most especially forest operations, such as felling and planting, and the development of windfarms in golden eagle areas. While the latter is supposedly quite tightly constrained, the former is not and there are times when, to be blunt, some people consider spruce trees to be more important than golden eagles. In one example, a certain enterprising forestry organisation that promotes its conservation credentials decided that it was sensible and good practice to send a team of workers to plant trees directly beside and in front of an eagle nest that was being refurbished in preparation for the breeding attempt ('that was the only time they could do it'); the foresters even stockpiled their white tree bags at the foot of the nest crag. In spite of an obvious breach of the 1981 Act, no legal action was subsequently taken because of the power and control exerted by the organisation involved. This is likely to become a greater problem with further expansion of the forest area and observers need

9

to be alert to the timing as well as the location of these practices if disturbance levels are to be controlled or countered.

The concept of disturbance is possibly further complicated by a failure to appreciate fully its dangers and by the length of time per year during which it is possible to cause disruptive, illegal and potentially damaging disturbance. While most people would be able to recognise the inherent dangers associated with disturbing birds during the incubation period, it is perfectly clear that most have no understanding of the dangers of disturbance at other times of year. Table 1 summarises the basic disturbance calendar.

Table 1: Summarised breeding periods and relevant threats from disturbance

Period	Duration[1]	Timing[2]	Annual Dangers
Pre-laying	7 weeks	1 February to egg laying	Use of substandard or less secure alternative nest; laying eggs away from nest
Incubation	7 weeks	Mid-March to mid-May	Desertion of eggs; eggs chilling and contents dying
Nestling period	11-12 weeks	Late April to early August	Nestling death; nestling weakened by delayed feeding; premature fledging
Post-fledging confinement	6 weeks	Mid-July to mid-September	Juveniles forced into more dangerous locations where injury is possible or where adults cannot attend
Total	32 weeks		

[1] approximate duration; [2] usual range of occurrence

It is not widely appreciated that disruptive disturbance with the potential to cause a failed breeding attempt can occur over a period of about 32 weeks per year, or that this is the period described by the Wildlife and Countryside Act (1981). It is likely that few people would consider disturbance prior to egg-laying to be potentially severely disruptive and, most of all, the majority of people are highly unlikely to think that disturbing a free-flying eagle (adults as well as juveniles) in August or September is either an offence or likely to have a harmful outcome. Unfortunately a great many conservationists are also of that opinion.

The problem is one of acceptance that disturbance can have detrimental effects over the greater part of the year. People simply do not appreciate the harm that can be caused by going to or closely approaching active breeding sites. Outlining this situation is also almost pointless because most people, including many raptor workers, refuse to accept that their actions are disruptive or else believe that they possess such a level of knowledge and experience that their actions cannot actually be causing disturbance.

Pre-laying period disturbance can result in eagles deserting their preferred selected nest for one they had chosen to disregard that year and can even result in eggs being laid away from nests. There are a number of such records in the literature and, while it is not often noted, there is no obvious reason for an eagle to lay an egg on a bare ledge or at its roost unless something untoward has happened at its preferred nest. When the use of an alternative nest is the result of disturbance, the breeding attempt usually fails. This is typically because the alternative site is usually less secure than the selected one, less prepared, often more prone to the influence of severe weather conditions and sometimes outside the usual main foraging areas. While golden eagles are capable of breeding successfully in any combination of these factors, it is when the combination results from disturbance rather than choice that breeding attempts seem to fail most frequently. This implies that stress may be involved and that cannot be seen or measured in the field.

The problems associated with disturbance during the incubation period are well known but it is worth reiterating that the incubating eagle does not have to leave the nest for it to have been disturbed and that its return to the nest is not proof of the absence of disruptive disturbance. While it is generally thought that eggs and embryos are most prone to the effects of disturbance during the final stages of incubation, this does not justify disturbance at an earlier point in the process. The idea that a small amount of disturbance would not be harmful has to be tempered by the fact that what has happened before or will happen later is usually not known to the people involved. With the licensing system being neither robust nor foolproof, the potential for the uncoordinated duplication of nest visits must be taken into consideration.

Nestlings are generally thought to be immune from the effects of disturbance but they can be harmed just as easily as eggs. With many hatching in April, the small chicks are extremely vulnerable to the effects of cold and wet conditions, but it does not have to be raining or snowing for nestlings to suffer from cold and biting winds that increase the wind-chill factor. While human visitors may assume that drier conditions are safer, there is a reason why small chicks are almost constantly brooded or sheltered by the adults for as much as three weeks after hatching; they are very weak, which is why most nestling mortality occurs during those first 21 days.

Nestlings at this stage are covered with down that can become waterlogged and retain the cold and, while it may offer sufficient protection when attended by an adult, any lengthy period without additional protection can weaken a chick or even result in its death. It is not known how long it takes for such conditions to be terminal, so all disruption should be avoided. There is no reason to visit a nest or cause disturbance at this time and while some observers seem to think that it is important to know how many eggs are laid or hatch, all that really matters is how many chicks fledge, and causing disturbance is only likely to reduce that number.

The nestlings are beginning to feather by the end of the close brooding period but the second three weeks is a danger time, as the chicks are still largely downy in appearance and therefore vulnerable to wet and cold. As the chicks are also rapidly increasing in size during this period, any disruption that prevents the adults delivering food can interfere with this process. It must be remembered that at this time, it is not simply the provision of food but feeding, too, that can be disrupted, as the nestlings are still mostly being fed beak-to-beak by the adults. There may well be food on the nest but it is of little value during this period unless the adults are there to present it to the nestlings. This problem can be exacerbated as observations suggest that it is at this time of year that golden eagles in general seem to have most difficulty in obtaining food.

The problem with disrupting the supply of food continues from this point and can be seen in the fault lines that can appear in the developing flight feathers. Whether or not these severely limit the bird's flying ability or survival is not really known so, again, it is best to avoid any potentially damaging situation.

Once the nestlings are well feathered, in no need of brooding and feeding themselves, there is less apparent danger from disturbance. Now, though, they are more mobile, increasing the risk of them trying to escape any potential threat. Until about seven weeks after hatching, the nestlings generally try to hide from anyone intruding close to the nest by lying low and remaining quiet. Some do put up a struggle when they are ringed but most of their threats are bluffs and the birds quickly settle without a fuss. When slightly older nestlings are marked (the attachment of telemetry devices requires the nestling to be closer to full body size) they are obviously more capable of independent movement, will flap their wings at the human, fall back and present talons and, more pertinently, try to escape.

It is at this time and beyond that premature fledging as a result of disturbance is a serious problem. Even though some recent sources that should be better informed, such as Holden and Houston (2009), persist in promoting the myth that eaglets can fledge only nine and a half weeks after hatching, nestlings of this age cannot fly. Any premature departure from the nest could result in death or serious injury or place the youngster at greater risk from predators. There are numerous examples of nestlings jumping from the nest when approached by humans and such birds can travel in an uncontrolled glide (and mostly downwards) some distance from their starting point. While adult eagles are unlikely to desert the youngster on such occasions, the risk of injury is a serious concern and the overall risks are greater if the humans involved have only a passing interest in the birds and no intention of correcting their actions.

Inexperienced observers may also be duped by the idea of magnificent first flights and simply give up on a prematurely fledged eaglet with the assumption that it has instantly become a master of the skies. This type of romantic notion can make it appear that there is no risk after fledging but this is followed by a largely unrecognised period of confinement and total dependency on the adults, very similar to that seen during the nestling period.

Newly fledged juveniles are largely immobile and restricted to a fairly small area because they are not powerful or even competent fliers. Because of this, the juveniles are entirely dependent at this time on the adults and while it is rare for the adult physically to feed the juvenile once off the nest, it continues to collect and provide almost all of the juvenile's food. Any disruption to this process can be harmful to survival.

Because young juveniles are poor fliers, and even worse at landing, disturbance can result, as during the nestling period, in a crash landing, especially as they appear to be easily exhausted at this time. The juvenile is likely to make a long, downhill and poorly controlled flight that could easily see it travel for more than a kilometre from its starting point and make it more likely to end its flight in a complex habitat from which it cannot easily extricate itself, even with the encouragement of the adults. If such an event occurs while the adults are absent from the nest area, fresh prey caught for the juvenile may be wasted and there is the possibility of the adults not being able to attend the youngster.

Poor landing ability is a key factor and it is not unrealistic to envisage a disturbed juvenile crashing into an area of clear-fell forestry with unmanaged entanglements of snapped branches, brambles and drainage ditches, hitting a fence or even a rocky outcrop. The last is by no means an exaggeration as the juvenile's flight (and perhaps its sense of perspective) is so poor during the confinement period that they do at times appear unable to recognise or fully comprehend the inherent dangers and difficulties presented by their surroundings. Juveniles have even been seen to hang upside down from branches as a result of failing to land safely in a tree.

Disturbance can also happen away from the nest site and outside the breeding season. Even a single observer walking the hills might disturb a golden eagle. It is not simply about the position in which the human appears: the bird might be flushed from food or prevented from foraging, the prey being targeted might be made more alert or chased from the area and a human presence can be disruptive over an area of several square kilometres. One person can literally make hundreds of mountain hare, rabbits, red grouse and ptarmigan unavailable to the eagles and because human movement is so slow, these species might be unavailable for the remainder of the day, a day on which food needs to be delivered to the nest or juvenile. Wild camping, if the pitching site is not selected considerately, can, in effect, prevent foraging on more than one day, and these problems persist throughout the year. It seems to be easily forgotten that food is just as important during the winter as when there are chicks in the nest and, with shorter daylight periods and longer, colder nights, even unintentional human influence on survival should not be underestimated.

Overall, the period of time during which disruptive disturbance can occur is widely underestimated and the potential harm resulting from such disturbance is far from fully appreciated. There often seems to be the belief that no harm can be caused if no harm was intended. These ideas result from people generally overestimating the extent of their knowledge and the quality of their fieldcraft. Because the golden eagle is considered to be a well-known species, it is also considered to be an easy species with which to work, resulting in sometimes irresponsible (and at times incompetent) site visits with observers believing that their actions will not be intrusive or influential.

FIELDWORK METHODOLOGY

There is surprisingly little published advice on how to perform competent golden eagle fieldwork, presumably because so many people believe it to be easy and straightforward and fail to recognise their mistakes. There is even less advice to be found on the interpretation of observations, probably because it is widely believed that a situation can only have one possible explanation. Unfortunately the guidance that is available promotes the impression that the work is easy, encourages the use of assumptions and (worst of all) is largely based on the assumptions of people with little investigative field experience. There is another bias involved, with even Hardey *et al* (2009) presuming a degree of familiarity and that the location is either already known to the observer or will be little different to any other location; effective guidance has to assume that the site is not known to the observer.

Monitoring has, unavoidably, long been a fairly haphazard affair, concentrating on the nestling period because of the comparative remoteness of many sites, the difficulty of accessing some sites outside the summer months and the time constraints endured by the voluntary fieldworkers who undertake most of the work. There has been little encouragement for fieldworkers to go beyond the monitoring of breeding performance and the reaching of simplistic conclusions about events at their sites.

Most guidance has typically been in the form of word-of-mouth advice from 'more experienced' observers, but these tend to be the very people who most adhere to the tradition of closely visiting nests, ringing chicks and/or applying their expectations. This can be seen from the advice included in Hardey *et al* (2009) which provides information on the plumage development of nestlings when this is of virtually no relevance whatsoever to raptor monitoring. Further evidence in the same source can be seen with the repetition of groundless, but widely believed, generalisations. An example to be discussed in greater detail later is the idea that flight displays are a special feature of eagle activity during the late winter period. This widespread belief is actually an unrecognised incorrect artefact of casual observation and selective sampling.

The approved methodology, as used during the national surveys of 1982, 1992 and 2003 (and as would be used in 2015), was evidently developed not to ensure the accuracy of results but to ensure the ease with which inexperienced observers could obtain some results. The methodology fails on both counts (and on a third, analysis) because it relies on assumptions and expectations. The preferred method is very simple and requires only three or four site visits during the year; one to check for occupancy, and/or one for a breeding attempt, one for hatching and one for fledging or the presence of a large chick. These visits often only amount to a few hours on one day in February, one in March or April, one in May or June and one (often not bothered with) in July or August. The observer either sees something or they do not and that record is interpreted as being indicative of certain outcomes. This will be discussed in more detail with real examples to illustrate clearly the ambiguities of field evidence that are rarely considered or highlighted but, put simply, the preferred or usual approach or methodology is virtually guaranteed to produce false results, and does so on a regular basis.

A different approach is needed in the modern era, one designed not only to recognise and acknowledge the unavoidable uncertainty that will be encountered, but one that is also more efficient when used by inexperienced observers and in less familiar or rarely visited locations. One of the problems with the current system and national surveys is that, because most established observers keep to their own study areas or the groups of sites they have monitored for a number of years, to maintain the record or sequence, it results in less experienced people operating in the areas about which the least is known.

For an experienced observer, one of the most frustrating aspects of this is just how easy it is to perform efficient fieldwork. An example from the 2003 national survey on Jura saw two employed fieldworkers, making separate visits to a site, fail to find an active nest that was later found by a third party in the same gorge as a nest checked during both earlier visits. The first two observers must have been within 50 metres of the nest when it contained eggs or at least one live chick and could only have been missed it because they were relying on inappropriate guidance.

Ironically, efficient and responsible fieldwork is very straightforward and not difficult but, unlike the standard approach, it begins with the acceptance of uncertainty. It begins with the acceptance that when a site is visited for the first time ever or for the first time in any given year, at any time of year and regardless of previous experience or knowledge, the observer does not know what is happening, they do not know what they will encounter, they do not know the importance of any given location and they do not know the status of any eagles that are seen. There must be no preconceived ideas about the location, the birds or the observed behaviour. This is an obvious and sensible starting point but it is commonly forgotten because of the degree of certainty with which most observers operate.

The main goal of efficient responsible fieldwork is to collect new and correct information without causing disturbance. This is achieved by following four basic rules which apply at all times of year and to everyone, regardless of experience: do not rely on previous experience, work from a distance, be patient and do not make assumptions.

1. Do not rely on previous experience. It should be accepted that what was seen and what happened at a site in previous years has no relevance to the current year. The same birds might not be present, so the observed habits might be different; the same nest might not

be used, so territory use and flight-lines might be different; there might be differences in food source availability, so habits and territory use might be different, even if the same birds are present; and what has been seen in one location may be in no way indicative of what will be seen in another.

2. Work from a distance. Use lower ground to your advantage to obtain a panoramic view. Because of the obsession with nests, most observers target known nesting areas and walk towards them without bothering to perform more than a cursory check beforehand but - and in spite of the idea of traditional nest sites - golden eagles regularly build and use new nests that might not be within the known group or the usual glen and, of course, there might not be an active nest to be found. Eagle nests are also not always in what might be considered the most likely places and even active nests can be easily missed. Conversely, unknown nests are easily stumbled upon. This can have a devastating effect on a breeding attempt and, if they are not at the nest, the birds themselves can be disturbed in a way that makes subsequent work that day uninformative and almost pointless. To target 'the most likely' locations is not only to apply preconceived ideas, but reduces the field of view and often results in the observer having no easy access to any possible alternative locations that may need to be checked.

This means that observers should not immediately access the site but should first take the time to sit and view glens, ridge sides and moorland from outside in order to increase the likelihood of contacting any birds before they commit themselves to a smaller search area. This open approach also means that any eagles in the area are likely to be aware of the observer's presence and, perhaps counter-intuitively, this can reduce the risk of disruptive disturbance.

Most eagle nests are actually quite easily viewed from a distance and many are more easily viewed from a distance than from closer at hand. In most cases, the closer the observer, the steeper the viewing angle and the more difficult it is to obtain the required information. It is, furthermore, less easy to retreat when disturbance is caused if watchers are scrambling about on the higher slopes to get level with, or above, the suspected nest. There have been too many cases of people carrying out physical, rather than visual, searches for nests.

Sea cliff sites are a special case as they are unlikely to be easily viewed from in front or even, in some cases, from the side. However, viewing from a safe distance is still the objective, even if it appears to be less efficient. An additional problem on sea cliffs is that there may be nests on sections of cliff that need to be viewed from opposite directions.

When addressing this problem, the great temptation is to walk along the cliff top, possibly with the idea of recovering feathers, pellets or prey remains, but it is often not appreciated that this can prolong a disturbance event that might not have been recognised, perhaps because observers fail to realise that the eagles can only perch to the side of the nests on sea cliffs rather than in front and across from them, as they do at most glen sites. What the observer sees may appear to be normal behaviour -an eagle sailing beside and then going to perch further along the cliff, for example - but this is, in fact, disturbance activity caused by the observer.

In these situations, it is also eminently possible not only to prevent an eagle from visiting the nest but also to prevent one from leaving. As the observer will undoubtedly have been seen by at least one of the eagles, this type of disturbance can be extremely prolonged, with the observer waiting for a changeover that will not happen. To avoid these situations when checking alternative nest sites on different sections of sea cliff, observers should always walk inland and around the site before returning to the cliff edge and a distant observation post from which the reverse angle view can be obtained.

3. Be patient. This is probably the feature with which most observers have most difficulty. Sufficient time must be devoted to the initial and subsequent wait-and-watch sessions to allow any eagles to reveal themselves and the locations in which they are most interested. Thereafter, the viewing angles should be changed by walking circuitously about or into a location before it is approached more directly or closely, whether or not an eagle has been seen. Golden eagles can be incredibly inconspicuous, as well as inactive, so each newly visible area should be viewed and reviewed before being approached. It is much better to sit and watch for activity than to blunder into a site in the hope of seeing something. This is especially true of gorges and narrow glens that can be difficult to view but easy to disturb. The outside of the site must be worked for visual evidence before the site itself is accessed. That said, when simply checking for occupancy or monitoring when the active site is known, or when simply trying to see eagles outside the breeding season, the known nesting area is more likely than not to produce the required sightings and can be more closely approached, but still from a distance, from in front and from the lower ground.

4. Do not make assumptions. The number of ambiguous situations and pitfalls that can produce misleading and/or mistaken results is too great for each to be listed here, but most will be addressed in the following sections. The problem is that the received wisdom and its presumed reliability is so ingrained that many observers rely on what they expect to see and see only what they expect to see, as well as believing that targeting the known nest sites will provide all the information they require. As already noted, though, while golden eagles are said to have traditional nest sites, that does not prevent them from having unknown nests or building and using new nests that are not close to the known ones, and the two birds seen might not be a pair, a male and female nor resident in that location. Many of the presumed indicative behaviours can also be performed by eagles of any status, in any location and when the preferred interpretation has no relevance.

That the golden eagle is believed to be an easy species with which to work is the main reason why the four simple rules are so commonly ignored and why so much of the received wisdom is of dubious value.

The outlined approach can, admittedly, feel time consuming and unproductive, but it is by far the most efficient and effective means of checking an eagle site at any time of year, before it is known what is happening, and of obtaining reliable information. It was this approach that in 1981 allowed an active Lake District nest to be found four and a half kilometres and in a different valley system from any nest used by the same birds in previous years, and that allowed the previously mentioned Jura nest to be found in 2003. In that case, as the nest gorge had been visited twice before in that year, it would seem unnecessary even to have viewed the area again, but the above approach allowed a distant panoramic overview to be taken without additional effort, and the sit-and-watch session revealed the nest that had been missed during two closer inspections of the site.

Once the status of any observed eagles has been correctly established, or a breeding attempt confirmed, the ensuing monitoring can, with care, be more direct but should still be done from a distance and without interfering with the eagles' activities, even outside the breeding season and when there has been failed or non-breeding. These latter situations are particularly problematical for the standard approach as the former is easily missed and it can be very difficult to prove the latter. Separating failures from non-breeding can also be problematical for the suggested approach and can often only be achieved by making almost daily site visits.

This advice is, of course, solely about monitoring sites, and is not about how to collect the accurate data needed to reach sound conclusions about other aspects of golden eagle ecology. And this has to be remembered; for example, accurate assessments of food availability cannot be obtained by visiting nest sites, by hill walking or by undertaking random transects within a site. As all others, it is a separate task that has to be undertaken as targeted fieldwork.

TIMING OF FIELDWORK

Regardless of the approach used, a remaining problem is the difficulty of seeing golden eagles and knowing that they are resident in that location. It is surprisingly easy to visit an occupied territory without actually seeing any eagles and it is by no means unknown for only an intruder to be seen. It is usually not too difficult to see eagles when there is an active breeding attempt but the nests are out of use for the greater part of the year and many pairs fail even to make a breeding attempt. For most of the time, in other words, observers do not have the short-cut provided by an active nest.

As noted above, the standard fieldwork approach involves three or four visits and while this seems to make sense, it is the absolute minimum effort required. Checking for occupancy at any time of year is fraught with difficulties, not least prior to egg laying, when it is most commonly specifically performed.

The national surveys have begun this work in February but that is too early to produce reliable results in sites that are without regular and frequent monitoring. Nest building activity is not always seen, any resident birds do not have to be present and most intrusions into nesting areas by other eagles take place during the first quarter of the year, so an intruder could be mistaken for a resident. As a result, it is eminently possible to believe that site occupancy has been confirmed when there are no resident eagles, or to confirm the presence of a resident pair when only one of the pair has been seen. It is more efficient to make two visits during the middle fortnight of March than to make one in each of February and March. This makes both visits closer to the likely laying date, nests are more likely to have been obviously repaired and it increases the likelihood of seeing resident birds displaying indicative behaviour such as making nest visits.

As implied, confirming a breeding attempt is not always straightforward and unless the usual laying date of the resident female is already known and targeted, it is very easy to miss an early failure, especially one which results from adverse weather conditions. Because of this, and variations in the laying date and the use of unknown nests, all records of non-breeding have to be queried and the evidence seen to be irrefutable, as many such reports are actually records of the observer failing to prove breeding rather than proving non-breeding.

Incubation is proven by seeing, ideally, two changeovers, each bird being replaced by the other which then sits until it is replaced. As the laying date is usually not known, confirming a hatch can be a hit and miss affair, although it is probably less crucial to do this as soon as possible and it can reasonably, and often best, be left until mid-May, unless there are specific requirements. Confirming breeding success is also straightforward, provided that it is remembered that success is not achieved until the young has/have left the nest alive and can fly. As there can be late breeding attempts, which have to be accommodated by varying the visit dates, confirmation is best obtained in early August, when the young should be off the nest but still in close proximity.

There has also long been a tendency to make observations preferentially during the morning, and often very early in the day, but, even in the nesting area at any time, it is actually easier to confirm occupancy and to see resident eagles during the last three hours of daylight. This is because eagles often depart the roosting/nesting area before sunrise but will usually return before sunset; also, the longer the observer spends from an early start without seeing an eagle, the more likely they are to see an intruder. Even when there is not an active nest, any eagles seen arriving at the evening roost inside a nesting area are almost certainly resident birds.

Confirming occupancy can be difficult and time consuming if there is no active nest. The birds might be present and active, or absent, throughout a visit; they may be present but out of sight; or they might be in view but not seen. Perched eagles can be extremely difficult to find and often remain perched for several hours if they have no incentive to move. The birds might also be flying high above the site, and a good way to gain an idea of how much flight activity is probably missed is to turn away from a high-flying eagle for about 20 seconds and then try to relocate it with the naked eye. Equally, eagles spend a great deal of time at low elevation while observers are probably scanning the skyline. Golden eagle fieldwork requires patience.

UNDERSTANDING FIELD RESULTS

The correct interpretation of eagle behaviour is by no means straightforward, as will be discussed, but the most important factor to be reiterated here is the often underestimated problem of separating resident from intruding eagles. Whether inside or away from the nesting area, the latter can be encountered at any time of day or year and how they are separated from residents is largely a question of what happens next, and even that may not provide definitive evidence. An intruder may behave identically to a resident when on the foraging grounds and then simply fly out of the viewing area without providing any additional evidence of its status. Equally, an eagle may be seen performing flight displays above a known nesting area but then leave without providing any real clues to its status. Flight displays are not always indicative of status.

The problem is that in most such cases, and in spite of the lack of evidence, these types of behaviour are too readily taken to be proof of residency. The eagle's status must be known before its behaviour can be correctly interpreted and given relevance, not vice versa, but that cannot be determined by simply looking at the bird. While an eagle that is incubating eggs is obviously a resident in that location there is, in broad terms, no guarantee that any other eagle seen in that territory is that bird's mate, or that an eagle seen in any part of the territory at any time is a territorial resident.

The reliability and understanding of field results depend on fieldwork being efficient and objective and on observers, recognising the limitations of the available evidence, being honest about the extent of their experience. The urge to provide confident explanations after brief sightings needs to be suppressed and it has to be accepted that there are a great many occasions on which an eagle's activity cannot be given correct relevance. This is why observers should record what they see and not what they think they are seeing; an eagle performing the sky dance is performing a display flight, and not necessarily performing a territorial display. There needs to be additional evidence available before that conclusion can be reached.

In short, there is often too little evidence on which to base a direct conclusion on most forms of eagle activity and the received wisdom is usually too limited to provide sufficient reliable advice or pointers. To fully and correctly understand what is seen in the field, these limitations must be recognised and that can only be accomplished by asking questions of what is thought to be known and by proving what is thought to be known with reliable evidence.

METEOROLOGICAL CONDITIONS

The way in which weather conditions affect golden eagle activity and our knowledge of the species has not been given due consideration. While it is probably accepted that there is likely to be little activity during severe weather events, it is observer effort that is most affected by normal conditions. Few informative records are collected away from nest sites during lengthy periods of continuous precipitation or clinging mist because it can be uncomfortable to operate at such times, and optical equipment becomes largely useless. It is a simple fact that observers are mostly active under conditions when they expect to see eagles.

It is also hard to gauge whether or not conditions have had a real impact, and ambiguities resulting from the impact are usually not being seen or experienced by the observer at the time. It is easy to blame a breeding failure on a severe weather event, but pairs may breed successfully under exactly the same conditions in another year. Equally, a severe event does not have to cause a total desertion of the eggs but may kill a developing embryo: all the observer sees is a clutch of eggs that failed to hatch. A dead chick on a nest without food might be blamed on food supply, but weather conditions may have prevented the adults from foraging at a time when food was otherwise readily available.

Watson *et al* (2003) reported a tendency for breeding performance to be influenced by temperature during some part of the preceding winter and by rainfall during the spring, but they found no long-term trends and, more tellingly, their results could not explain differences between pairs or between years with the same pair; not surprisingly, they ultimately suggested that the variations were linked to food supply. With a generalist such as the golden eagle, the impact of topics such as this are best considered on an individual basis.

The effect of climate on golden eagles is much more difficult to prove, discuss and understand and is unlikely to be very discernible during fieldwork, even if a long-term involvement can allow it to be said that springs are generally wetter and autumns milder than they were twenty years ago. Climate must have an impact on golden eagles because it must affect habitat quality and that must influence food availability, but the certainty of its impact can be disguised or exaggerated by other changes that are taking place, which might be more immediately important but not recognised as such at the time. It is probable that most observers do not measure the changing numbers of other animals in the eagle territories monitored and may not even notice change until a species is largely absent. How that change came about is usually only retrospectively considered, when the evidence is no longer available.

Field observers are more likely to see the impact of weather conditions, or the aftermath of weather events, and there can be severe weather events at almost any time of year. A major problem when considering the effects of weather on breeding performance is that the most damaging events can be very brief, were maybe not seen at all, or might even be considered unlikely to have had any real impact. As noted, the effects of the same event can also vary considerably and be given too much relevance; a severe snow storm in March 2013, for example, might be thought to have caused many breeding failures, but one pair of eagles hatched two eggs in a nest facing east-north-east into the storm, so there is no real reason for the event to have been directly responsible for many breeding failures.

Without detailed monitoring at the right time, failures might be linked to certain events simply because they are expected to have been damaging. In this way, while deciphering what actually causes a breeding failure is not straightforward, it can appear to be easily explained in an acceptable manner. Resorting to questioning the food supply in relation to a failure, as so often happens, could also see habitat quality called into question when it has no relevance to what actually happened.

WIND

Golden eagle activity in relation to the wind has usually been considered in terms of the species' ability to cope with storm and perhaps hurricane force winds (Gordon 1955), and its ability to progress on cold, windless days when it is presumed to labour. Such considerations are largely irrelevant as most eagle activity is linked to necessity rather than whim; an eagle that has not recently eaten is more likely to fly than one that has eaten, regardless of conditions.

Of more interest is how the wind influences eagle activity. Golden eagles clearly use the wind to gain height and hold station over the territory far more commonly than they use thermals. This can be deduced by the opening and closing of the flight feathers as the bird circles with, against or across the wind; a bird on thermals does not have to do this. Wind speed appears to have little relevance to this and, while some flapping may be necessary when the wind is light, eagles can gain height rapidly in both strong and light winds. They can also hold their position at any elevation regardless of wind strength.

Although the importance of ridges has been highlighted by some sources as creating updrafts (Watson 2010) this is very dependent on wind direction; a down valley wind will produce fewer updrafts than one blowing up the glen because it is not distorted by the closed head of the glen. Contrary to the standard idea, eagles do not rely on ridges or hills for the wind or for their movements and are as likely to be seen performing height-gaining circling, and high circling, above open moorland, valley floors and at elevations where topography is unlikely to deflect the wind. Similarly, eagles can be seen to circle, or soar, above open water, both inland and over the sea.

Perhaps the eagle's most impressive use of the wind is shown by its ability to remain motionless in the air without flapping its wings. This can be seen close to a ridge or nest, and very often when the bird is being buffeted by a strong wind, but is probably most impressive when performed over open country. Here the bird, having circled to high elevation, literally stops a circle when facing into the wind and does not move. There have been numerous occasions on which a telescope has been locked on to an eagle in flight and left untouched for many minutes without the bird moving from the centre of the field of view. On these occasions the eagles were, in effect, perched in mid-air (it is also not unusual for eagles to gain height in this way, using vertical lift rather than by circling). Although this might not be seen as hovering, that is what they were doing and, contrary to some sources, golden eagles will, at times, actively hover by flapping their wings, as can be seen during slow foraging flights.

As it could be said that flight is effectively controlled falling, when using a sequence of circling and gliding to move between locations, upwind progress is usually direct and elevation is largely maintained but downwind progress usually involves a loss of elevation. This increases the need for more frequent circling and, because circling is often mistaken for a display, can give the impression of the flight being of a more specific type than is actually the case. Eagles will use flapping flight in either situation, especially if more speed is required, and a good sign of the presence of an intruding eagle is a straight-line flight with flapping and partially closed wings that ignores wind direction.

Perhaps as a means of maintaining elevation when at any height above the ground, golden eagles often seem to prefer using (or adjusting their flight to create) a crosswind and can often be seen making what could be called a sliding flight. The bird's flight configuration does not alter, but it travels at an angle across the wind direction, rather than head-on to the direction of travel. This can be quite deceptive to watch as the bird's flight attitude does not appear to reflect the location of the start or finish points, or its route.

The way in which the wind influences ranging activity and territory use has not been given a great deal of attention. Even so, there has long been the idea that some areas can become less available to resident eagles because of wind direction and strength. This is probably something that could be proven statistically if the other contributing factors, such as food source distribution and requirements, were ignored. However, the idea is unlikely to be correct. If eagles were limited by the wind in this way it would be apparent from the orientation of territories, or the location of the core area in relation to the nest sites. As will be discussed in a later section, the nest groups are generally not located centrally within territories and eagles do not radiate their movements evenly around the compass face; because the location of foraging areas and food sources change little between years, there is much regularity in the direction of flight lines regardless of wind conditions.

The wind's greatest impact comes in how it carries rain and snow, and the most used and preferred night-time roosts in an established territory are almost invariably sheltered from, and from some deviation to, the prevailing wind. Eagles will also have roosts that are protected from alternative wind directions but the main roosts, away from extreme and unusual conditions, usually seem to suffice. The wind itself does not appear to be the problem, as during the daylight period eagles can be seen to perch in extremely exposed locations and remain there for long periods, even when a howling gale is forcing them to crouch so low that they appear to be clinging on to the vegetation or even sitting on the ground.

It might be thought that nests would be as sheltered from the prevailing conditions as are roosts, especially as severe weather events are common during the incubation period, but that is simply not the case. Although Watson and Dennis (1992) found more nests facing roughly north-east than roughly south-west, most severe weather events have a more northerly origin during the early part of the breeding season and so most nests are commonly exposed to very poor conditions when they are in use. Watson and Dennis (1992) is also a single-year study looking at active nests, but most if not all of the territories involved will have had alternative nests with a different orientation to that used in 1982, the study year. In reality, there are many nests that are fully exposed to the extremes of wind and weather conditions and from which young can be successfully fledged, not least of being those on sea cliffs on the western seaboard.

REDUCED VISIBILITY

Dense mist is one of the conditions most likely to influence golden eagle activity, although its actual influence must be considered in relation to the observer's ability to see what is happening. While it is easy to assume that an eagle perched in dense mist is becalmed or limited by conditions, it is not unusual, when on a ridge, for an observer to hear but not see what could only be an eagle passing by in flight.

The idea that golden eagle activity is severely affected by reduced visibility is further contradicted by some everyday occurrences. Eagles commonly fly horizontally into and through clouds and, even more so, circle into and through cloud as they gain height. They are also not always seen to emerge from the other side, suggesting that they may travel within the cloud. This may seem unlikely but clouds are not a solid mass and often contain air pockets and even tunnels; on one occasion, an observer in dense cloud on one ridge could suddenly and briefly see the opposite side of the valley but no other ground or any sky as the tunnel passed, travelling down the valley. When low cloud shrouds the nest site during the breeding season, but remains above the glen bottom, eagles sweep into the cloud - and often directly towards the ridge - as if unhindered. That the same or the relieved bird later emerges in some other location points to it having flown in cloud or mist that might be quite dense.

Golden eagles can clearly make progress in conditions of very poor visibility and must be able to travel and forage with few clues to their position. It should not be assumed that there will be little or no activity at such times, especially when there is a nestling to be tended.

In the same way it must also not be assumed that the golden eagle is affected by darkness in the same way as the observer. While eagles are often still on the roost at first light, a bird that was seen to arrive the previous evening is by no means always there when the perch becomes visible the next morning. Equally, a bird not seen to go to roost may well be on that perch at first light the next day. Eagles have been watched feeding from a relatively short distance until it was too dark even to see the location, let alone the bird (more than forty minutes after sunset time) so the eagle must have accessed its roost in what would be called total darkness (Walker 2009). In a similar way there are many occasions when an eagle will return to its roost when only visible as a silhouette against the sky.

PRECIPITATION

Wind and visibility can influence eagle activity to some degree but this is more obvious when they are coupled with rain, sleet, hail or snow. Even so, it is probably only the most severe of conditions that prevent eagles from flying, as they can be encountered at most other times. Grey, drizzly days, when prey animals are less alert, may indeed be to the eagle's advantage when foraging, and an observer will generally find it better to look for eagles on such days than on those with clear blue skies. It is certainly more productive to look for eagles immediately after severe weather than during long periods of good weather. It should also be remembered that, when tending for a nestling, there is little that will prevent an eagle from flying, and little that will encourage them to fly when there is no necessity.

The prevailing conditions can produce subtle changes to the eagle's patterns of behaviour and these are most apparent when snow is involved. As it tends to be cold when snow falls, and the lying snow has the propensity to cover carrion carcasses and make live prey less available, golden eagles will often reduce their flight activity to the vicinity of a food source in a way that they do not when it is simply raining. This can result in the birds also roosting away from their usual and preferred locations. This can be on a short-term basis, as a result of the conditions, as well as becoming a longer-term habit that can develop during lengthy periods of severe weather or prolonged snow cover. The latter can produce situations in which the resident eagles habitually show strong seasonal variation in the use of different parts of their territory (Gordon 1955) or where the nesting area may be abandoned for several weeks in some years but not in others (Walker 2004).

As the highest slopes receive the most snow and are covered for the longest periods, as well as being shrouded in cloud most often, and as snow can force the food species on to lower ground, eagle foraging is often limited to below the snow line, even where species such as ptarmigan are available. When there is total snow cover, foraging activity becomes more expansive as the more obvious prey species, such as red grouse, become more wary, carrion- producing species commonly congregate on the lowest ground and often gravitate towards woodland, and corvids can become less apparent.

Neither rain nor snow is likely to prevent a breeding attempt but both can have a direct impact on breeding performance. The numerous records of eagles keeping the nest cup free from snow prior to laying might suggest that the eagles have a solution to this problem, but it is not always proven that egg-laying has immediately followed this action. Eagles also do not habitually prevent snow from building up on the nest, because it can easily do so during the night when it is left unattended, and there are records of eagles making repairs and building on top of snow and waiting for snow to melt before laying the first or second egg.

Incubating golden eagles seem willing to sit out any amount of rain, but prolonged heavy snowfall poses a threat to the survival of an eagle sitting largely motionless on its nest for hours on end and, perhaps especially, overnight. In the Lake District a pair of eagles failed in two consecutive years because of snow during the incubation period and this probably happens much more often in Scotland than is suspected. The idea that the majority of breeding failures result from a lack of live prey (Haworth and Fielding 2013), when severe snow storms may occur at any point during an incubation period that can encompass March, April and May, shows how little real consideration is given to the influence of weather conditions.

The vulnerability of eagle breeding attempts during such events is illustrated by one of these snow storm failures almost certainly occurring on the day the second egg was laid, and the other happening approximately 36 days into the 43-day incubation period (Walker 2009). The former can also be used to raise questions about the reliability of some non-breeding records; early season breeding failures are not easily recognised and are easily missed.

Rainfall is more likely to cause breeding failures during the nestling period because small chicks are probably more vulnerable than eggs. Chicks will be brooded or at least sheltered by the adults, especially the female, throughout the entire nestling period, not only when they are small but while they are still vulnerable. Nestlings can quickly become waterlogged and chilled, so downy chicks are brooded almost continuously at first and commonly for the first three weeks of life. This is not unbroken brooding, and feeding bouts will almost certainly result in wet chicks if there is not the opportunity to feed during dry periods. It is likely that quite a few chicks die as a result of this, possibly after also being weakened by the adult's initial reluctance to expose and feed them during poor conditions.

Extensive wet periods can also cause problems by limiting the adult's foraging efficiency. The fault lines that can sometimes be seen in the nestling's growing flight feathers have usually been associated with food shortages but they might be better seen in the context of the adults' inability to provide food because of the weather conditions. It is also possible that the deaths of larger nestlings may be associated with rainfall affecting the adults' foraging ability and/or because they were soaked and weakened as a result.

Rainfall and its associated low cloud can also affect eagles during the confinement phase of the post-fledging period. In the Lake District - the only location from which detailed observations are available – the adult male eagle was almost unable to provide the fledgling with freshly killed food in one year. As a result, that juvenile began feeding on carrion and ultimately left the territory at an earlier age than the others studied. In that year, 1986, 36 of the expected 42-day post-fledging confinement period were affected by lingering low cloud and rain during which the adult could not forage effectively (Walker 1988).

How precipitation affects single, failed and non-breeding eagles of all ages and status is less well known, but as such birds seldom struggle to find food or shelter it is probably not a major concern: these birds probably spend most periods of inclement weather perched in as sheltered a location as required. This is certainly true outside of the breeding season when it is not at all unusual to see eagles still on their night-time roosts long into the daylight period. The youngest birds are probably always those at most risk and the 1986 Lake District juvenile died on overhead power cables during a period of blizzards in its first November.

COLD AND HEAT

Cold conditions, even extremely low temperatures, seem not to have a great effect on golden eagle activity and eagles are often to be found perched, apparently quite happily, even out of the direct sunlight, on the bitterest of days. Alternatively they go about their daily business unimpeded by conditions. When it is remembered that night-time temperatures are usually lower than those of the daytime and that the winter nights can involve 16 or 17 hours of darkness, it is likely that whatever an eagle faces during the daylight period is less oppressive than what it suffers at night.

Although it is probably widely believed that winter food supplies are much lower than those during the summer months, there may be little difference in the comparative availability of biomass between the two seasons. In fact, as a result of their productivity, the resident species' biomass is usually greater during the winter than during the nestling period, and carrion availability is also likely to be greater.

However, where carrion is most important, there is the problem of frozen carcasses, and while there may, technically, be an excess of biomass, the practical availability of carrion can be greatly reduced by low temperatures, even if the carcasses are not buried by snow. Although the poor breeding histories of some territories have been attributed to low live prey availability (Watson *et al* 1992) the impact of cold conditions on the practical availability of carrion should not be overlooked or underestimated as an influence on breeding condition and the ability to produce viable eggs.

Golden eagles in Britain only rarely encounter extreme heat but these conditions probably have a greater impact on their behaviour than does the cold. An active nest in a sunny location may be pleasant during the incubation period but is a cause of concern during the nestling period. The breeding female will often be seen standing over – and so not brooding – a nestling, or simply standing in front of it, casting her shadow as the only means of keeping it out of direct sunlight, and it is incredible how hot it can become in an eagle's nest in Scotland. Chicks will stop calling and lie flat, often with their wings spread, and appear to be clearly distressed by the heat. Watson (2010) makes mention of nestling deaths due to heat stress in the USA and, while it may seem unlikely, it is perfectly feasible for this to happen in Scotland as well. It may well be a cause of some late-season breeding failures.

Adult eagles are also susceptible and will typically become very inactive at times of excessive heat, even if there is a nestling to be attended. They can spend long periods on a high perch in the sunlight, but often not only in the shade but deep in a tree canopy, where the air might be cooler. They will find shelter wherever possible and can be incredibly difficult to see at such times; hours may pass before any flight activity is seen. The same problems apply to juvenile, immature-plumaged, single and non-breeding birds and huge tracts of Scotland can seem to be without eagles during the summer months, even when they are known to be occupied. Birds have also been seen to hide under boulders or lie flattened on ledges with their wings spread out and, of course, golden eagles have been seen to bathe during hot conditions in Scotland.

Unfortunately, because most fieldwork is undertaken in conditions that are favourable to the observer, the effects of weather on golden eagle activity are generally not seen or fully appreciated. While it probably is true that only the most extreme conditions genuinely impact on golden eagle activity and breeding performance, the weather will have some effect every day and that can influence what is thought to be known about many aspects of golden eagle ecology.

STATUS

The golden eagle's historical, or even current, status in the British Isles might seem to have little relevance to fieldwork but it is worthy of some consideration because population size and trends are important aspects of conservation. An awareness of how these are determined can also help to illustrate problems with several aspects of golden eagle ornithology.

The golden eagle's historical status has always been of some interest to conservationists, even if only because it can be used as a tool in the fight against persecution. The problem is that the historical distribution and population size are not known and there are no even reasonably reliable population estimates from before the first national survey in 1982 (Dennis *et al* 1984). Even so, there are the established assumptions that the population was at some time much larger than it is now and that, in recent times, it was much smaller than it is now. There will always be uncertainty over what happened in the past and there is always likely to be over-confidence in the reliability of the assumptions that can be based on the available evidence.

An additional problem with the historical status - unlike that within living memory - and the way in which it is used is that it has no relevance to the current situation. Unfortunately, recovery and reintroduction projects tend to highlight the species' historical presence in the target areas as part of the justification for its future presence, while generally failing to appreciate fully the negative changes that have occurred and which would influence a location's attractiveness to the present time. This is why such projects are more about involvement and manipulation than conservation. For example, even though the title is widely used, the Irish Golden Eagle Reintroduction Project is actually a golden eagle removal project; as far as Scotland is concerned, it is of no benefit to golden eagle conservation.

The problem with the species' historical status is that it cannot be accurately estimated in spite of repeated attempts to do so, such as by Holloway (1996) and Evans *et al* (2012), because there are simply too many unknowns and assumptions to be included. For example, while there are numerous crags and locations named for the eagle, there is no evidence that they were all used by golden eagles, that they were all occupied simultaneously or that eagles were more or less restricted to locations bearing their name. In fact, most of the old breeding sites and their times of use are unknown, so a historical review that might be produced to give support to another project provides neither detailed nor usable evidence, only an assumption that the situation is now different from how it used to be.

With these points in mind, it must be remembered that while habitat suitability and prey availability must have been different in the past, there is also no proof that it was better for golden eagles. The species is not truly a forest species so the native woodland that was apparently extensive until the late 18th century (Fraser Darling 1947) could have limited its numbers. For example, Watson (2010) refers to two works which show forest population density in continental Europe at fewer than five pairs per 1000 km², while suggesting that population density in Western Scotland, where there is little forest cover, stands at more than twenty pairs per 1000 km². If there was greater forest cover in the past, the population density and size was probably lower than it is now, just as greater forest cover in the future will probably reduce the number of pairs.

It has also become easy, or convenient, to imagine that much of Scotland must have been alive with prey species such as red grouse and mountain hare during the earlier periods, but any forests would also have limited their numbers and reduced their availability, just as it does today. Red grouse numbers are generally fairly low in the absence of favourable habitat management because the heather has little age structure and this must have been the general situation prior to the introduction of management designed to increase grouse numbers, which really only began in the middle of the 19th century (Vasey-Fitzgerald 1953). While other prey species such as black grouse and hill waders may also have been more widely available, their numbers would have been affected by habitat quality in a similar way.

Carrion availability is also likely to have been different in the past because they were times with fewer sheep, and even red deer carrion may not have been as available as it is now. After all, the modern and controversial increased red deer cull is because their numbers are said to have never been as great as they are today. It must also be remembered that there would have been greater competition for food and breeding habitat in earlier times, with more predators and scavengers - including white-tailed eagles and wolves - occupying the same or similar habitats and feeding on the same food sources.

When the factors potentially limiting the size of the historical population are considered, it becomes increasingly apparent that the relevant questions cannot be satisfactorily answered, either on a national or local scale. It has to be accepted that exercises such as historical reviews have no relevance to present day management and that they should not be used to justify manipulation of the current situation. Unfortunately, reviews using at least some of these basic ideas are presented as robust conservation documents when they are not, and they are usually biased towards the preferred outcome. The influence of other recent factors, such as the idea that gamekeepers leaving the hills to fight in wars allowed a population recovery to occur, are also without foundation. There are no reliable national population figures or large scale studies from these times against which the modern situation can be compared.

POPULATION ESTIMATES

Table 2: Summarised breeding performance from three national golden eagle surveys (data from Dennis *et al* 1984; Green 1996a; Eaton *et al* 2007).

Year	1982	1992	2003
Number of pairs	402[1]	422	442
Breeding pairs	260	n/a[2]	262
Successful pairs	182	119	145
Young fledged	210	133	160
Mean productivity[3]	0.52	0.32	0.36
% of pairs failing	54.73	71.80	67.19

[1] 424 pairs were reported for 1982/83 but comparable data were only provided for 1982. [2] the number of breeding pairs was not presented in the 1992 results. [3] mean number of young fledged per pair.

Nicholson (1957) appears to have provided the first considered estimate and suggested a population of about 190 pairs at that time. Everett (1971) suggested that the population was 'probably well over 200 pairs', and referred to an estimate of 213 pairs for 1968 and also to one of 300 pairs. Sharrock (1976) suggested there to be about 236 breeding pairs. The three national golden eagle surveys, in 1982/83 (Dennis *et al* 1984), 1992 (Green 1996a) and 2003 (Eaton *et al* 2007) each reported a broadly similar number of pairs: 424, 422 and 442 respectively (Table 2).

These numbers provide an interesting discussion point because if any credence is given to them, it would suggest the eagle population to have increased by about 123% during a period of only 25 years (1957-1982). There are a number of reasons why this must be unrealistic and why the earlier population size must have been greater than suggested or believed. Everett (1971) was a review devised after declining productivity had been reported by Lockie and Ratcliffe (1964), suggesting that the implied 123% increase included a period of lower than usual productivity; it must also be remembered that during that 25-year period (1957-1982) there was more direct persecution than at 1982, more egg collecting, egg-shell thinning through environmental contaminates and greater loss of habitat through new upland afforestation. It is unrealistic to believe that the golden eagle population could have more than doubled at this time under these circumstances.

The evidence to support continued expansion to 1982 is also weak. While the golden eagle re-establishing itself in south-west Scotland during the 1950s (Marquiss *et al* 1985), returning to Northern Ireland in 1952 (Deane 1962) and then reoccupying northern England (Sharrock 1976) does appear to suggest an increasing population, the number of pairs in each of these areas had actually declined before 1983. While the range expansion may have been genuine it was probably small-scale, short-lived and restricted in nature, and it cannot be used to explain the huge implied population increase. Not only must the earlier 20th-century golden eagle population have been greater than the recent estimates suggest: it was also almost certainly greater than that reported for 1982. The losses from the reoccupied areas prior to 1983 further imply that the golden eagle population was in decline before that year.

To make matters worse, the reliability of the three professionally-organised national surveys must be questioned. The idea that such surveys can be accurate to a single digit is implausible and the 2003 survey only reported 442 pairs because some sites at which only one eagle was seen were counted as pairs if a refurbished nest was also found. There are several reasons why this is an unacceptable assumption, not least of which is that single eagles build and repair nests. In fact, it is probably safe to say that the published results of all three surveys are unreliable overestimates because of problems with the methodology, fieldwork and analysis.

Dennis *et al* (1984) provide two population figures, one for 1982 and one for 1982–1983, but the greater, commonly used, second figure (424) was achieved without changing the number of breeding pairs in the first. It would seem likely that at least some of the extra pairs made breeding attempts but they are simply added to the total after apparently having been found in a year without a national survey, and without really confirming that they were definitely missed in 1982. Furthermore, at least one pair – probably more – was lost before the 1983 breeding season but there is no indication of whether these birds were subtracted when the extra pairs were added to the survey total.

There is a simple mistake in Green (1996a) regarding the category of breeding pairs: until the correction was published (Green 1996b) there appeared to be no pairs in which one or both of the partners was in immature plumage, but this was not the case. However, according to Eaton *et al* (2007), there were even greater problems with the 1982 and 1992 totals. They suggest that both of those totals are too low because of incomplete coverage. This is certainly possible, as one of the main failings of the surveys' organisation is that they typically see the least experienced observers working in the areas about which least is known, because most experienced workers have long-term monitoring study areas and records they do not want to compromise. It is a fact that observers with literally no experience of golden eagles have been employed to take part in the surveys.

When raising the point of coverage, Eaton *et al* (2007) suggest that a recorded increase in one area was not a real increase in numbers but was due to better coverage, but this has unforeseen consequences. If the suggestion is correct - and there seems to be no solid evidence to support it – there must have been more pairs than recorded in 1982–83 and 1992. All three sets of survey results must therefore be wrong. The problem is that we do not know by how much they are wrong and their unreliability is probably linked to more than one factor.

However, the problem with this type of re-interpretation is that not all of the information is available for consideration and the reliability of the base information is unknown. With the incorrect idea that a built-up nest equals a pair of eagles being included in the published results from 2003, there is the likelihood that other misinterpretations and assumptions have been included, not least of which are those arising from the already mentioned problem of uncertainty: the failure to recognise potentially ambiguous situations or results, and the fact that the interpretation of events is largely based on expectations.

In fact, given that the earliest population estimates are unlikely to be accurate and likely to be too low, there is a strong argument to be made to the effect that the Scottish golden eagle population has suffered a decline within living memory, and that the decline is continuing. However, because of the unfounded certainty that exists, the problems with the usual methodology and the failings of the consultation process, the 2015 survey is unlikely to reveal a declining trend in population size; it is much more likely to show, again, near stability, because that is what it is geared to find. It needs to be added at this point that the idea of the population being in decline would not be popular among professional conservationists, as it would argue against the type of manipulation project mentioned earlier in this section, and much of the already available advice.

As an aside, the published results of the national surveys also demonstrate the fallacy of the peer-review process. Each of the survey papers was written, peer-reviewed, refereed and edited for publication in respected ornithological journals without even the most obvious of the errors being spotted; at least 15 people failed to spot the lack of paired immature-plumaged birds in the 1992 results and the 2003 results show that eagle specialists were not even consulted prior to publication of the paper. If they had been, a built-up nest would not have been counted as a pair of eagles.

It is probably only safe to say that Scotland had a golden eagle population of about 400 pairs in the survey years, plus an unknown and variable number of singletons. When the annual population of free flying eagles is at its highest, in August, there may be only about 1,100 golden eagles in Scotland, and by the end of each winter there could be fewer than 1,000. With only about 30% of the population breeding successfully during the last two survey years and low overall productivity – about 0.36 young per pair in 2003, or 160 young fledged (Eaton *et* al 2007) – how the golden eagle remains only Amber Listed as a species of conservation concern rather than Red Listed is something of a mystery.

Although they are presented as reliable information, the survey results almost certainly overestimate the number of pairs and underestimate the number of breeding attempts. Some of the reported successes will be failures and some reported failures will be successes. Equally, some of the non-breeding pairs will actually be failed breeders and some of the remainder will not even be pairs. In fact, most non-breeding records are probably better described as a failure to prove breeding.

Non-breeding and pairs which fail early in their breeding attempts are easily overlooked during basic monitoring and the national surveys are unavoidably the most basic and superficial type of monitoring, with too few observation sessions per site to guarantee accuracy in all locations. It seems entirely plausible that these unsuccessful parts of the population will have been grossly underestimated in the past, and especially so prior to 1982.

There are also the problems of observer effort and reliability to consider. Put simply - but as will be discussed in more detail later - an eagle's status cannot be determined simply by looking at it: a visible size difference between two eagles is not proof that they are a male and female and two birds sky-dancing inside a known nesting glen in March do not have to be a resident pair or even a male and a female. And, as already noted, occupancy records from January and February are unlikely to be wholly reliable or truly indicative of status at sites that do not receive frequent coverage. Unfortunately, the easiest convenient explanation is usually the one selected, with the result that too many conclusions in the past have been reached using superficial evidence, with observers seeing only what they expect to see. But worst of all are the final results: national surveys should report the minimum number of definite pairs and not use contrived evidence to find as many as possible.

When all of these points are combined, only an unsettling conclusion can be reached; although it is not evident from the published results, each survey year probably had fewer pairs than the last. There is probably a documented decline in the number of golden eagles and this probably began before 1982.

LIMITATIONS TO DISTRIBUTION AND POPULATION SIZE

The golden eagle's population size and distribution is primarily limited by the extent of human activity. There is no shortage of suitable habitat, nest sites or food that could be utilised. Within this the eagle's distribution has a clear trend, with numbers and population density broadly increasing towards the west and north-west. The paucity of its numbers in England and in southern and eastern Scotland reflects long-term progressive changes in land use and habitat suitability, the size and distribution of the human population and the effects of persecution. The species' apparent regression to the more remote north and west is an indication that the process of external influence and decline, which probably began most noticeably during the 19th century, is still relevant.

Some 'new' pairs of eagles are found in most years and because these records tend to be given more prominence than any reported losses, because it generally takes longer to confirm that a pair has been lost, this can give a misleading impression of overall numbers. However, because eagles are often seen in 'abandoned' territories and the true status of any eagle is easily mistaken, it might be best only to claim a new pair after their presence has been confirmed for two or three years. At least on the mainland, changes of land use, such as those resulting from forest expansion, suggest that in reality there will only be an overall loss of pairs as time progresses.

The cessation of persecution would almost certainly see an increase in eagle numbers but this is unlikely to be great, and probably not as great as some would suggest. It is likely that for persecution to stop, the reasons for persecution would also have to be removed. As this would mean, in particular, the virtual cessation of driven grouse shooting it would also almost certainly result in the conversion of good quality habitat with good food resources to sheep grazing, spruce forest or windfarms. It must also be remembered that increasing the number of pairs would also increase the number of failed breeding attempts and, given the other factors involved, overall productivity might actually decrease with a greater number of pairs if habitat quality is also declining.

The golden eagle's status is therefore not as healthy as it may appear. The species is unlikely to naturally recolonise England or the south and east of Scotland, apart from the occasional pair. Attempts to manipulate this situation - such as what I call the Irish removal project and the impending south of Scotland manipulation project - are undertaken to the detriment of an existing population that can be seen to have low productivity. Rose-tinted recovery-style projects for areas that are noted for their suspected high level of raptor persecution, combined with windfarms and extensive commercial forest, have no real relevance to golden eagle conservation, especially as they are unlikely to follow an intensive and objective assessment, and should be shelved in favour of investigating and addressing the reasons for low productivity in the majority of the population. Unfortunately, that is a less attractive prospect than handling nestling eaglets. If this problem were addressed, the golden eagle would have a healthier population and a brighter future than would be achieved by further reducing their numbers with misguided intervention projects.

INDIVIDUAL RECOGNITION

The reliability of recording and the correct interpretation of golden eagle behaviour and activity are greatly dependent on correctly determining the status of the observed bird. Achieving this is by no means as easy as many observers seem to believe; in broad terms, and except when with an active nest, an eagle's status cannot be correctly determined simply by looking at it.

To reach the correct conclusion about a sighting, the observer must be able to recognise, or accept that they cannot recognise, the birds they are watching. The failure to do this, which is very common, is one of the main causes of misinterpretation and the drawing of false conclusions about what is seen. Perhaps one of the simplest examples of this involves pair stability: there are surprisingly few reliable records of the members of a pair being known to change without persecution being involved, even changes involving birds in immature plumage. This is usually explained by the eagle's longevity and birds 'pairing for life' but it is almost certainly more likely to result from a failure to recognise that change has occurred.

It needs to be stressed that 'recognition' is not about being able to recognise an eagle wherever it is seen; recognition is more precisely about knowing if the eagle in view is a resident or a non-resident in that location, an established bird or a replacement. Contrary to what some people believe, it is eminently possible to recognise the adult members of a pair as individuals, by using their plumage characteristics, habits and even behaviour, and thereby follow them from year to year. However, the certainty with which this can be achieved, and the reliability of the results, depends on the frequency of observation, and there are too many cases where pair stability has been assumed even though there were several months between sightings. That is not to say that the same birds would not be seen in such a situation, but simply that they should not be assumed to be the same birds.

When the general similarities between the plumages of adult golden eagles are considered, along with the frequency with which such birds intrude into adjoining territories and the general paucity of intensive or investigative fieldwork, the need for caution becomes very apparent. Add single and non-territorial birds into the equation and it would seem almost impossible genuinely to recognise an individual golden eagle away from an active nest site. Certain recognition can be achieved but the quality of the evidence has to be considered objectively.

As golden eagles are known to visit and cross the territories of other eagles, it is easy for observers to believe that they are looking at a resident when they are not. What is thought to be a known bird could easily be a similar-looking bird visiting from another location, and its 'recognition' is often confirmed by false assumptions about the purpose of its behaviour, the idea that only a resident territorial eagle would behave in a certain way.

The recognition of individual eagles in immature plumage is extremely difficult, if not impossible, in practical terms. As juveniles can wander widely as soon as their dependency on the natal territory slackens, and because adults often tolerate visiting juveniles in their territory, there can be little certainty after October that an observed juvenile is the bird fledged in that location unless it has been artificially marked. As some juveniles begin to explore more widely at an earlier date than others, it is also possible that the presence of such a bird could lead to a wrong conclusion about breeding performance. This may seem to be unlikely, but most territories are not monitored with sufficient intensity to be certain of non-breeding, and there are examples of a family party of eagles - both adults and the juvenile - in the heart of what was known to be a vacant territory. With only casual monitoring in such a situation, it would be easy to conclude that the vacant territory was actually occupied by a pair which had bred successfully.

In broad terms there are fewer differences between eagles in immature plumage than there are between those in adult plumage. As a result it can be easy to believe that the same immature-plumaged bird is being seen when, in reality, a succession of different birds is seen in the same location. For example, immature-plumaged eagles were seen annually in an 'abandoned' Argyll territory over a ten-year period; it could not possibly have been the same bird every year and was more likely to have been four or five birds than one or two, but it may have also involved the same bird in non-consecutive years.

This situation becomes more complicated because there is plumage variation between individuals of the same age and because the immature plumage patterning changes with each moult. And, due to the often-overlooked 'near-adult' plumage phase, it is possible for the same bird to have three distinct plumages over a three-year period, and therefore possibly be 'recognised' as three different birds.

This is why it is important to record distinctive plumage characteristics each year, but even this can become problematical because of the way in which lighting and weather conditions alter a bird's appearance. A wet plumage looks darker than a dry one and lighting from the side, top, back and front can alter how a bird looks. Ideally, blocks of patterning should be recorded diagrammatically - rather than the plumage being drawn in minute detail - showing, for example, their position and angle on the upper surface of the open wing and, if possible, on the closed wing while perched. One of the stand-out plumage features helping to confirm a change of eagle at an English site was that a paler patch on the closed wing of the new bird was lower than a similar patch on its predecessor, but this was not apparent when the bird was in flight.

PAIR STABILITY

It can be noted here, as it is also relevant to recognition, that the idea of eagles pairing for life does not mean that a bird which has lost its mate will not take a new partner. There are also records of living and apparently healthy eagles leaving or being ousted from a pair. It is important to understand this because, in most cases, the members of a pair will not be the same age and might not be close in age. As a result, it is possible that many pairings may last for fewer than ten years rather than continuing in the long term.

The place of a lost or replaced member of a pair is not always taken by one in immature plumage and if the replacement is without white plumage patches and/or is at a site that receives only general monitoring, there is a high likelihood of a change in partner not being recognised. It should never be assumed that the eagles seen are the same as those seen the previous year or even on the previous visit. Confirmation should be acquired on each visit.

AGEING

A curiosity of recording is the number of times that three-year-old female eagles are reported; few people seem to see two-year-old males. This suggests that the field signs are being misread and that assumptions are being made, not least about the size of the bird in view. Part of the problem is the belief that there is a simple sequential progression from juvenile to adult plumage that is readable in the field. There is no such sequence; birds of the same age can look both very similar and very different. The amount of white in the immature plumage does not simply progressively reduce with age.

The over-riding problem arises at the outset; juvenile eagles do not all fledge with the same amount of white in their plumages. While all seem to have extensive white areas on the tail-base, many juveniles show very little white in the wings and these might be mistaken for birds of a greater age. It is also likely that birds fledging with little white in the plumage will lose all of it before same-aged birds that fledged with more white, again making them appear older than is actually the case.

Young eagles also tend to show larger white patches on the underside of the wing than they do on the upper side, so even the viewing angle can give a misleading impression. The underside patches tend to be longer and thinner than those on the upper side - which can often appear as a single spot patch - when seen in the field. It can also be seen that the true extent of the wing patches is only really apparent when the wings are fully open. Any flexing of the wings reduces the apparent amount of white feathering and it is often only when the bird tilts its flying angle that any white can be seen. It is also the case that a typically-marked juvenile might not show any white feathering when it is perched.

The white base of the tail feathers appears to be less variable in extent than the white wing patches but the underside of the tail can still appear very different to the upper side. Care must be taken to ensure that it is the tail base that is being seen as many eagles, even those in adult plumage, show very pale undertail coverts that can give the impression of a white tail base.

In spite of these practical problems, many observers believe that they can accurately age unfamiliar immature-plumaged eagles to a specific year on the basis of their patterning. To further encourage over-confidence in this, Watson (2010) discusses what are thought to be age-related changes in the wing coverts of immatures. While noting that the white wing and tail patches change little during the first three years of life (something that is not generally appreciated and making their use for ageing eagles absolutely without value), the upper wing coverts apparently change from dark to pale and then dark again during this period, before becoming pale in the fourth year. So after the second moult the bird presumably looks more or less identical to a juvenile. Because observers seldom have ideal views in the field, and because the coverts are generally paler than the other coloured feathers to begin with, such details - even if correct - are of little value in the field. In simple terms there is very little likelihood of an immature-plumaged eagle being correctly aged in the field unless it is known to be a juvenile, i.e. a bird that is less than one year old.

At best it might be possible to suggest that an eagle has passed its third moult because the mixture of feathering (some, perhaps most, young eagles might at some point be carrying juvenile, immature and adult feathers) does seem to produce a more speckled appearance on the upper side of some birds. Although the age of most of these birds has not been known, the modern use of satellite tracking technology has allowed fully reliable field evidence to be collected on this point; with their backpacks visible, birds of a known age can be seen in the wild that match this suggestion. There is also the possibility that birds of this age have a brighter appearance, although this may be related to their gender, the adult male plumage being brighter than that of the adult female.

Plumage anomalies are also to be seen. A bird breeding successfully in Tayside in 1992 did so with what could be called one adult and one immature-patterned wing. The age ascribed to this bird by an unwary observer might depend on in which direction the bird was travelling, and if it flew out of view, paused, and then returned it could be mistaken for two birds. Some birds also seem to retain white patches beyond the age of adulthood, possibly most often in the tail, and one bird has been seen with sandy-brown rather than white patches which it retained well into adulthood and which led, on more than one occasion, to the adult bird being wrongly aged as an immature.

As noted above, an eagle may have no white patches in its plumage but also not be in adult plumage. This is the often overlooked 'near-adult' plumage, which is typically darker than the full-adult plumage; the full-adult patterning may have been achieved, but not the tonal shading. This intermediate plumage appears to be carried for only one year, and has been seen at more than one location where a replacement member of a pair, being observed with sufficient frequency to be certain of residency, moulted from a plumage with some white into a plumage without white and then into paler plumage, which it then retained after subsequent moults.

It must also be remembered that immaturity of plumage does not equal sexual immaturity and that immature-plumaged birds have been seen to breed successfully both when paired together and when paired to an adult. The presence of an immature-plumaged bird does not preclude territoriality, pairing, breeding or successful breeding and such a bird should never be assumed to be a visitor, or a bird fledged in that location.

Once in adult plumage there appears to be no way of ageing a golden eagle to a specific year by appearance alone. A recognisable bird can be followed from year to year and so its age can be said to be the number of years it is seen plus about five for the pre-adult plumage period, but it cannot be recognised as, say, a 15-year-old bird. As a result, an unknown adult-plumaged eagle can only be said to be at least five years old.

Within this work, a juvenile is a bird known to be less than a year old; an immature is any bird with white wing and/or tail patches that is not known to be a juvenile; and an adult is a bird without white patches.

GENDER

This is the point at which a great amount of field recording loses its reliability, and where the limitations of the available evidence become most obvious and begin to have a major impact on knowledge and species management.

While it is accepted that female golden eagles are larger (heavier and longer winged) than males, the differences are not as great as is often thought, or implied by such terms as sexual size dimorphism. It is also commonly forgotten that there is size variation within the genders. In other words, two eagles with a visible size difference are not necessarily a male and a female. It should be immediately apparent how this can influence ideas about territory occupancy and population size. Observers not uncommonly report pairs of eagles when they have only definitely seen two eagles and also not uncommonly sex single eagles on the basis of their apparent size.

The reliability of the idea that the larger of two eagles must be a female was put into fine context some years ago in Argyll when the protracted presence of three birds became evident in a territory. This meant that an observer could see three possible pairings: the pair, the female with a bird that was not its mate, and the male with a bird that was not its mate. One of these pairings had to be two eagles of the same gender. However, the third bird was of intermediate size so the possible pairings were actually the pair, the female with a smaller bird that was not the male, and the male with a larger bird that was not the female.

In spite of what is widely believed and put into practice by almost all observers, there was no way of determining the gender of the third bird in this example on the basis of its apparent or comparative size. If gender could not be determined when more than one eagle was in view here, it cannot be possible knowingly and correctly to determine the gender when only one unfamiliar eagle is in view. A great many observers, though, still 'know' the gender of the bird they have in view.

This was a real situation and it is a situation that is potentially more common than might be expected. When observers encounter two eagles with a visible size difference inside a known nesting area, they typically record that they are looking at a resident pair and that they have confirmed occupancy of the site without considering the other possibilities. They see what they expect to see.

There is an additional point to be made about using apparent size to determine the gender of golden eagles. It is not uncommon for the eagle's size to be judged in comparison with another species, most typically raven or buzzard. This does not produce reliable results because - it would seem from all the examples witnessed - the observer, amongst other things, never determines the gender of the other species. Male ravens, though, are larger than female ravens and female buzzards are larger than male buzzards. The size difference between a female eagle and a female buzzard may differ little from that between a male eagle and a male buzzard and so be of no value. The apparent size of an eagle is not a reliable means of determining gender.

Watson (1997) reports on plumage differences, suggesting that female eagles may have a less barred tail than males. This is extremely difficult to see with any certainty in the field and some observations would suggest that, if this were correct, females have bred successfully while paired to other females.

The problems when determining gender also apply to juvenile and immature eagles. Firstly, the flight feathers are not fully formed when the bird leaves the nest, so the bird can appear to be on the small side and therefore probably a male; secondly, once they are fully grown, the flight feathers are fresh and unworn, unlike the adult's feathers, so juveniles can appear to be larger than adults of the same gender, and so be taken for females; and thirdly, as the moults are incomplete, not only can this situation continue for more than one year, but the worn and abraded flight feathers of the immature bird in its second year are likely to appear shorter than the fresh feathers of an adult of the same gender, suggesting that it is probably a male. That moult and feather replacement is apparently not precisely synchronised across the population merely adds to the difficulty of determining gender in the field, and suggests that it should not be attempted in any situation that might be said to be of some importance, such as when determining territory occupancy.

There are two additional tentative methods of sexing adult eagles in the field, neither of which is confirmed and both of which require great caution, and healthy scepticism, if they are to be used, and neither of which should be used with any degree of confidence if only one bird is in view. Firstly, female eagles sometimes give the impression of having a more bulbous trailing edge to the fully-extended wings than do males. This is best seen when the pair are together but it is a very subtle difference and may be more individualistic than is apparent.

Secondly, in this study, paired females in full-adult plumage were invariably darker than their mates; although this is also suggested by a photograph in Watson (2010), MacNally (1977) reported a female that was paler than its mate. This tonal or colour difference has not been widely reported but it is probably also not being considered. As usual, other factors such as light quality and weather conditions can affect what is seen in the field but the dark female/pale male separation appears to be reliable once the members of a pair have been separated by other and additional means. This plumage variation is an insufficient basis on which to reach conclusions about eagles seen singly.

None of these situations or methods is improved by the fact that eagles of the same age and gender also show differences in general appearance. This is especially obvious when a paired adult has been replaced by another adult. If the pair is well known, the observer's first impression is usually concerned with differences in the bird's structural appearance and involves thoughts of apparent wing length and body size. These can be quite obvious and it is by no means unusual to have an immediate sense of there being differences when the new pairing is seen together for the first time. While this can help point to the replacement of a paired bird, differences in the plumage may not be immediately or quickly apparent and, of course, the observer may still actually be looking at a resident interacting with an intruder. There can be very obvious behavioural differences between the new and the lost member of a pair (Walker 2009) but, in most cases, there will be no usable information available to highlight this point.

There are, typically, too few observations being made to be absolutely certain of pair stability from year to year and, unless an immature plumaged bird is confirmed to be the member of a pair, it is often just assumed that the pair remains unaltered from the previous year. The make-up of a pair must change at some point but it is remarkable - and quite telling - that these changes seldom seem to be recorded.

To summarise these headings, and support the conclusion of Watson (1997) in the hope that recording will improve, the ageing and sexing of golden eagles in the field is not as easy as is often suggested, and is put into practice based on misguided beliefs.

HABITAT

The golden eagle is, in the popular imagination, inextricably linked to mountain and moorland habitat and these areas hold what are usually considered to be the best nest sites and the most important food sources: sheep, red deer, mountain hare, red grouse and ptarmigan.

The reality is that, even today, golden eagles can also be found breeding in low-lying areas, relatively close to human habitation, using nests that are clearly visible from public roads, on sea cliffs and within forestry plantations. A single territory might even include most of these features. Non-paired and young eagles can be seen almost anywhere within the species' range, right down to the seashore, from major roads and, not unusually, above enclosed farmland. As a result their diet does not have to include hares and grouse and can largely consist of sheep or deer carrion, corvids or a wide variety of less expected species; a pair on Lewis bred successfully with a diet including many mink and fulmar. In other words, the golden eagle is a generalist species capable of making the most of what is available.

However, there is still a tendency to think in terms of 'typical' situations and to judge potential habitat quality on the basis of what is thought to be most suitable. Golden eagles can therefore be easily overlooked, as some productive sites do not provide what are thought to be the species' requirements and, as a result, area or habitat assessments can easily under- or overestimate the suitability of a location.

Although golden eagles can be found using and taking advantage of most types of natural habitat, from the strand line on the seashore to the tops of the highest hills, they are unlikely to be found nesting in the extreme locations and Watson (2010) states that nests are most likely to be found at about half the maximum height of the surrounding land. This idea is not entirely useful in practical terms as a great many nests are situated well below the mid-point elevation and some others, such as those at coastal sites, are, in effect, always below the base elevation of the adjacent land. Nests are commonly found well below the higher elevations simply because the range of food sources increases as elevation decreases and food is more easily delivered to a lower nest than to a higher one.

Most carrion occurs on the lower ground, as do most rabbit warrens, and if golden eagles are watched over a long period of time, and in a way that avoids any disturbance, it quickly becomes clear that the lower ground receives a great deal of use. This even applies in the most mountainous areas because the golden eagle is not really a species of the high tops, it prefers the middle and lower slopes simply because of food source availability. This ground is also less likely to suffer from as many extreme weather events.

These points contradict at least some of the ideas used in guidance for changes of land use, such as that for increasing the area of woodland, which implies that glen bottoms receive relatively little use by golden eagles and essentially offer no important food sources (Haworth and Fielding 2013). This suggestion is a classic example of expectations based on the received wisdom being used to reduce the need for a detailed assessment.

When determining use and value it must be remembered that eagles will always be above the target area and will be viewing a broad swathe of land rather than simply the ground directly ahead or below it; a bird sailing at mid-height will be scrutinising land at lower elevation and a bird on a high perch may be foraging all the way down to the lowest ground and the furthest visible point. It is because of such factors that great care is required when the frequency of use is taken into consideration; the fact that one location produces fewer contact records than another does not have to mean that it is of less value than the other. It must also be remembered that remote tracking systems (radio and satellite telemetry) provide only locations and do not explain the purpose of a bird's presence or differentiate between active and inactive use of the location. An eagle's presence is also not proof of habitat suitability.

HABITAT SUITABILITY

Because of the ingrained ideas about golden eagles, it first has to be noted that food source availability is more important than the type of habitat present in a location. There is little point in highlighting the value of heather moorland if it supports no red grouse or of dismissing grass moor as being of little value when it may provide sheep and/or deer carrion and young. In fact, in this way, many large areas of rough grass moor are more important to golden eagles than similar-sized areas of heather moorland that is not managed for red grouse. Away from the managed moorlands, much of the heather is rank, cropped short or fragmented, none of which are conducive to high numbers of red grouse. Habitat is not of high or low value simply because it is dominated by a particular type of vegetation and, in fact, there is usually a greater diversity of food sources and higher value where the habitat is more varied. Given their size, most eagle territories will offer a variety of habitats of differing value, but specific areas should not be assumed to have be of greater or lesser value than others to eagles on the basis of vegetation.

The different types of habitat can obviously provide different food sources and it is this that makes comparing the apparent qualities of different territories, or comparing them to an idealised norm, largely redundant. Unfortunately such comparisons are still commonplace and, because much of the received wisdom is still based on ideas from a small number of sources, territories without extensive heather moorland or without large numbers of hares and grouse are almost by tradition considered to be of lower quality. However, the absence of large areas of the supposedly best habitat can be countered by variety.

OPEN HABITATS

It is easy to view open ground simply as dominated by heather or by grass and to determine its value in this way. It is, of course, not that straightforward, nor simply about differences linked to degrees of deliberate management. Heather moorland managed for red grouse will support more grouse than unmanaged heather, but the latter can form extensive continuous areas, large fragmented areas, patches or be spread fairly uniformly and fairly equally across large areas without it supporting grouse. Grass moor can be described as rough grazing or semi-improved, amongst other headings, and can vary in appearance and supposed value along with the species of dominant grass; as well as containing heather patches, grass moor might also include areas with bracken. The upper slopes and high tops might be dominated neither by heather nor grass and may only have mosses or lichen or, indeed, be composed largely of bare rock. With the last in mind, the substrate, acidity and soil types may need to be considered when determining the value of land to golden eagles.

Such is the certainty of what is thought to be correct that such divisions and what they mean to food availability and eagle usage seem to be seldom considered. Here, only broad values can be discussed, but what these differences do show quite clearly is that simplistic assessments are of little value to eagle management or conservation.

The presumed importance of heather moorland has long seen the undervaluation of other open habitats but, as implied above, these can be equally productive foraging grounds for golden eagles. Deer forest, especially in western Scotland, is typically grass-dominated and the presence of large herbivores, red deer and/or sheep, can easily sustain successful breeding at sites largely devoid of hare and grouse. Grazing by deer and sheep is also linked to habitat deterioration, usually linked to the loss or fragmentation of heather, but this is still essentially presuming any heather to be of value. What also appears to be overlooked in such situations, in a potentially damaging fashion, is that red deer and sheep are a source of live prey as well as a source of carrion; reducing their numbers to 'improve' the habitat - such as in modern attempts to re-establish or increase the area of native forest – by removing or reducing the numbers of large herbivores is also to reduce the winter and breeding season food supply of many golden eagles.

Invasive bracken appears to have been an increasing problem in many areas in recent decades and while it can be a nuisance for farmers and walkers it should not be dismissed as unusable as readily as has been attempted (Haworth and Fielding 2013). Found mostly on the lower ground, bracken cover is thought to have helped increase rabbit numbers in some territories by providing cover and protection against predators such as foxes, is commonly used by red deer to hide their calves and can be a source of carrion. It cannot simply be dismissed.

The value of wetland areas and water bodies should also not be underestimated and to exclude water bodies from assessments or estimates of territory area is to forget that eagles willingly forage above water and will take gulls, wildfowl and waders as prey. Rivers and streams are also commonly edged by trees or bushes that often hold corvid nests; water courses are commonly followed by potential prey items and mossy bogs and drainage ditches often hold sheep carcasses. It should also not be assumed that lochs and water courses form separation points between pairs, or barriers to ranging activity; there are known to be pairs with nests on opposing sides of freshwater and sea lochs. Some eagles commonly cross large lochs in their territories and birds have been seen to cross from island to island and from an island to the mainland on the western seaboard. That the author once saw a red deer swim from Jura to Islay also suggests that loch shores could be a source of carrion. As golden eagles also drink and bathe, the presence of water should never be undervalued.

While some deer forest and some managed-heather territories have fairly uniform habitat, the size of most territories ensures that there is always some variation that the resident eagles will exploit at different times of the year or under different conditions. Because of this, there should be no such concept as exclusion on the grounds of habitat in any territory assessment.

SCRUBLAND

While it might be thought to be closer to woodland, scrubland is best considered close to open habitat, because rank heather is closer to scrub than to woodland and does not really provide perching spots. Scrubland such as that formed by gorse, willow or young conifers can be highly valuable to foraging golden eagles, as it often holds such species as hare, rabbit and black grouse; red grouse are not unknown in young plantations and, in the worst of conditions, even ptarmigan sometimes move down to the scrubby forest edge. The varied structure of scrubland does not only help to break up a blanket covering of snow: it provides shelter from storms and offers roosting spots for the prey species without making them unavailable to eagles. Although eagle nests have been found in bushy woodland, the scrub is really of value as foraging land and a great many territories would probably benefit from the addition of open scrub, even if only by managing the plantation fringe to create an edge of varied age, density and growth, rather than a wall of trees.

COASTAL SITES

The fact that golden eagles breed on sea cliffs helps to dispel the idea that the species has a typical and easily predictable habitat. However, it must remembered that, while eagles will make kills above the sea, the vast majority of a coastal territory still lies behind the cliff, and is still an inland territory. A side effect of this is that sea-cliff nests are not located centrally, so the idea of a territory centre calculated from the mean grid reference of nest locations becomes meaningless and of no value to estimating the territory area.

Not surprisingly, coastal sites are often particularly rich in food sources (even though there appear to be few records of auks in the eagle's diet) and many such sites are among the most productive, or at least among the most regularly successful. Sea cliffs pose a problem when considering habitat because the territory may be linear in form, and so relatively thin, or extending more narrowly inland from the cliff because of neighbours. There may be no inland neighbours. As there are sea-cliff sites with blanket plantation forest right up to the cliff edge, it is not at all straightforward to determine the boundaries and the relative importance of different parts of a coastal site, and it not sound to assume at such sites that the cliff is the territory or that only seabirds are taken as prey or used as food.

It might also be the case that coastal sites have a much greater seasonal element to their existence than do fully inland sites. As the majority of such sites probably have a western or south-western exposure, they will be prone to the worst of the Atlantic storms, through which the resident eagles are unlikely to remain perched on exposed bare ledges. The inland expanse of a coastal territory will probably have much greater value than might be thought, not least because some coastal prey species might not be available at any time during the winter.

As an aside, while it has often been suggested that the golden eagle's use of sea-cliffs may have resulted from, or been made easier by, the absence of white-tailed eagles (Love 1983), it is possibly more likely to have resulted from the expansion of the fulmar's distribution. The historic record and modern interpretations of it are by no means fully reliable, but the white-tailed eagle's general demise appears to have come about too early for it to have been a major factor, while the fulmar's colonisation from the north appears to be more coincidental with the golden eagle's use of sea-cliffs (Sharrock 1976). Of course, earlier observers might also have been less aware of the number of coastal sites.

FARMLAND

Even though most of the eagle's Scottish range is farmed in one way or another, the image of farmland tends to be that of a habitat unavailable to golden eagles. This is not in any way a reliable conclusion to draw, and 'farmland' is used far more by golden eagles than is generally presumed.

Enclosed pasture, in particular, is commonly dismissed as being of little value to golden eagles because of its presumed lack of food sources and the implied proximity to human activity, but most farmland is enclosed in some way and it is by no means unusual to see eagles in such locations. The use of such areas is also too easily or readily dismissed as evidence of a low- quality territory or desperation on the part of the eagles. Golden eagles certainly can be seen above such ground when foraging potential elsewhere has been reduced by seasonal variations in availability, or as a result of severe weather conditions, but it can also be deliberately selected for foraging during the height of the breeding season.

For example, in late autumn, when there should be no natural food shortages, a pair of eagles was watched from a car parked next to a barn alongside a public road as they foraged along hedgerows at less than ten metres above the ground, at times coming to within 100 metres of the car and 300 metres of the occupied farmhouse. On another occasion, elsewhere, a resident adult eagle was seen to kill a hooded crow and land with it in an area of low-lying, improved enclosed pasture while the local gamekeeper was working in an adjoining field. These examples are not as exceptional as they might at first appear to be, and territorial eagles can be seen in such locations during casual ranging activity at almost any time of year. Immature-plumaged and non-territory holding birds also often wander above enclosed farmland at low elevation. As with other habitats, enclosed and even improved pasture cannot be dismissed from a territory assessment nor said to fail to provide foraging opportunities. They are always, at least, an alternative source of food.

WOODLAND

Although the golden eagle is usually presented as a species of open habitat, woodland in its varying forms is an important part of many eagle territories. It can provide food sources, shelter and nest sites and should not be casually dismissed in site assessments.

THE NATIVE PINE FOREST

This is often presumed to be the best quality woodland for golden eagles, largely because it is mostly mature and is known to be used for breeding sites. It generally has a fairly open structure, which permits easier flight between the trees, and can be rich in wildlife and potential prey, with red grouse found in some such woodland as well as black grouse and hares. That said, foraging in any woodland is more difficult for a large bird than foraging in more open habitat and most food is still obtained from outside the forest.

One problem is that woodland of any type provides cover into which the potential prey can escape and the trees themselves form obstacles which the eagle must negotiate when in pursuit, and around which the potential prey item can more easily manoeuvre. Deer and sheep carrion (sickly deer and sheep often seek shelter before dying) would be available among the trees and used, if they are not excluded on conservation grounds, but in practical terms, because of the difficulty in locating carcasses, the forest, again, probably makes foraging more difficult.

There is, of course, little remaining mature native pine forest, and few extensive areas of immature forest, and its attractiveness to human recreational activities probably reduces the value to eagles of much that does remain. Human interests have seen attempts to increase the area of the native pine forest in many areas, but the methodology can be seen to be not in the best interests of golden eagles. The forest is not ideal golden eagle habitat to begin with, and to achieve the expansion, in at least some areas, all of the sheep have been removed and the red deer cull increased. This conservation effort has not only removed foraging habitat, but has actually reduced food availability in some Golden Eagle Special Protection Area territories that were already largely or entirely without red grouse and mountain hare. The argument that forest expansion will eventually improve species diversity and live prey availability (Haworth and Fielding 2013) holds no water, as it would require implausible levels of resources and effort, and the timescale involved would certainly result in eagles being lost before the improvement could be achieved.

DECIDUOUS WOODLAND

Surprisingly, even native or natural deciduous woodland is generally not immediately considered as potential golden eagle habitat, even though there are many nests positioned in the birch and rowan woodland on ridge sides. It is used in the same ways as the pine forest, even if that is only mostly for nest sites and roosts. However, the general thinking has had an interesting influence and further reveals some of the biases in the received wisdom. It is generally suggested that most golden eagle tree nests are in north-east Scotland (Watson 2010) even though there is no lack of such nests elsewhere in Scotland. This has led to the native pine forest being given greater importance, even though the evidence suggests that eagles will nest in any suitable tree if that is their desire. For example, in the west of Scotland, including some of the islands, tree nests have been found in oak, ash and birch, as well as in pine, larch and spruce.

Mature deciduous woodland can have as varied a structure as the pine forest and, in both, the eagle nests are not always to be found in the most open areas. One old oak tree nest on an island seemed to need vertical access from above and a mainland nest in an ash tree probably needed such an approach from below. When it comes to foraging, mature deciduous woodland offers the same advantages and shortcomings as the pine forest, as it does when it comes to breeding, perching and roosting.

To sum up, then, and underline the problem posed by fixed ideas, a golden eagle breeding attempt was once made at a site where the nest was in an oak tree on the edge of improved pasture and alongside a farm track that was in regular use. The breeding attempt failed but the location was not a hindrance to the eagle's choice.

PLANTATION FOREST

The value of plantation forest needs more careful consideration as it is planned, managed and has a structure that changes more rapidly than that of 'natural' woodland. The golden eagle does not have a simple relationship with this habitat and while the plantation forest is commonly seen to be a dense, dark blanket that obliterates foraging opportunity and destroys territory viability, this view does not paint the whole picture. Even the established idea and expectation that the forest area becomes essentially valueless after the pre-thicket stage (with trees of up to about 12 years of age) - and can be treated as an exclusion zone in assessments - can give an entirely false impression of what is happening, not least because eagles will forage above plantation forest.

However, what is most often overlooked on this point is that habitat quality and foraging opportunity are reduced before the trees are even planted, as the ground preparation (usually a type of ridge-and-furrow approach with drainage ditches) introduces habitat fragmentation that immediately reduces food source availability and attractiveness. This means that impact assessments commonly consider the effects of converting open habitat to closed canopy forest to be a gradual process when, in fact, it has an almost immediate effect. This was seen in Argyll where a regularly-used area of open hill supporting red grouse ceased to produce eagle records only three years after it was made ready for spruce trees. In other parts of the same territory, eagle use also declined sooner than expected after planting because the food sources had been destroyed at an earlier date. The age of the trees is not really relevant here: what matters is the impact of the process of afforestation on food sources.

There is also an often-overlooked side effect of tree planting: it is not only the planted area that loses value and foraging opportunity, it can also be the adjacent unplanted areas. Observations in the main Argyll study site and elsewhere revealed not only the timing of the reduced use and near-abandonment of forested areas, but also revealed that unchanged adjacent open habitat recorded reduced use by the resident eagles at the same time. This was because removing the food sources from the forested land also removed any possibility of the food species involved dispersing on to the adjoining land during the autumn and winter. Although the adjoining land remained entirely unchanged, it ceased to produce even annual contacts with the resident eagles. Something similar may well have happened on Mull, where Whitfield *et al* (2009) reported a territory that had been abandoned with a smaller plantation area than one which remained occupied in spite of having a greater forest area; the location of the planted area was probably of more importance than its size.

It is probably the middle-aged plantation that is of least value to golden eagles, as it supports only remnant prey populations and does not provide good perching, roosting or nesting opportunities. Golden eagles do forage along the rides and roads in such forests and will, of course, forage above all plantations.

It does not seem to be widely appreciated that mature coniferous plantations are by no means unattractive to golden eagles and probably provide the most usable form of this type of habitat. Mature plantations can offer reasonable amounts of food in the form of corvids, pigeons, other birds of prey and carrion as well as safe roosting, perching and nesting sites. There are probably more eagle nests inside the forest boundary than is generally appreciated, including some that have been built in plantation trees.

Mature plantations can also provide safe havens for immature eagles as they are probably less prone to disturbance in these habitats than in any other, and even quite small shelter belts may be used in this way. Such situations may also allow tentative pairings and associations to be formed which might result in some speculative breeding attempts. How many of these are likely to be found is largely limited by the way in which plantation forest is so easily dismissed from assessments.

In spite of these points, it can be deduced that plantation coniferous forest is not ideal golden eagle habitat and any expansion of its area is likely to be detrimental to golden eagles. The main problems are that forestry tends to planted in unsuitable locations, with too much uniformity, with a general disregard to its impact on the wildlife community and in too close proximity to known golden eagle breeding sites, and is managed in a way that does not greatly benefit wildlife. Perhaps the most overlooked problems, though, are associated with the felling and extraction of the timber. Not only is this an extremely disruptive process, but it generally appears to be done with little forward planning, meaning that extraction routes and new roads commonly have to be created through mature woodland rather than at the planting stage. Felling, of course, also leaves the horrendous clearfell areas that are of virtually no value to any animal of substance.

It has to be said that commercial forestry organisations, with their lack of forethought, inconsiderate planting regimes, over-culling of deer and the often thoughtless manner in which they proceed, pose a much under-rated problem for golden eagles. The fact that some published forest guidance is so inadequate as to be potentially very damaging probably shows that the presence of golden eagles will always be viewed as a nuisance, to be grudgingly accommodated in some areas.

HABITAT DETERIORATION

It has been shown in many territories that habitat quality does not decline simply because of tree growth and the loss of heather, resulting from a combination of grazing pressure, weather conditions and climate, as well as other possible factors. Red grouse, and perhaps other food sources, are often absent before the habitat is lost, as its quality deteriorates below the point at which it can support a species. This is seen to be a particular problem on the western mainland and has been linked to the eagle's low productivity in such areas but, because the idea of overgrazing is so ingrained, this has not been examined in sufficient detail to allow solid conclusions to be reached. Some eagles continue to breed successfully in 'overgrazed' habitats with few of the expected live prey species, and it is often overlooked that overgrazing, especially by red deer and sheep, should increase carrion amounts and, with lambs and deer calves, increase the available live biomass during the nestling period. It is not often seen in this way because of the misplaced importance that is attributed to grouse and hares and the general reluctance to view sheep and red deer as sources of live prey.

That is not to diminish or detract from what is a major concern in the uplands, but it is a matter that requires much closer and more detailed investigation. Most habitat deterioration is a continuous process that can only be quantified in the long term and changes can be so slow as to go largely unnoticed until it is too late. Part of the reason why many changes are likely to go unrecognised is the concentration of effort on the nesting area. There are probably very few territories that are even roughly surveyed on a regular basis and in a way that would allow the process of change to be identified before it has a detrimental effect on golden eagles.

CHANGES OF LAND USE

While habitat quality can deteriorate almost imperceptibly and have an impact on golden eagles that may go unnoticed, other changes can have a much more immediate effect. The influence of commercial plantation forest has already been mentioned and the burgeoning upland windfarm industry cannot be ignored. While this is a more regulated industry than forestry, it is an advancing one and windfarms have been permitted inside and close to occupied eagle territories regardless of the fact that their real and potential impacts are largely unknown and only predicted in environmental impact assessments which are also, typically, fairly superficial in nature. It is in these assessments that the use of distance constraints is most easily seen, applied without any consideration of actual food source distribution and real territory use, and where the subjective use of received wisdom is most apparent. This situation is unlikely to change and may worsen, given the desire for renewable energy.

One complicating and little-mentioned effect is that, while conservation concerns may prevent or result in the relocation of a windfarm, developments in areas without golden eagles will probably reduce the likelihood of the species expanding its range. This may be of particular relevance to the south of Scotland, an area where there are already coniferous plantations and where there is likely to be more. Some locations there, known to have held single and what might be called prospecting eagles in fairly recent times, now have windfarms in them and an infrastructure that has made the location unsuitable for eagles.

The windfarm industry presents three major problems, excluding raising the standard of analysis and interpretation which applies to all aspects of eagle ornithology, that need to be better addressed if it is not to have a major impact on golden eagles. Firstly, the results produced from windfarm sites can be ambiguous when viewed in the light of received wisdom, so there is a need for much more detailed investigation at these sites before, during and after construction. Secondly, concerns over commercial confidentiality, which mean that there is little sharing of information, need to be put to one side. Locations have often been investigated more than once without the investigators being aware of earlier assessments. It is, in fact, not unusual for more than one team of fieldworkers to be working simultaneously on the same site and not to be sharing results. This raises the third problem: the duplication of effort that can cause disturbance and disruption to breeding attempts. The imperative to obtain results probably also sees unrecognised disruption, such as that caused in foraging areas, because the site has not been properly assessed before fieldwork begins. Schedule 1 licences also sometimes seem to be issued regardless of pre-existing coverage provided by the raptor study groups. These problems are all easy to address, but the governing bodies seem reluctant to do so.

HABITAT USE

How golden eagles use the habitats that form their territories is extremely difficult to predict or easily summarise, because it is so greatly influenced by other factors. There can be annual and seasonal variations in the importance of different habitats because of fluctuations in the availability of different food sources and the prevailing weather conditions, as well as outside influences such as changes in human activity levels. A change of bird in a pair may also result in a changed use of the local habitat and the eagle's typically casual approach to its daily activity can give misleading indications of its associations with its location.

It is not necessarily simply the presence of reliable food sources or of potential nest sites that sees golden eagles use any given area, and there is often no obvious definable relationship between habitat, use and breeding performance. Eagles do not simply ignore, fly high above or fly around supposedly less attractive habitat: they will forage over it. As a result, no assessment of suitability should make assumptions about the potential value of habitat or of a particular location. If the relevance of habitat is taken to mean the provision of nest sites or the provision of food sources, then all types of habitat have to be considered and included in an assessment. The same applies in the field: nothing should be dismissed or called unsuitable. The value to juvenile eagles of apparently little-used areas must also not be underestimated as, while the adults might not obtain much food from them, they form what could be called nursery areas that may be essential to juvenile development.

It can be seen, therefore, that some of the established ideas about habitat quality and suitability are best not applied wholesale to the species. The rich habitats of north-east Scotland, which support large numbers of grouse and hare, are not necessarily better eagle habitat than the western mainland areas from which these special habitats and species are largely absent. There should be no preconceived ideas when dealing with golden eagle habitat, as it is too easy to reach the wrong conclusion and so provide the wrong advice.

TERRITORY

A detailed understanding of all the elements relevant to golden eagle territories is essential to our knowledge of the species and to its conservation but, in spite of this level of importance, it is still a topic that has not really been examined in any detail and is overly simplified for convenience. Most of the available information is the result of casual observations or assumptions and its application is generally little more than a guess or prediction, or a 'best fit' based on generic ideas. The failure to recognise these limitations reduces the value and reliability of data collected on other aspects of golden eagle ecology. For example, the influence of food supply on breeding performance cannot be reliably determined if the area from which the food is obtained is not known.

This is an important point to understand because it has become very easy for species managers to simplify decision making by applying convenient values without recognising their wider implications. For example, in relation to eagles in the south of Scotland, Fielding and Haworth (2014) imply that the maximum range (territory) radius is six kilometres from the mean nest location. This is not only incorrect, but is misleading in a way that could be detrimental to eagles even when the idea is used by conservationists: it is effectively saying that nothing of importance is found beyond that distance and that eagles radiate their movements around a central point.

There is no reliable shortcut to determining a territory area, its delineation or how it is used by the resident eagles. A territory is not the average area available to each pair of eagles within a population, and neither is it accurately represented by the arithmetically most efficient means of dividing the available land between the pairs that are present or by imposing distance constraints around a contrived location, the mean nest location grid reference or 'territory centre', as it is misleadingly called. Determining a territory area is not at all straightforward; it is time consuming, it cannot be reliably achieved as a desk exercise and, in the field, data collection is hindered by problems such as the difficulty of recognising the status of the eagles seen and of correctly interpreting their behaviour.

TERRITORY, HOME RANGE OR RANGING AREA

It's important, first of all, to establish what is meant by the idea of territory and to arrive at an acceptable definition, because different terms are used as if interchangeable when they might mean different things to different people. The terms 'territory', 'home range' and 'ranging area' have all been used to designate the same piece of land; 'core', 'primary' and 'secondary' hunting (or foraging) areas are used to highlight units within a territory; and the misleading term 'core range' has been used.

It has to be said that much of the confusion over what is meant by the various terms seems to originate with attempts to make a special case out of the golden eagle. Brown (1976) stated that he disliked the use of the word territory because it implied 'a defended area' and eagles, he said, do not obviously defend their 'territory'. As a result, 'home range' has been popularised and is widely considered to be the most appropriate term to use with this species; and the underlying sentiment about territoriality has been incorporated into the general approach to golden eagle issues. However, these views are not the result of detailed studies, and in spite of them it is still accepted that golden eagles occupy exclusive areas, perform territorial displays, defend their breeding areas, chase intruders and indulge in physical combat with neighbours and intruders. Golden eagles, therefore, are indeed territorial and so can be said to occupy territories.

The term 'ranging area' is probably the most appropriate alternative to 'territory' but it denotes something greater than the area needed by a pair of eagles to survive and make successful breeding attempts. For example, adult male eagles accompany their juveniles into areas with which they have no real association and which they might only visit in successful breeding years. Those places are inside the 'ranging area' but they are not a part of the territory or the implied home range as they are not essential to successful breeding. Because of such ambiguities, 'territory' should be the preferred term, with 'ranging area' only used in general discussions; 'home range' is both too vague and, simultaneously, too apparently definitive to have real value.

There is one final introductory point to be made. It must be remembered that a territory is not a truly exclusive area and that territorial behaviour does not prevent intrusions by other members of the same species. Territorial behaviour is a response to the presence of other members of the same species, either within the defended area or simply within sight of the resident birds, and can involve flight displays, confrontations or the simple physical presence of an eagle. It must also be remembered that intrusions are not always seen by the resident birds (or by the observer) because of the variable terrain in almost all territories, so when it comes to the interpretation of behaviour, some territorial activity will not be recognised, and much of what is thought to be territorial behaviour could have an alternative purpose or explanation. It is also apparently often forgotten that territorial behaviour can be an attraction as well as a deterrent; a displaying eagle is not necessarily defending its territory.

TERRITORY ESTABLISHMENT

As the location of newly occupied sites is generally a closely guarded secret, only very sketchy information is available for the consideration of this topic. Most eagles have also probably already been present for some time before they are settled and will probably be thought of as visitors before their true status is recognised and examined. This influences the interpretation of what is seen.

While it is easy to suggest that habitat, food and nest sites are the main requirements for any territory it is not easy to recognise the value of these requirements in the field and there are locations for which the presence or absence of eagles appears to be almost inexplicable. This is undoubtedly because of the inappropriate way in which suitability has been traditionally determined and not least because of the assumptions made about food sources and their availability.

While it might be expected that the formation of entirely new territories would involve pairs of immature-plumaged or near-adult eagles, these are probably the least stable associations and the least likely to form territories. A new territory may be suggested because it might be thought that the same birds are being seen on a succession of site visits, but the difficulty of confirming this means that it should not be assumed. As there is likely to be an age difference between the two birds in any pairing and because juveniles (sexually immature birds) are unlikely to commit themselves to a location, there is always the possibility of an older, or simply more dominant, bird usurping a younger one. As a result, what may appear to be a new pair may have no stability at all and may have involved several different birds rather than just two. To add to the difficulty of confirming events, it is clear that young eagles associating with one another might begin to build new nests very early in the association or in their presence in a location, and of course there might in fact be only one active bird and a passive visitor rather than a pairing. These points may at least partly explain why many such sites are not occupied in the long term and usually fail to produce breeding attempts.

Golden eagles arriving in previously unoccupied locations, or in those from which the species has been absent for many years, generally use an area that is much larger than would be expected to equate to a territory. There appears to be a process by which the potential area is investigated, developed and condensed, sometimes over a number of years, with the eagles identifying suitable and unsuitable areas and adapting their ranging activity accordingly. The same, though perhaps to a lesser extent, can be seen when a replacement eagle enters a pair. The new bird is unfamiliar with its surroundings and has to address this before settling into its routine and into an area smaller than that which it first uses.

This may seem to be an impossible task inside an established population, but intrusions into neighbouring territories are common and can be observed when changes occur within a local population that is subject to detailed assessment, and new residents probably more commonly intrude into adjacent sites than do established birds. Individual eagles, and especially replacements, also show different patterns of behaviour and are attracted to different areas than are established birds, in a way that would also seem to alter territory use and the location of boundaries. They can also show differences in their preferred food types or their willingness, or ability, to utilise food sources in the same way as their predecessor. Each of these also allows an eagle to discover its surroundings and potentially occupy the area in a different way to its predecessor without actually changing the territory boundaries in the longer term.

The situation is still more complicated because eagles that are new to a location are not absent one day and permanently present from the next: they familiarise themselves with the area and what it offers and may move on if it becomes unsuitable, but perhaps not doing so until several months after arriving. They are also sometimes absent for several days during their time on-site before returning, possibly giving the impression that they are visitors rather than residents.

As new pairs tend not to breed in their first year of presence, it is likely that overall suitability is still being determined. This may help to explain why it is also not unusual for sites to hold birds for two or three years (with nest building and even a breeding attempt) and then be deserted. This adjustment process probably continues for several years after establishment, or may be continuous, given the observed annual variations in established territories. During the establishment period, nests may not be built, and those that are built may be scattered about a larger area rather than being locally grouped. Nest building and/or breeding attempts may seem to be made in almost random locations, often in what observers might call inappropriate or unexpected ones, which makes determining the layout of a new territory even more difficult.

A distinction must also be made between areas that are capable of supporting eagles and those which can sustain successful breeding. Some existing occupied territories do not appear to be capable of the latter with any great regularity, while some unoccupied areas appear to be eminently suitable for eagles. Similarly, territories of apparently low quality (as suggested by the basic criteria) often produce young, while those of apparently higher quality regularly fail to do so, even in the absence of human interference. There are, of course, many potential causes of failure or non-breeding and these can be difficult to assess or even to recognise as influential at any given time. A location should therefore never be said to be suitable or unsuitable for golden eagles without an intensive long-term review, because of the variables that can influence occupancy and breeding success;

there are also large tracts of countryside that appear to be capable of supporting eagles but which probably will not support successful breeding.

TERRITORY QUALITY

It is an unfortunate fact that assessments of territory quality are almost invariably highly subjective and based on breeding performance, the site history or a simple expectation resulting from the presence of certain food sources. Territory quality cannot be determined in this way, by predictive means, in desk studies or by traditional methodology and analysis. Territory quality judged on perceived ideas about habitat importance, food availability and breeding performance can be shown to be too simplistic an approach.

For example, an Argyll study site produced only one chick in 19 years; during that time land, foraging opportunity and food sources were lost to forest expansion and growth and to a 46- turbine windfarm constructed on a known foraging area that held red grouse. The territory was also without red deer, mountain hare and ptarmigan and held relatively very few rabbits and red grouse. The comparative ways in which these factors are usually applied point to the territory being of low quality and provides an explanation of the low productivity. Five young were then fledged during the next five years, including the first known instance (with monitoring dating back to the 1970s) of a two-chick brood being fledged (M. Gregory *pers. comm.*). Contrary to the simplistic conclusion based on expectations, the territory is actually of high quality and must have been fully viable during the 19 years of very low productivity. The poor site history was the result of something other than food and habitat, the factors most commonly used to determine territory quality.

In a similar way, while mountain hare and red grouse have been implied by some sources to be of almost overriding importance to golden eagles, their almost total absence from territories does not necessarily prevent the occupying eagles from breeding successfully. After more than 25 years of monitoring, neither of these species, nor rabbits, has been recorded in the most successful (c.0.7 young per year) north Argyll territory, from which all the sheep were also removed during the 1990s.

Too many locations are described as being suitable, or not, for golden eagles on the basis of a superficial assessment that has used an inappropriate means, if any at all, of determining quality. For example, the presence of red grouse is not proof that the location is suitable for golden eagles, because their practical availability cannot be determined by an observer simply walking the hills. Unfortunately, it is a simple fact that most observers' knowledge of the food resources within a territory has been acquired in this casual way.

Food availability will always be seen as the overriding constraint on golden eagles, even though Brown and Watson (1964) noted that there would not be a fundamental shortage at any time in any territory, a conclusion supported by a more recent and more detailed assessment (Walker *et al* 2014). Food source availability may have relevance, according to the idea that different sources have peak availability at different times, but this is probably usually addressed by the size of most eagle territories; they are large enough to provide the variety that produces the necessary food requirement when it is needed.

Food availability has also always been directly linked to habitat, and forest expansion, habitat degradation due to grazing pressure and, probably, climatic factors do reduce food source availability. However, basic assessments and inferences are usually made in comparison with a theoretical ideal, while golden eagles are capable of breeding successfully where all of these factors fail to match the best areas.

Most other considerations are of less importance. The idea, for example, that nest site availability may limit golden eagle distribution (Watson and Dennis 1992) is entirely groundless. Golden eagles breed successfully in nests on the ground, in trees, on sea cliffs and on small, medium and large scale crags. The species' distribution and territory quality is largely governed by human activity rather than by physical features.

TERRITORY DELINEATION

Golden eagle territories can be very large, often exceeding 50km² in area, and many are probably larger than estimates suggest. This is because eagle territories are not of uniform shape and do not fit neatly into the available land, and habitats that are commonly excluded from assessments are often actually integral parts of the site.

Determining the boundaries of a golden eagle territory is not at all straightforward; it cannot be easily achieved without detailed year-round observations or with a simplistic interpretation of behaviour. The boundaries cannot be accurately ascribed by using the mid-point nearest-neighbour distance between breeding sites or by dividing the available land by the number of pairs (such as Watson 1957); they cannot be correctly predicted by using statistical models (such as MacLeod *et al* 2003); and they cannot be reliably produced using the application of distance constraints or by subjective assessments of habitat and topography. Unfortunately, all of these methods have been used in conservation management, and sometimes used in combination, even though their inappropriateness has been made clearly apparent in relation to windfarm developments and expansion of the plantation forest area.

The reliability of predictive methods of territory delineation has been exaggerated and they have not been properly tested in the field; that their inclusion is almost a requirement of environmental impact assessments is not proof that they are reliable. Work from the Lake District (Walker 2004; 2009) and Argyll (Walker *et al* 2005; 2014) provides the only available detailed year-round studies and show that the areas used by the relevant eagles do not fall into simplistic predictable patterns (Figures 1 and 2). In neither case was the nest group located centrally; the resident eagles in both preferentially ranged in certain directions more than in others; and, in both, the habitat and topography could not be used to identify boundaries to activity.

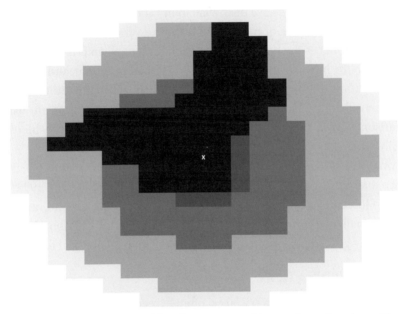

Figure 1: A schematic representation of the Haweswater golden eagle territory's position in relation to land 3km, 6km and 9km from the mean nest location (marked 'x').

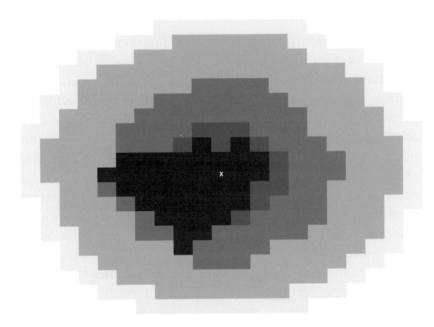

Figure 2: A schematic representation of an Argyll golden eagle territory's position in relation to land 3km, 6km and 9km from the mean nest location (marked 'x').

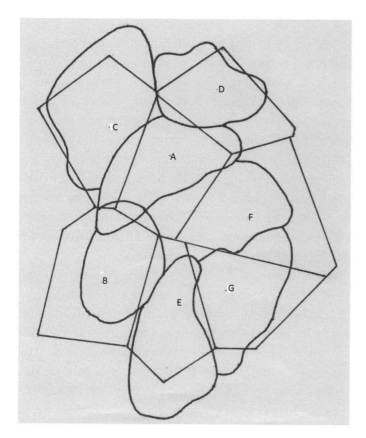

Figure 3: Territory delineation within the north Argyll population of golden eagles using two methods: 1. direct observation and interpretation of eagle activity (curved lines); 2. nearest-neighbour distance (straight lines).

Although the Argyll and Haweswater sites were two relatively isolated territories, exactly the same situation was found to be the case in an assessment of territories or area division within the north Argyll population. This assessment was performed in detail during the 1992 National Survey but incorporated year-round data collected during 1986 – 2012 (see Figure 3).

The north Argyll study targeted one territory because it was known to have about average productivity, while being surrounded by other occupied territories which were, in turn, surrounded by other territories or unsuitable/vacant habitat. The study territory (territory A) was therefore the one most likely to have limitations imposed on its size and shape. The results provide a good insight into the problems of predictive methodology, applying expectations and how these might impact on species conservation.

Comparing the two sets of results showed that the observed territories varied between c.14% larger and c.36% smaller than predicted; c.22% of the predicted territory A area lay within the observed territory of a neighbouring pair, of which c.30% lay within the predicted territory A area. The predicted territory A area also overlapped with the observed areas of four of its other neighbours. Also, some of the predicted boundaries dissected nesting glens that were known to be exclusive to one pair with, in the surrounding population, c.46% of one nesting glen being ascribed to another pair, and a pair apparently having favourite perches c.2.5km inside a neighbour's territory.

Put simply, the predictive methods were not only unreliable but were so misleading as to be potentially damaging to species management. Furthermore, while MacLeod *et al* (2003) advise that boundaries can be adjusted to major terrain features wherever there might be anomalies such as boundaries dividing nest glens, this negates the value of a predictive model, with the Lake District and Argyll results showing that major features did not form simple or definitive barriers or boundaries. The boundaries between pairs were often minor features or much broader locations, meaning that a boundary was not a simple line on the ground but might be up to three kilometres in breadth; it would be a valley, rather than a ridge. It was only where the nesting sites of adjacent pairs abutted that there was a simple division between pairs.

As the nest groups were not located centrally in the study territories, these points also mean that there were times when eagles were closer to the nests of other pairs than to their own, and closer to that group than were the eagles to which it belonged. This may seem to be unlikely but that is only because of expectations and the idea of central nest groups; nest groups are not as far apart as possible and territories are not of regular size or shape, fitting into the landscape as a complex jigsaw rather than a neat pattern. This clearly has major implications for anyone trying to associate an eagle with a location when it is seen away from the nest group, and why the interpretation of behaviour has to be approached with much more caution than is generally the case.

Territories can also not be assessed in terms of physical features, because golden eagles occupy a wide variety of habitats in variable terrain. A territory does not have to have a certain amount of bare rock, ridges, hills or moorland, nor do any of these things have to be within a certain distance of the nest, and the nest, indeed, does not have to be in what is considered the most appropriate location.

Deciphering territory delineation in the field is largely a matter of interpreting behaviour over a huge area, most of which will not be visible from any single position within the site. As the bulk of fieldwork is targeted towards nest sites, most observers actually spend little time in the fringe areas where the delineating behaviour is most likely to occur. This situation has led to a number of misleading generalisations, principally that territories are defined by flight displays and that eagles are 'central place foragers' (Watson 2010). Golden eagles appear to be central place foragers because most observations are made in the nesting area and that is assumed to be located centrally.

It is possible to delineate golden eagle territories but their boundaries, size and shape are neither predictable nor easily deduced from basic field observations. Where a high degree of reliability has been achieved using field investigation, the dimensions of territories have not been what was expected. Two territories in the Lake District were found to be very different in all aspects of their make-up and did not match predictions based on nest location (Walker 1991); an Argyll territory also failed to conform to expectations (Walker *et al* 2005); and the territory layout within the north Argyll population bore little resemblance to that suggested by nest group location, terrain or distance constraints. The main reason for this is that, regardless of what is implied by statistical models, all territories are different and offer different resources in an unpredictable manner.

TERRITORY UNITS

In spite of evidence to the contrary (Gordon 1955) and the recognition that some parts of a territory will offer greater food availability than others, there remains the underlying idea that golden eagle territories have fairly uniform value. This is strongly implied by models which utilise distance constraints (such as McGrady *et al* 1997 and MacLeod *et al* 2003), the basic implication of which is that the value of land decreases with distance from the mean nest location (the 'territory centre'). This idea is wholly unreliable and yet the principle has been put into practice and changes and disruptions brought about in some areas simply because a location lies beyond a certain distance from the nest, rather than because it has been shown to be of low value to golden eagles.

A major part of the problem is that the 'core area' has been defined as that producing 50% of contacts with resident eagles and typically lying within three kilometres of the territory centre (McGrady *et al* 1997). By implication, the remaining 50% of contacts are more scattered and made in a much larger area, but what seems to have been ignored is that both areas produce the same number of contacts and are therefore of equal value. This is not a flippant argument: the smaller core area only produces relatively more contacts because it holds the nests and the main roosts which, obviously, means that eagles are more likely to be seen here than elsewhere in the territory. In real terms, land outside the core area can be more important than land inside the core when total requirements and seasonal considerations are taken into account.

Walker (1991) provided a better definition of the core area (calling it the 'primary hunting area') by showing that, as well as having intrinsic value because of the nests and roosts, it offered the most reliable and accessible pre-laying and nestling-period food sources. This meant that the resident eagles could attain breeding condition and provision their nestlings with the minimum of foraging effort. This practical importance has subsequently been recognised (and is easily seen) in other territories and it seems likely that all nest groups are located in, or no further than on the fringe of, the most reliable food source. This need not be in the form of live prey, as might be expected, but will be the best combination of sources. This is also why it is not unusual to find eagles nesting in grass-dominated areas rather than as close as possible to heather with grouse; it must be remembered that the practical availability of live prey such as red grouse declines during the pre-laying and incubation periods and is greatest during the autumn and winter. The situation is probably different in red grouse management areas where live prey availability is artificially high throughout the year.

These points also mean that assessments based on the idea of core areas being located centrally within territories, of eagles being central place foragers and of the nest group being at the geographical centre of the territory (Watson 2010) are all too simplistic. It also helps to explain why territorial eagles do not radiate their ranging activity uniformly around a central location (see Figure 4).

That the core areas actually relate to food source distribution also means that they will vary in shape and orientation in different territories. It also means that nest sites may not be in the most expected locations (and eagle nests are often not on the largest crags or in the most rugged part of a territory) and that there will be situations in which neighbouring pairs nest in quite close proximity and range away from one another, as can be inferred from Figure 3.

What is also not recognised by modelling techniques, but which is still well known, is the likelihood of there being secondary core areas in at least some territories. Gordon (1955) implied this when noting a pair of eagles which, in effect, occupied wintering grounds, and Walker (1991) found something similar. In the latter study, and again contrary to expectations, the secondary area provided red grouse while the primary (core) area provided none. This means that a standard assessment based on the presumed overriding importance of live prey would identify the secondary area as the most important part of the territory, even though it held no nests and had little, if any, relevance to the production of viable eggs. This also shows how territory use can be seasonal in a way that would not be recognised by statistical models.

The existence of primary and secondary core areas means that territories must also have areas of lesser use. However, this does not mean less value or importance to the whole, as they are still within the territory. Walker (1991) noted that a territory's two foraging areas did not form a contiguous area and that the land outside them provided connecting routes, flight corridors, some minor foraging opportunity in the form of carrion and corvids, and nursery areas for juveniles fledged at the site. Given that these areas were predominantly heavily-grazed grass moor with no live prey concentrations and lay more than three kilometres from the 'territory centre', predictive assessments would almost certainly ascribe them little value and potentially make them available for damaging changes of land use, even though they were essential to the resident eagles.

The relevance of distance from the so-called territory centre is of great importance and needs to be challenged. In the Lake District and Argyll studies, some foraging areas were located beyond areas without specific food sources and at a distance (up to nine kilometres from the nest) that would seem to preclude them from being part of the territory. Conversely, at the same time, there were areas much closer to the nests, less than three kilometres away, that were of little value to the eagles and which received very few or no visits over the course of a year. This will almost certainly be the case in other territories, and not only in isolated or larger ones. The idea of distance constraints that can be applied in management is a contrivance and an artefact of inappropriate assessment techniques.

That c.95% of the contacts with resident eagles are apparently made within six kilometres of the territory centre still largely results from nest and roost use. The value and importance of the core area are unquestionable, but the value of more remote areas cannot be determined by the comparative frequency of use. The core area will always produce at least twice as many contacts as other areas simply because the eagles breed, roost and loaf there.

Factor into the equation habitat and terrain variation, with their different fauna and foraging opportunities, and it becomes apparent that it is extremely difficult to produce accurate territory plans, and that determining use and value within these is neither predictable nor easily accomplished. To assume that these things are straightforward and to act on that basis will almost certainly destroy the viability of some golden eagle territories. The core area, in particular, must be correctly identified in the field before any decision is made about changes of land use.

SHARED AREAS

And so arises the complicating problem of overlapping territories, or shared foraging areas. Even though they have long been recognised (Watson 1957) and are probably much more common than is generally recognised or easily identifiable, they tend not to be considered in relation to land value or during fieldwork.

Overlapping territories do not exist simply where there is high population density and are probably most likely to occur, in fact, where there is low population density, as the birds probably wander more widely. This might suggest that eagle activity expands to utilise the available area but it can be seen that even isolated established territories have a finite size and definable area; the resident birds do not simply range out until they meet another, but range as far as is necessary. That said, it is probably the case that all territory boundaries are buffer zones rather than hard and fast separation points, and also that there is some fluidity to the boundaries.

It might be thought that areas of clear overlap would be of low value because they are not worth claiming or defending, but those examined appear to be of intermediate foraging value, being neither the best nor the worst available. This would suggest that the shared areas are integral to each of the relevant territories and that their use may be dependent on localised or seasonal variations in food availability or breeding performance. Territory use varies considerably between the different periods of a breeding season and is also different in successful, failed and non-breeding years at the same site, so shared land could be fully available without conflict to different pairs at different times.

The main difficulty in recognising shared areas is the ease with which eagles cover large areas, coupled with the frequency with which they make intrusions into neighbouring territories and the fact that the observed eagles are unlikely to be recognisable as individuals. The simple presence of an eagle in the same location on several days is not proof that the same eagle, or an eagle from the same pair, is being seen; that different eagles might be seen is also not proof of sharing. However, that non-territorial and immature-plumaged eagles actively use the known territories of established pairs does point to sharing being quite common and in a way that does not affect territoriality.

It should also be noted that sharing might not just involve two pairs and various immature-plumaged single birds. Because the available land is not neatly divided between pairs, it is not unusual for the birds of three different sites to use the same piece of ground. Though unusual, it is not impossible for six or more eagles to be seen simultaneously in such circumstances. This also shows why simple assumptions of status and association must be avoided; the chances of knowing the definitive relationship to that location of any of the eagles involved are very slim.

An associated problem is that of territory amalgamation. While it might seem logical that a remaining pair would usurp a neighbouring abandoned territory, the fact that the two territories had previously existed in isolation suggests that this would be unnecessary and unlikely, not least because the best foraging areas might not form a continuous area. Eagles, as already noted, commonly visit other territories, and seeing an eagle from one site inside another does not prove that the territories have been united. An example of this was seen in mid-Argyll, where birds from two adjoining territories, including family parties, were recorded inside an 'abandoned' site. Detailed observation, though, showed that the territory had not been amalgamated into either or shared between the others, but was just being visited or possibly even used as it may have been while still occupied. There may actually be very little difference in the amount and type of use given to the area by the remaining birds because total abandonment, rather than temporary vacancy, probably means that the site is no longer viable or attractive to eagles. Territory amalgamation is a conclusion that should only be reached after detailed and intensive field investigation; it cannot be determined on the basis of monitoring visits or by using the type of information collected during national surveys.

This point was highlighted during the 1992 national survey. During occupancy checks in February that year, all the relevant boxes were ticked in two adjoining territories but, in each, one of the birds was seen to be wing-tagged. The first question was, therefore, whether there were two pairs, one pair in two territories or one pair plus a resident with an intruder and, if so, which was which? Detailed searches proved that there was only one pair and after breeding began at one site, no more contacts were made with eagles at the second one. While the wing-tagged bird's presence at both sites may suggest territory amalgamation, one sighting is insufficient evidence on which to reach such a conclusion, and the lack of additional sightings further acts against it. Without a feature as obvious as a wing tag, the chances of unambiguously knowing that the same birds are definitely being seen in different locations are very slim, and most claims of territory amalgamation probably fail to consider all of the points relevant to shared, amalgamated sites and general intrusions.

TERRITORIAL ACTIVITY

Golden eagle territories can be very large and most will be made up of a complex combination of hills, ridges, glens, moorland and, possibly, coastline. As a result of size and terrain, most of the territory is usually out of sight of the resident eagles (and the observer) and perhaps most clearly so during the incubation period, when breeding eagles can have greatly reduced activity levels. Although eagles are more than capable of visiting all parts of their territory every day, it is generally impractical and unnecessary for them to do so and would also be unwise at certain times of year. For lengthy periods each year, during incubation and the nestling periods at successful sites, there is also usually only one resident eagle available to perform the territorial duties. This means that it is surprisingly easy for eagles to intrude and operate inside the territories of others and even for them to come quite close to the active nests of other pairs without being challenged, confronted or even known about.

As well as offering a possible explanation of why some people do not believe the golden eagle to be highly territorial, this also makes it very difficult to recognise territorial activity for what it is, a problem exacerbated by the fact that the amount and intensity of territorial activity varies across the year. In addition, and quite beside the problem of eagles sometimes being closer to their neighbours' nests than to their own, it is also difficult to know whether it is a resident or intruder that is being watched and whether or not the location in question is actually a relevant part of a territory at that time of year. Furthermore, territorial behaviour is not what many people believe it to be and what is taken as such often has no such relevance. An eagle's apparent behaviour is not always a good indicator of its status and most territorial behaviour involves little more than the bird's presence.

Flight displays such as the sky dance and high soaring are usually described as being, or primarily being, territorial displays (Watson 2010) but this is not the case and most territorial activity does not involve display flights. Such flights are certainly used to advertise territory occupancy but most performances are about pair bonding and are performed in situations where they would not be seen by other eagles. An additional problem with the idea that flight displays are indicative of territorial activity is that itinerant, unmated and non-territorial eagles perform exactly the same flight displays as territory-holding adults and will perform them inside the core areas of occupied territories, with or without the resident birds, without any signs of animosity, as well as inside vacant territories and in areas that are not territories; eagles from neighbouring pairs will also display inside their neighbour's territory. These situations also arise most commonly, but not exclusively, during the pre-laying period when most observers are trying to confirm site occupancy by seeing two eagles performing flight displays. Displays are used as territorial behaviour but they are not proof of it, nor of status; it should not be assumed that a displaying eagle is a territorial bird performing inside its own territory. These problems apply to both the sky dance and to soaring displays, with the latter, contrary to popular belief, also being extremely difficult to separate from soaring or high circling for other reasons.

The birds from more than one pair must be visible to the observer before any display can even be considered as territorial in nature. To apply this criterion quickly makes it apparent just how infrequently soaring or high circling can justifiably be called territorial, even when it is performed above the nesting area. Soaring display flights are more likely to be seen when the eagles from neighbouring pairs are close to their separation point but that does not necessarily mean that the boundary is midway between the two pairs. As soaring flights can occur in any part of a territory, they cannot be assumed to be occurring close to the separation point or related to territoriality.

Something similar can be said about the sky dance. While it is the most demonstrative display, it is mostly used close to the nest sites and when it cannot be seen by other eagles. When it is performed for the benefit of other eagles, it is also usually as advertisement rather than activity, and when it is performed with intruders it does not appear to be aggressive. It is also not a step of higher intensity than soaring; the territorial response is not incremental, or it might be the opposite of what may be expected. Distant intruders can appear to have elicited a robust response while those close to a nest might be almost ignored. Walker (2009) describes a spring incident where, after sky dancing with a resident, an intruder was ignored once it had passed over the nest ridge, even though it was clearly still within the core area. By contrast, in an autumn example from the same site, the residents directed a lengthy and intense bout of displaying at two eagles that were more than four kilometres away and outside the territory.

In effect, it is just an accepted assumption that flight displays are an integral and easily explained part of territorial activity. However, in reality, most truly territorial behaviour is very low key in nature and easily mistaken for other activity. One of the commonest forms of territorial behaviour is a simple straight-line flight which takes the resident towards, but not as far as, the intruder, usually because the latter withdraws before the former arrives. These can be called half-flights because, once the intruder begins to move away, the resident usually returns to its starting point, either to a perch or to circle over a central part of the territory.

Flights of this type are extremely common but a problem with recognising them for what they are (rather than viewing them simply as the actions of an eagle that changes its mind, perhaps having misjudged a foraging opportunity) is that observers tend to concentrate on the first bird they see, rather than looking for the stimulus of its actions. The observer needs to ignore the first bird and consider why it is travelling in a particular direction. In a similar way, other apparently simple ranging flights across the territory can have territorial connotations, the bird's presence often being a sufficient means of defence. This type of activity is often seen outside successful breeding seasons but a problem with its recognition is that few records are collected in outlying parts of the territory and/or when eagles fail to breed successfully.

It is not surprising that most territorial activity is low key and unobtrusive rather than being clearly demonstrative. As the golden eagle is a truly resident, long-lived and largely site-faithful species, the members of a population must be familiar with one another, must be aware of their active status (breeding or not breeding; successful or failed) and must have developed a working relationship to reduce the time spent in active conflict. The main reason why golden eagles have been thought not to actively defend their territories is probably because they do not have to continuously defend them against their nearest neighbours.

Territorial confrontations and even physical combat do occur, though, but this seems mostly to be associated with dominance within the population and confronting itinerant birds looking for partners. Confrontational encounters are actually quite commonplace but their intensity appears to vary with the age of the birds involved. Young immature-plumaged birds are generally tolerated, or elicit little response, unless they were reared in the site being visited. It is not at all unusual to see immature-plumaged birds in occupied territories during the breeding season and one was once watched as it flew past the active nest sites of three adjoining pairs without causing a reaction from any of the residents. However, uniquely marked (satellite-tagged) juveniles have been seen to be aggressively pursued by their parents when visiting the natal site in the spring after their birth. The more aggressive approach towards their own young probably results from the recognition that such birds have knowledge of the adults' routine and of the perches and roosts. This knowledge would make it easier for their presence to be disruptive and so merits a greater response. This was seen in Argyll where the disruptive presence of such young possibly caused non-breeding in two years.

Resident eagles often engage in lengthy encounters with older immature-plumaged birds but this is usually because the youngsters' status means that they do not have to retreat. With these birds also probably being sexually mature, they may be looking for vacancies and can afford to be disruptive in the long term.

TERRITORY USE

Even with the recognition that a territory will be divided into units of different value, its use by the resident golden eagles is still considered too simplistically. It is not something that can be determined on the basis of casual observations, by using predictive models or by applying subjective values. It is also not easily summarised because, to a large extent, use will be different in all territories. Use in relation to foraging will vary in line with food source availability seasonally, annually and on a day-to-day basis and so is highly dependent on the distribution of different food sources within the site.

The activity of territorial eagles may well be centred on the core area, on identifiable foraging areas that may be targeted for use and on food source availability, but all parts of the territory are used and a greater ranging area will be used over the course of a longer period of time. In line with the difficulty of correctly delineating territory boundaries, usage can vary on an annual and seasonal basis with not all of the known territory always being used in every year or in a way that is easily explained by considering habitat or food source distribution. Territories in which there appears to be little year-to-year change in circumstances still show variations in use.

As already noted, a change of bird in the pair can produce variations in territory use, as can breeding performance. It has been suggested that eagles breeding successfully use smaller areas than those which fail (Haworth *et al* 2006) but this is not supported by more detailed long term, year-round studies such as those in Argyll and England. For example, a greater than usual area is clearly used during the post-fledging period (Walker 1991), which is part of a successful breeding season, and some parts are used more intensively at such times than when breeding has failed. The annual use maps from Argyll also show there to be no pattern in this sense, with failed breeding years producing both the largest and the smallest recorded annual area, as well as there being overall annual differences and successful years producing different-sized areas. The preferred areas also had different amounts of use per year, because of variations in food source availability.

There are also likely to be subtler variations in use that only become apparent in long-term studies. Perhaps prime among these is gender variation in territory use. Long-term studies strongly imply that established territorial male eagles range more widely than their established mates and use outlying parts of the territory to a greater extent and with greater regularity. The female is more closely associated with the nest group at all times of year and regardless of breeding performance. This is partly the result of the differing roles played during the breeding season, of course, but it extends beyond this and to when no breeding attempt has been made or is in progress. In this way, while a territory or ranging area is usually taken to be the area used by a pair of eagles, it is, at least to some extent, the area used primarily by the male (Walker 1991). The female will use the total area but not to the same extent as its mate.

These points could influence the conclusions of studies relying on the number or frequency of contacts because while only one bird might be using the outer parts of a territory, its intensity of use, and therefore the value of the location, will probably be greater than may be inferred from the frequency of use.

It may appear that territory use is primarily associated with foraging activity but it is by no means uncommon to see eagles that have recently eaten (as shown by their distended crops) ranging over the greater territory area in a largely non-specific fashion, and birds returning to the roosting area outside the breeding season will often not follow a direct route but instead take in a broader area. This is probably a low-key form of territorial behaviour that allows the pair to demonstrate their presence over the greater area in a way that might deter casual intruders; although it may be thought that territories are most important during the breeding season, their security has to be maintained throughout the year.

Much of the territory use shown by juveniles and the accompanying adult also has little to do with the distribution of foraging areas and food sources; a juvenile's movements appear almost random, to be more investigative than selective. The greater territory area is also required to allow the semi-independent juvenile the opportunity to develop without interference from other eagles. What may appear to be little-used areas or areas with little real value may actually be vital to the development and long-term survival of juveniles.

What must also be taken into consideration when undertaking site assessments is that, while an established pair of eagles will cover all or almost all of their territory over the course of a year, they do not travel haphazardly within the site; there are flight corridors connecting the nesting area to the foraging grounds, and between the foraging grounds, that the eagles will follow with great regularity. When deliberately departing for an intended lengthy absence, eagles typically leave the nesting area in a particular direction or over a particular part of a ridge. There may be more than one such point, with use determined by the targeted foraging area, but they can be seen to be used with much greater frequency than other nearby points on the same ridge. The same routes are also commonly used when returning to the nesting area and often in preference to a more direct route. As a result, the point over which a bird will return with food can be predicted with some reliability if the routes are known to the observer.

To avoid the inclusion of in-and-out flights, such as when chasing other species, a minimum absence of ten minutes was used to produce Figure 4. In this, flights to the north-east took the departing eagle deeper into the core area where the main food sources were sheep, red deer and corvids, while those to the east and south-east took it to the nearest red grouse populations. It can be inferred from this that the mean nest location was not located centrally within the territory and that the birds ranged away from one corner of the site, even though there were no neighbours to constrain their movements.

Considering the departure routes can also lead to understanding the relative importance of the different foraging areas and eagles can be seen following these routes in an apparently casual fashion before more obviously foraging when they arrive at their

73

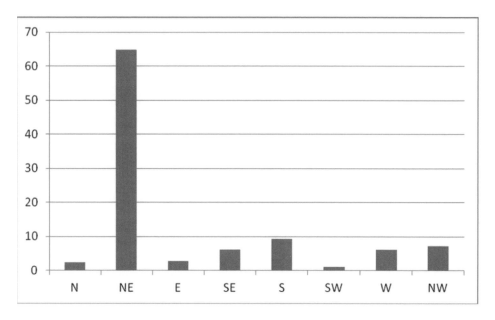

Figure 4: The directional proportion (% of annual total) of golden eagle movements away from the nesting valley over a six-year period in a Lake District territory.

destination. Distinctive routes can also link separate foraging areas but these are not always simple here-to-there routes. It is not unusual for an eagle to retrace its route, as if to a central or focal starting point, and then proceed along the next route rather than simply flying directly to the next area to be searched. There are a number of likely practical reasons for this: each starting point may provide a more advantageous approach, their presence may be less obvious prior to the next bout of foraging, and it may return the bird to a location from which the security of the nesting area can be determined.

A detailed assessment of activity shows that eagle movements are not random and demonstrates that it is possible to build up a detailed understanding of territory use in a way that explains what is being recorded. If a reliable site assessment is to be produced, it is insufficient simply to look at the distribution of food sources or the type of habitat involved. A great deal of territory use is not immediately linked to the actual food sources that are involved, even if use is ultimately linked to their distribution. Areas of apparently little value can form highly important access routes and juvenile development ground which, if lost or altered by changes in land use, could have a detrimental impact on territory quality and breeding performance.

DOMINANCE

The question of dominance is important but its existence is not generally recognised; almost all studies and fieldwork assume that eagles are of equal status, but this is not the case. An area in north Argyll was used by the eagles from three pairs, A, B and C (see Figure 3), its centre being roughly equidistant from the nest groups of A and B and slightly further from that of C. Observations suggested that Pair A dominated the others when in this location but was more dominant over Pair C than over Pair B. Pair B dominated Pair C but while subordinate to Pair A was not entirely subjugated by them. Birds from all three pairs could be seen in the location but while a Pair C bird always departed with the arrival of one of the others or was chased and sometimes engaged in physical combat if it did not (and always lost), Pair A and B birds often reacted to the others' presence by circling roughly one kilometre apart (regardless of their location) until Pair B eventually turned away. This type of dominance was also seen when examining the relationships between the other pairs within this population.

While subordinate eagles might be expected to have lower productivity than dominant pairs, the reality is more complex than that, as there is unlikely to be one pair with either over-riding dominance or total subordination. Here, while Pair A dominated the group, they did not dominate the adjoining Pair D and were only apparently equal to Pair E, which was subordinate to Pair B. In spite of apparently being the weakest of the group, Pair C had higher productivity than Pair E.

Dominance can obviously be down to the individual involved and a change of partner or any delay in replacing a partner could influence both the pair's status and the size and delineation of the territory. Although it did not necessarily allow them to breed more, or less, successfully, the strength of a relationship between neighbouring pairs certainly influenced the location of boundaries in Argyll, with some areas that would probably be expected to belong to one pair, the nearest, actually being dominated by another.

TERRITORY STABILITY

There is an interesting conclusion to be reached from the basic ideas about golden eagle territories. It is well known that many nesting areas have been in use for many decades, and golden eagles are said to occupy traditional locations. That their nests are usually in groups rather than being scattered at random means that these are also fairly traditional and because of this their distribution and the distribution of golden eagles could also be said to be traditional; by implication, then, territory delineation and use must also be fairly traditional.

While it might be thought that the situation is not this simple, it is difficult to present a counter argument based on the available evidence. Habitat and food source distribution, in the main, change very slowly and so do not necessitate great or regular change on the part of the eagles; breeding sites are abandoned when they cease to be viable and are not really incorporated into other sites; the nest groups rarely definitely become alternatives for a neighbouring pair; and if nest use does not change to any great extent, why should the ranging area change? When considering such points there is, of course, the ever-present problem of fieldwork concentrating on nest sites rather than on territories; there are very few locations in which territory use is sufficiently well known to allow any variations to be recognised.

There is evidence to counter this stability argument, however, and Table 3 provides an insight into how much variation can be recorded in a ranging area, with the implication of how much variation there might be within the established pattern of territory delineation. Here, only between c.35% and c.48% of the total recorded area was used per year and it could be argued that the other parts were available for use by other eagles, either in the form of shared areas or as dominated land. This may well be the case as only 38 out of 83 one-kilometre squares (c. 46% of total) produced regular records and could be said to equate to the actual territory. That said, there were also only twelve squares that actually produced records in every year, the core area.

Table 3: Number of 1-km squares used by resident golden eagles during a 12-year period in Argyll.

	# squares
Total	83
Regular use (overall)	38
Regular use (2nd six years)	31
12-yr mean	35
Used in all years	12
Only used in one year	20
Most per year	40
Fewest per year	29

However, none of the summarised numbers truly represented the territory because the annual maps, the pattern of area use per year, were all different. Beyond the core area there was no uniformity of use and annual use varied in a wholly unpredictable way and in a way that could not be linked to habitat type or food source distribution. There were longer-term changes to territory use as a result of these two factors but these had no influence during the final six years of the period when the annual area used was different in each year regardless of breeding performance. There were differences in use even when there were no differences in circumstance.

This is of great relevance to species and habitat management because no single year, nor any run of two, three or five consecutive years, provided a true record of total use, mean use, regular use or valued use; the area used in any year was not predictable. If this were also true within populations, the total area used by all the pairs would be different in every year. However, environmental impact assessments for developments such as windfarms are typically completed, and reach conclusions about eagle territories, after sometimes only three years of fairly superficial fieldwork.

Seasonal factors other than food availability are also influential in territory use, with successful breeding seasons at the Argyll study site resulting in the post-fledging use of ten one-kilometre squares that did not produce any other records during a six-year period. However, the same post-fledging squares were not used in all the successful years and breeding success or failure could not be used to predict the area used in any year, or at any time of year. Both the largest and smallest recorded areas involved failed breeding seasons and the areas used in successful seasons varied in both size and location outside the core area.

Figure 5 shows how these variations can be simplistically plotted and gives an idea of how the frequency of use and how annual and total value of a location is neither predictable nor easily recognised. It also shows that territory use did not radiate evenly around the 'territory centre' (in finer detail, the 'territory centre' is not even actually in the core area based on food source availability although, as suggested above, it does lie on the very edge of this).

Figure 5: Schematic representation of a golden eagle ranging area showing the number of years in which each 1-km grid square was visited by the resident pair during a twelve-year period. One record equals one year. The shaded square holds the mean nest location.

									1				
								1	1				
								1	1	1			
								1	1				
								1	1				
							4	4	5	1	1		
						1	5	11	10	5	4		
							11	12	12	11	7	2	
					4	5	7	10	12	12	12	11	3
1	4	2	3	5	9	11	12	12	**12**	10	1		
1	0	3	4	6	10	11	12	12	12	12	5		
		3	4	5	6	7	4	7	2	10	8	2	
1	3	4	2	3	4	3	3	2					
							1		2	1			
									1				

As the variations in annual use seen in this study largely took place within the area of regular use, it is probably safe to conclude that similar variations will occur in other territories. This supports the idea that territory areas and boundaries are more fluid and more dependent on annual circumstances than is generally realised. It also means that it will be almost impossible to predict reliably the likely impact of any intrusive change of land use outside the core area, where it would be hugely detrimental.

In fact, the majority of territories will see almost annual changes in their make-up and use and will have seen major changes over their lifetime of occupancy. Even the apparently least changed territories, perhaps those in the deer forests of the western mainland, will be different now from how they were 20 or 30 years ago, as has been seen in the north Argyll study area. Because change can be a slow process, it is not always easily recognised and is sometimes not noticed until it has passed beyond a critical point; without proper surveys it cannot always be said that a food source is declining until it has almost disappeared, because a drop in availability may, at first, be thought to be a cyclical event, something that might correct itself.

It is often only the most obvious of things that is noted and this can lead to the wrong conclusion. For example, while Gregory (2011) claimed that an Argyll territory was abandoned because of a windfarm, that territory was apparently without resident eagles before the windfarm was constructed (Gregory *et al* 2003). In this case, the problem that caused the original vacancy can no longer be identified because it was not seen to be influential or examined when it was relevant; that the territory was reoccupied after construction of the windfarm only complicates the matter even further.

As long-lived birds, golden eagles will see many changes to their territories and can undoubtedly adapt to some of these in a way that permits successful breeding to be continued. This can happen in the face of quite major changes of land use, fragmentation of the territory or with greatly increased human activity, which might suggest that the changes had little impact. Experience is almost certainly a key factor in this so, as well as influencing breeding performance, a change of partner may also alter territory use and delineation. Not only does the new bird have little or no experience of the location when it settles, but it will be unaware of its boundaries and may range differently to its predecessor. In Argyll, the replacement of a male coincided with a smaller total area being used and similar effects - a decrease in the regular use of certain territory units - have been recorded elsewhere following a change of partner. Such changes could result in ground being lost to neighbouring pairs and reduced breeding performance. The impact of a change may also be dependent on the replacement bird's age, gender and general physicality, all of which can influence status within the population.

How the various changes act on both occupancy and breeding performance can be seen or inferred but they must not be assumed and it must not be thought that only major or clearly intrusive changes can have damaging impacts. It is quite clear that if located unsympathetically, even comparatively small changes of land use can have detrimental effects, as implied by Whitfield *et al* (2009). Similar situations have arisen elsewhere, with some vacated territories appearing little changed from when they were occupied and successful. In these, it is probably the importance of the affected location rather than the scale of the change that is most influential.

It can be seen that, contrary to the general impression, and while they may have some permanence, golden eagle territories are not easily predictable: they are not determined by distances from an arbitrary location, by direction, habitat or topography. To believe that they are unchanging or only changing when change is seen is almost to condemn them to negative change and almost certainly to allow major and intrusive changes to occur without a suitable appraisal of their likely impact.

OTHER SITUATIONS

Some consideration must also be given to single and non-territorial eagles. Neither category is composed entirely of immature-plumaged birds or of birds that do not demonstrate some residency; both will include birds that have lost their mates and those in adult plumage that have never paired.

It is usual for the surviving member of a pair to retain its territory, mostly because abandoning it, even in search of a new mate, is to risk being usurped or missing breeding opportunities. Observations of known birds in the Lake District and Argyll suggest that survivors will visit other areas as if searching for a new mate but also that the survivor will spend most of its time in its home base. At the time of writing, a Lake District male eagle which is not known to have made any breeding attempts and has been without a mate for more than eleven years, is almost constantly present in the territory and appears to use it in exactly the same way as when it had a mate. Something very similar was seen in Argyll, where a female was without a mate for 18 months but continued to occupy and use the territory as if paired.

Given that the Lake District eagle would appear to have little chance of gaining a mate in such an isolated location, the fact that it has not left to seek out a vacancy within the easily reachable population probably shows that the bond is with the territory, rather than to a mate. That the Argyll site was visited by at least five other eagles when the resident was without a mate also suggests that the incomer makes the decision to stay because of the territory rather than because of the other eagle. The incomer probably makes a decision on what it encounters during what might be a prospecting settling-in period.

In addition to these, some eagles occupy locations as territories without ever having had a mate. Surveys in the south of Scotland in the 1980s and 1990s produced evidence of golden eagles, including birds in full adult plumage, in several locations that were not and did not become paired territories. These may be initially thought of as the pioneers of a failed population expansion, or the result of there being too few eagles for all to be paired, but they (and those known about in other areas) actually appear to be birds that had decided to settle in locations that were not suitable for pairs. While these eagles behave as if in established territories (with roosts and sometimes nests) they do not attract partners or partners that remain in the long term.

These birds are different to those in immature plumage which may temporarily occupy a location and develop regular roosts. Such birds not unusually use vacant territories as safe havens, as these generally provide some foraging opportunity as well as security from other eagles. One such location, a territory without breeding attempts since the late 1980s which is now predominantly plantation forest, has been found to be in use (with roosts) by a succession of immature-plumaged eagles in every year since 1997 without breeding being confirmed. This is one reason why a territory used for breeding in the recent past should never be said to be abandoned: in the face of potential changes of land use, the fact that there is not a resident pair or breeding attempts does not mean that the location is of no value to golden eagles, nor that there will be no breeding attempts in the future, as has happened in more than one 'long-abandoned' territory.

Immature-plumaged eagles that are not a part of the breeding population may have more than one safe haven in the area over which they range. This is because such birds tend to utilise much larger areas than do established pairs, with their ranging areas perhaps the equivalent of four or five breeding territories once they have settled after an initial year or so of wandering more widely after independence. These are the birds that are most difficult to study and for which the use of satellite telemetry should provide a greater insight, provided it is accepted that the results are about the bird's location and not the reasons for its presence; that can only be determined in the field.

The eagles in all of these categories and situations exploit the available land and food sources and often concentrate their activities as if in a core area. They can also be seen performing flight displays, including high circling above the roosting area or when other eagles are sighted, and sky dancing both alone (in a way that may be thought of as trying to attract a mate) or with any other eagle that may be present. They commonly start and sometimes complete nests and there are even occasional breeding attempts but, because there is usually a turnover of birds and because the location is not good enough for successful breeding in the long term, these seldom amount to anything and are typically not repeated with any frequency. Such temporary territories are not at all unusual and have been recorded in many areas.

In other words, from about a year or so after leaving the nest, most, if not all, golden eagles behave as if they are occupying territories. Their chosen or preferred location may be larger than a typical breeding territory and some birds may never wander far from there during the remainder of their lives and, as a result, may never make a breeding attempt.

In summary, the factors relating to territories are by no means clear cut and easily explained. There is a general perception that 'territories' are understood and that generalised conclusions can be applied in all situations but that is not the case, and detailed site-specific investigation is required before reliable conclusions can be reached. This is especially important when any change of land use is being proposed.

FOOD AND FORAGING

It has already been noted that the golden eagle is a hunter-gatherer rather than a true predator. A failure to recognise this point increases the subjectivity of assessments and interpretations and can result in mismanagement of the species. Accepting the eagle as a hunter-gatherer increases objectivity and can, at the very least, help to explain some of the apparent anomalies that may be encountered, such as why some pairs of eagles repeatedly breed successfully in territories that appear to be of low quality. This point requires more careful consideration than is usually the case if only because, while red deer and sheep are often thought to be simply sources of carrion, they are actually also sources of live prey. To view them predominantly as carrion, as in Watson *et al* (1992), or to largely dismiss them as food sources, as in Haworth and Fielding (2013), is to undervalue their potential importance to territory quality and breeding performance. Unfortunately, such misunderstandings are common and as a result food, and more especially the availability of certain live prey species, has always acted as a catch-all explanation for the recorded breeding performance and even for territory occupancy.

Food and foraging is one of the most commonly recorded elements of golden eagle ecology but the type of information collected also makes it one of the topics about which there are most preconceived ideas, assumptions and subjectivity. This is because most of the accumulated data and opinions are of a casual or incidental nature and typically the result of selective sampling in one form or another. It is also one of the most contentious issues and the reason for most of the persecution suffered by golden eagles.

It must be remembered that food remains recorded at nests during successful nestling periods mostly represent the nestling's diet rather than that of the adults; they do not represent what the adults require to enable them to breed successfully nor what the adults depend on at other times of year, and not what allows the territory to be occupied with breeding attempts. A record of diet collected during successful breeding attempts also does not and cannot be used to explain breeding failures or low productivity.

In spite of the impression given by the received wisdom and the confidence of many pronouncements it is surprising just how little is actually known about the way in which food influences the various aspects of golden eagle ecology. Most people would agree that food supply influences breeding performance (Newton 1979), but it is not known at what levels this influence occurs or what influences the different breeding results, even in the same territory. Our knowledge also fails to explain how food supply influences everything from why juvenile eagles leave the natal territory at a certain time and later settle in one location and not another, through territory occupancy and use to nesting density and survival. In spite of this, when considering territory quality, a subjective and superficial interpretation of food supply has usually proven to be sufficient grounds on which to reach a conclusion.

It needs to be recognised that the value of even apparently robust scientific research is typically limited by selective monitoring, small sample size, a failure to consider food source availability or depletion by other species and by the inappropriate use of the eagle's recorded diet.

Failing to acknowledge these limitations can have major consequences for species management and conservation because it leads to the conclusion that territories with low productivity must have fewer resources and therefore be less valuable than productive sites. But these ideas are not necessarily correct (and have been shown to be quite the opposite in some cases) because the reasons for most breeding failures and low productivity are not known. However, the assumption that the link is with food is very strong so workers often fall into the trap of seeing what they expect to see in a way that supports what they presume to be correct.

It is probably in relation to changes of land use that the reliance on received wisdom is most apparent, with environmental impact assessments seldom, if ever, looking at actual food availability but almost inevitably reaching conclusions about the impacts of change and the suitability of locations in relation to food supply or foraging activity. This generic approach is potentially very damaging to golden eagle conservation because it ultimately results in inexperienced people providing inappropriate guidance for use in management policy that cannot be challenged. A simple example of this would be Haworth and Fielding (2013) and Fielding and Haworth (2014) both using the term 'prey' instead of 'food'. In doing this, they reduce the apparent value of carrion and the species and habitats that produce carrion in ways that could make it easier for territories or particular locations within sites to be deemed suitable for intrusive changes of land use.

When considering food, it must first and foremost be recognised that very few reliable conclusions can be reached about any element of eagle ecology on the basis of what is seen during normal breeding season fieldwork.

ASSESSMENT

While the food eaten by golden eagles, as demonstrated by pellet analysis and the counting of prey remains at nests, has been widely reported this, the recorded diet, is not a measure of food availability nor of the influence that food has on breeding performance. It is a simple record of exploitation. The fact that a certain species is present in the diet does not make that species important or irreplaceable.

Although some of the biases associated with pellets and prey remains have long been recognised, they continue to be major sources of information and fieldworkers often make determined efforts to collect and record them. This type of information is actually of little real value because it will not represent an accurate cross-section of the diet nor be a true indication of the scale of exploitation. For example, a hare might be killed by the male eagle which then partially eats it before carrying the carcass to the nest where it is eaten by both the female and the nestlings. As a result, that single prey item can be represented in the pellets produced by four different birds and also found as pluckings, carcass and skeletal remains. Although careful studies use the minimum possible number of items in a set of results, there could still be a reluctance to reduce seven pieces of evidence to only one item.

Something very similar applies to carrion; the number of feeds taken from a carcass, and the number of birds feeding from it, cannot be determined by looking at it. Also, the amount of indigestible material consumed varies with the different feeds (an eagle opening a carcass eats more wool, fur or hair than one feeding where the flesh has been exposed) so the same carcass can be represented in numerous pellets, or none at all if only meat or organs are consumed. Such points are still widely overlooked and have undoubtedly influenced the results of numerous studies and the way in which the importance of carrion is considered.

A pair of eagles will have more or less the same food requirements in all years but breeding success clearly requires additional food to be obtained during April to September. However, as breeding success (the first step being the production of viable eggs) is ultimately determined prior to egg laying (Newton 1979), the influence of food on breeding can really only be determined by detailed pre-laying studies. No such detailed studies have been undertaken until very recently and earlier ones which have claimed to consider this point are actually some of the most selective and superficial, limiting the species considered, walking transects rather than performing surveys, not being territory-specific and combining the pre-laying and incubation period results. When assessing carrion availability, Watson *et al* (1992) even deliberately avoided the locations most likely to produce carrion. As correctly determining the location of foraging areas is by no means straightforward and as food source distribution within territories is not predictable, it is easy to see how a study presumed to be reliable can be influential while simultaneously almost meaningless.

It must be stressed and understood that walking the hills does not produce a reliable assessment of food or food source availability. For example, the number of grouse flushed during a walk may provide no indication of the numbers actually present; the observer might flush the only six grouse in a territory or only six of a thousand. Flushing the so-called main prey species encourages the belief that they are important, but availability can be very different from what may be perceived during ordinary fieldwork, not least because the observer might actually see more crows than grouse but pay them little attention.

Such failings mean that sample size is also an important limiting factor that is often overlooked or disguised. Haworth *et al* (2009, discussed in Watson 2010) report on more than 2,000 prey items in what appears to be a major study, but the data come from more than 90 territories – a mean sample, in other words, of only about 22 items per site if it was only a one-year study. Were it a more suitable three- or five-year study, the sample could be as little as five items per site per year, when the resident pair alone are likely to feed on more than 700 occasions per year, so the sample size is far too small to be truly representative. With the key findings of this superficial work, as reported in Watson (2010), including the fact that eagles will eat whatever may be available and that most breeding failures occur during the egg stage, this report, commissioned by Scottish Natural Heritage, did not produce ground-breaking revelations or, indeed, tell us anything that was not already known.

It must also be recognised that food sources can be concentrated rather than spread evenly or thinly across a territory, meaning that they can be missed during site visits. While Haworth and Fielding (2013) suggest that prey concentrations are unusual and mainly restricted to rabbit warrens and seabird colonies, the reality is that most food sources are found in concentrations. For example, red grouse are concentrated in heather-dominated areas (and can be noticeably localised in some areas) and ptarmigan on the higher ground, while hill waders such as curlew and golden plover can provide both spatial and seasonal concentrations. Some red deer calving grounds could also be described as concentrated food sources.

The same applies to carrion; while little carrion will occur on land that is not grazed by sheep or red deer, it will occur on grazed land and there are seasonal concentrations due to peaks and troughs in availability. While sheep and deer also often appear to die in fairly random locations, there are places in which more deaths occur than might be expected. These can be certain points along precipitous paths from which animals fall, certain mossy bog-holes and ditches in which animals become stuck and even sheltered gathering or herding points. These dying-zones are not necessarily easy to find and their locations are not easily predicted; the point at which most crag-fall deaths occur might not be the location that seems to be the most dangerous to humans (because they have grasping hands that give confidence in tricky situations) and a gathering point may simply be a slight hollow on a hillside that provides some additional shelter from poor weather conditions. This also makes assessing carrion availability much more difficult than is generally appreciated, because the concentration point is not always along the route most likely to be followed by the observer.

There is another major problem with reaching conclusions about the influence of food on breeding performance when using a simplistic approach: many female eagles appear to lay their first egg of the year on more or less the same date in most years. For example, at Haweswater in the Lake District (where the onset of incubation was known with absolute certainty, thanks to the efforts of the RSPB wardens) the first egg-laying date, with one exception, varied by only a day or two around 24 March throughout the period 1982-1997. However, that bird's predecessor appeared to lay on about 27 March and the female at a second Lake District pair laid on or about 16 March each year. Similar examples of this near- regularity have been noted at Scottish sites for which a series of accurate laying dates are known. This stability in a female's laying date, which does not appear to influence breeding results, suggests that food may have little real relevance to the onset of breeding. If food was really influential in that way, each female's laying date would be much more variable because of variations in food availability.

An additional consideration under this heading that has the potential to influence the interpretation of results is that the cause of many, if not most, breeding failures is not known. Even the effects of persecution are not always easily identified and it is usually the case that a failure is not noted until some time after the event. Because of expectations, when there is no obvious cause of failure, the reason is usually assumed to be food supply, especially if it can be linked to the apparent availability of live prey, but there are many other potential causes of failure.

Another problem is that, in spite of the accepted importance of the pre-laying food supply, most assessments deal with annual biomass. There may, however, be insurmountable problems associated with assessments of seasonal availability, not least of which being that all live animals are available as prey until they die and most individuals will remain available throughout the year. Seasonal and daily food availability is therefore always likely to be in excess of requirements, even without the inclusion of carrion. This point may even make assessments of food supply in established territories redundant and a complete waste of time.

All these points, and those to be raised in more specific terms, must be borne in mind if a competent assessment of food availability is to be attempted. If assessments are to be attempted they must target individual territories to have any real value, because area assessments have no relevance, and they must encompass entire territories, all habitats and all potential food sources, not just the core area or where food is expected to be found. Food availability varies within and between years so assessments must continuously consider availability over a number of years; and each food source or species must be surveyed using an appropriate species-specific method. Most of all, food availability should not be linked to breeding failure or low productivity unless the connection has been proven.

LIVE PREY

The importance of live prey to golden eagles has been overstated; the idea of its great importance largely results from calling the eagle a predator rather than a hunter-gatherer, by selective sampling that has focussed attention on certain species and by concentrating recording effort during successful nestling periods. This overstated importance has resulted in numerous misconceptions and the failure to recognise other potentially influencing factors. For example, Haworth and Fielding (2013) suggest that a lack of live prey is the most likely explanation for the golden eagle's generally low breeding performance, when there are many other and varied potential causes of failure that might affect the same territory in different years, but which might seem more difficult to prove.

Although commonly included in studies, there is little point in listing the species known to have been killed by golden eagles. Prey lists can be extremely misleading as they are usually biased towards what is found at or close to a successful nest (or highlight what might be considered to be unusual prey) and so may only show the results of targeted or opportunistic rather than general foraging. There have also been too few extensive year-round studies to give prey lists any meaningful value. Suffice to say that golden eagles are capable of killing the adults and/or young of just about any land animal they are likely to encounter in Scotland.

In spite of these things, it has commonly been said that species such as mountain hare, rabbit and red grouse are typical golden eagle prey species but this, clearly, can only be the case where they exist in relatively large numbers. There are many Scottish eagles that have little, if any, access to one, two or all three of these species. In fact, during about 25 years of monitoring the most productive site in north Argyll, these species were never seen alive in the territory, as prey in the nest or as remains in pellets. These species are only considered to be typical prey because much more fieldwork has been performed where they are numerous than where they are not. As a result, their general absence has been used to explain low productivity, even though their absence does not prevent successful breeding.

The presumed value of certain species is also influenced by inappropriate survey methods which effectively reduce the value of assessments as many commonly-taken species, such as hooded crow, are generally excluded from surveys. These exclusions (and the failure to recognise sheep and red deer as sources of live prey) further reduce the apparent availability of live prey in a way that can be used to explain low breeding performance and which can ultimately act as justification for a change of land use. However, while the locations supporting the so-called most important prey species may be protected against change, more damage may be caused by altering land use in other parts of the territory. If the other potential prey species are excluded or undervalued in assessments, the way in which food supply is expected to influence breeding performance becomes much easier to see. The other potential live prey species are also not alternative food sources because they are often the primary live prey sources; grouse and hares are often the additional sources where they are not present in large numbers.

The idea of live prey being more or less essential to successful breeding, or even that eagles preferentially kill prey for their nestlings, is, while not a complete fallacy, certainly misleading. Many golden eagles feed extensively on carrion prior to laying viable eggs and take carrion to their nestlings. The former is often overlooked and the latter usually missed or denied because it is less easy to recognise than is the evidence of killed prey.

Walker (1987) implied that the value of live prey became most obvious during the confinement period after fledging, with juveniles effectively only being provided with freshly-killed prey even though carrion was available and easily accessed. Additional work at this site (Walker 1988; 2004) showed later juveniles feeding extensively on carrion when there was lower live prey availability and them subsequently reaching independence at an earlier age than their predecessors. Even so, this use of carrion was the simple exploitation of a food source and there was nothing to suggest that the later juveniles were weaker or had lower survival chances than those fed exclusively on freshly-killed prey.

Live prey availability also shows strong seasonal variations; when considering the influence of the so-called important species, their available biomass peaks in the late summer and early autumn rather than during pre-laying or the nestling period. Their practical availability actually declines towards the eagle's laying and hatching dates, meaning that they can have little value even when present. This helps to show why resident species that are often considered to be of low importance can be much more influential than may be presumed and why certain species cannot be said to be more essential than others to breeding success, they are all simply a part of the available biomass.

Summer visitors, such as curlew and golden plover, add to the live prey availability in some areas but will have little influence on a territory's suitability for breeding. By contrast, the seasonally-available young of red deer are probably essential for breeding success in some territories. At the above-mentioned North Argyll site, and in some of its neighbours, they were probably the most numerous medium- to large-sized prey item available during the nestling period. As already noted, this last source of live prey is often overlooked, with even major studies failing to consider red deer as anything other than carrion.

Small mammals and small birds also often fail to be considered on the grounds that they are not important, even though it is well known that eagles eat voles and pipits.

While they will not be a defining part of the diet, they can still help to achieve the daily requirement and Walker (1991) described how they can be virtually farmed in order to keep the nestling placated. Just as it should not be believed that certain species are fundamentally more important than others, so value should also not be related to size. The daily food requirement does not have to be achieved with a single kill or one feed, but can be achieved with several small kills and feeds.

CARRION

Many, and probably most, golden eagles feed extensively on carrion, most usually in the form of dead sheep and dead red deer, but other animal carcasses are also used, with even dog and horse being recorded (Walker 2004). While it might be thought or implied that carrion is mostly used during the late winter and incubation periods, this does not preclude its use at other times of year, including during successful breeding attempts. It is not at all unusual for a breeding pair to feed from carrion, the female commonly doing so when relieved from the nest during the incubation period, and both adults might do so when there is a chick in the nest. In spite of this, Watson (2010) states that eagles take little carrion during the summer months and, if this is taken at face value, carrion feeding could be seen to imply poor territory quality, but it is really only evidence of eagles using a food source.

Carrion is available throughout the year but, as with live prey species, it also shows annual and seasonal variations in amounts and availability. There may be thought to be more carrion available during the pre-laying period but it is well known that red deer mortality actually peaks in about April and into May (coincidental with the eagle's late incubation and early nestling periods), and that sheep mortality has a minor peak in the autumn months. Given the number of problems that can result in large herbivore deaths, there are usually few lengthy periods in a year when carrion is not available and when it is not used.

It must also be recognised that, as well as seasonal and annual variations in carrion availability, there can also be more precise temporal variations that may have a major influence on breeding performance. Walker (2004) not only noted that pre-laying carrion amounts varied between years but also that the temporal distribution of carcasses varied within years, with the implied result that the eagles in question were more likely to lay fertile eggs when the weekly fresh carrion amounts increased towards the usual laying date than when weekly amounts declined towards that date. Such variations in availability and their effects are likely to go unnoticed at most sites and this example also shows how simply counting and estimating the age of carcasses on one day is an insufficient means of measuring carrion availability or value. The period with the lowest carrion availability is mid-summer and it is the month of June when many eagles appear to have the greatest difficulty in obtaining food of any type.

As already noted, and contrary to what has often been said, carrion is deliberately taken to nestlings. Stillborn and other dead deer calves and lambs are readily gathered and even the limbs from adult carcasses may be taken to the nest. Eagles may seem to prefer to take freshly- killed prey to the nestling but carrion is neither ignored nor apparently detrimental to the health, growth or survival of their young.

Although there is a tendency to believe that live prey is the be all and end all of golden eagle ecology, this is simply not the case and eagles can survive and breed successfully where their diet includes a large proportion of carrion. Too many unreliable conclusions have been reached about territory quality and breeding performance in the belief that carrion is a second-rate food source.

FOOD SOURCES

There is a general progression of food source availability across the year which golden eagles exploit when appropriate. While eagles will exploit resident species at all times, it could be said, simply, that the timing of different availability allows sheep sources to be replaced by deer sources (adults, then young, in both cases), followed by summer visitors such as waders, followed by the young and surplus members of resident species such as hare and grouse, which are principally available from mid-summer and into the winter. Other resident species, including crows and raven, or fulmar and gulls where appropriate, are taken throughout the year, along with those often considered to be of little importance or of only opportunistic value, such as fox. Given the importance that is conferred on the hare and grouse species, it is worth repeating that their numbers and practical availability decrease towards the eagles' laying date; in other words, they have lower availability when food is most required to attain breeding condition. By contrast, the commonly ignored hooded crow can be highly visible and available during the pre-laying period.

Food sources are selected and utilised because they are available, not because they are in some way better than others, and the presence of so-called 'unusual' species in the diet should not be interpreted as having any great relevance. The mindset at work with these ideas is illustrated in Watson (2010) where a section headed 'unusual prey' states that field voles and fox cubs are not uncommon as prey. This contradiction shows the unwillingness to accept that such species can have genuine value to golden eagles as an integral part of the diet and that their use is not evidence of desperation, food shortage or unusual behaviour. Part of the problem is again the lack of detailed evidence and the assumption that broad statements based on casual observations must be reliable.

It must be appreciated that the proportion of each food type or species in the diet of any pair of eagles will also vary with time. This is not simply the result of the type of cyclical population fluctuations associated with hares and grouse as the numbers and availability of all species change between and within years. Golden eagles will exploit whichever food source is most exploitable; they do not stop breeding simply because one species is less available in some years than it is in others. For example, at an Argyll study site, red grouse was the most numerous nest area remains in one year that produced two chicks, while the most numerous in another two-chick year was rabbit. Whether the diet was 'dominated' by grouse or rabbit (if that was actually the case) made no difference to the eagles.

Although all species reproduce each year, the way in which that alters food availability and exploitation across the year is also commonly overlooked. For example, when a species becomes more numerous because of juveniles, it becomes more easily exploited so, where appropriate, red grouse predation increases as the year progresses because there are more red grouse, not because red grouse are an essential food source; when available, other species can be targeted in preference. Put more simply, the fact that a species is present in an eagle territory is not proof that the eagles depend on it at any time.

Furthermore, given the comparative scarcity of the so-called important food sources in the Argyll study site (red deer, mountain hare and ptarmigan being absent and red grouse and rabbits being available only in relatively small numbers), along with habitat factors and a history of low productivity, a typical assessment of this territory, such as that suggested by Whitfield *et al* (2008), would conclude it to be of low quality and close to abandonment, but that could not be the case, as it produced two broods of two young in a three-year period, and six young in seven years overall. Why these eagles failed to rear young in other years, and failed even to lay eggs in some years, cannot be linked to food because the same sources were available in about the same amounts in all of the years under consideration.

This illustrates one of the major problems with snapshot assessments that rely on standard knowledge: they are simply too superficial to allow reliable conclusions to be reached. The food remains found during nest visits to ring the Argyll site chicks was not representative of the eagles' diet nor of food availability in the territory, and had the nest been visited a week earlier or later, the observed remains would probably have been different.

FOOD REQUIREMENTS

As with so many contentious issues, a consideration of the amount of food eaten by golden eagles has led to much debate, speculation, many unreliable claims and not a small amount of ambiguity. The main reason for this is that the issue of food requirements has never been properly investigated in spite of the degree of certainty with which it is discussed.

There have been no real attempts accurately to assess the amount of food that wild golden eagles require to survive, to occupy a location, to make breeding attempts or to breed successfully. Even so, the figure given by Brown and Watson (1964), based on records from captive birds, remains the accepted standard upon which numerous conclusions are based. Not knowing the true figure means that territory assessments, explanations for territory occupancy and the reasons for variable breeding performance are not only all likely to be based on unreliable evidence, but also on an interpretation that is unlikely to be correct.

This situation is exacerbated by attempts to convert the estimated requirement into food items. Initially presented by Brown and Watson (1964) but repeated by Watson (2010) the annual requirement has been said to be the equivalent of two dead sheep, 70 mountain hare and 140 red grouse or, alternatively, one red deer stag, 110 rabbits and 160 ptarmigan; to these suggestions can be added the equivalent of less than one elephant.

Suggesting the number of items that equal requirements is entirely irrelevant, misleading, results in biased assessments and is potentially very damaging to golden eagle conservation. The insistence on using the typically preselected food sources in these examples immediately ascribes them greater than likely importance, devalues other food sources and reduces the potential that may be apparent in the field. Conversely, the implied number of required items may also lead to habitat potential being overestimated; if a territory need only supply the numbers suggested, then it is easy to conclude that a location is suitable for golden eagles when it is not. This has great relevance to management such as reintroduction or recovery projects that are already likely to have an overly optimistic outlook; the collected evidence will always support the desired outcome.

The previously published assessments also give the impression that eagles might not try to feed every day and this supports the common belief that eagles choose to feed and fast. The latter term is grossly misleading. Golden eagles do not fast. There may be days on which they do not feed but most spells without feeding are periods of enforced starvation, not fasting. Indeed, rather than fasting after a large feed, eagles have been seen to gorge on carrion on a series of consecutive days (Walker 2009). The concept of fasting is a romantic notion based on assumptions and inadequate observation time. During detailed, intensive year-round studies it is highly unusual not to see eagles feeding, or showing signs of having recently fed (such as having a distended crop) on any day away from prolonged periods of severe weather that physically limit their foraging opportunities.

The idea of gorging and fasting is also impractical and not a suitable survival strategy; deliberate fasting is to risk harmful starvation in the belief that more and sufficient food would be easily available whenever it is required, but during the winter the need to feed after a period of fasting could easily coincide with the onset of several days of severe weather during which they cannot feed. It seems more likely (and winter observations and the numerous observed short feeds at all times of year would suggest this) that eagles feed often enough to remain constantly well fed, and are probably only occasionally truly in need of food.

The daily food requirement is the mean figure of what an eagle needs to survive but, of course, the amount actually consumed is likely to vary on a daily and seasonal basis. Brown and Watson (1964) concluded that each eagle requires about 230 gm (c.5% of body weight) of food per day (c.84 kg per bird or c.168 kg per pair per year). Also working largely with 'captive' birds, studies of the bald eagle (Stalmaster and Gessaman 1982) and the white-tailed eagle (Love 1983) have suggested greater requirements. It is implied that smaller species, such as the golden eagle, would require proportionately more food and this suggests that golden eagle food requirements are probably closer to c.10% of mean body weight, or c.440 gm per bird per day, c.160kg per bird per year, or c.320 kg per pair per year.

Direct observations also suggest that the figure of 230 gm is far too low (Walker 1991). This is evidenced by many examples of watching the same birds taking two complete feeds on carrion per day, seeing the same bird making and feeding from two crow kills per day and by seeing eagles killing prey and feeding after having fed on carrion, and seeing them feed on most days. Detailed observations from a wide variety of locations also show that eagles kill and feed with much greater regularity than has been implied. That most observers seem to see very few kills (Gordon 1955; Crane and Nellist 1999 and Watson 2010) is the result of the fieldwork methodology rather than the absence of predation or feeding.

To add to the argument against the figure of 230 gm a day is a calculation of what that might equate to: it is roughly the equivalent of one half of a crow, one third of a grouse, one fifth of a rabbit and about one tenth of a mountain hare, after wastage has been excluded. Based on this, and many hundreds of observed kills and feeds, the often repeated figure is simply unbelievable, golden eagles must require more than 230 gm of food per day. With this in mind, it is interesting to note that uninterrupted eagle feeds from carrion commonly last for about 25 minutes, as does feeding on red grouse and rabbit; crow feeds tend to be of shorter duration. The time taken to complete an uninterrupted feed provides an indication of the amount eaten and this shows that the typical daily requirement is definitely more than half a crow.

Because a golden eagle's actual food requirements are likely to vary according to the time of year, an annual assessment would again probably be of little value. However, it would be expected that requirements would be greatest during the harshest and coldest periods of winter weather when, even on clear days, there might only be eight or nine hours of daylight. This would still seem to be sufficient time in which to find food even if there are fewer live prey species and individuals and less carrion available at this time of year. The daily winter requirement may well be twice the accepted or mean figure but that should not be taken as evidence to support the influence that food or live prey is presumed to have on breeding performance, because food availability is always likely to be much higher than is thought.

FOOD AVAILABILITY

Raising the estimated food requirement not only increases the amount of food the eagles have to find, but also increases the amount of food a territory has to supply to be viable. This may seem to be a useful idea, given the general difficulty in explaining why eagle pairs are unproductive or why a breeding attempt has failed, but most failures and non-breeding are probably not linked to food supply. It is probably safe to say that all territories will provide a sufficient food supply or they would not be permanently occupied, but the subject is still clouded by uncertainties.

What may be forgotten is that there will be cut-off points that determine whether or not an area is suitable for golden eagles, whether there is sufficient food for survival, egg laying, producing fertile eggs, hatching young, nestling survival and juvenile survival. Unfortunately, none of these figures is known and the value of basic assessments which produce annual biomass figures is further reduced as they fail to recognise (no matter how obvious it may be) that successfully completing each of these steps requires more food at the relevant time.

Also, while a simple association between live prey and breeding success has been made (Watson *et al* 1992), occupying a territory with apparently low live prey availability does not preclude the possibility of successful breeding. The problem here is again too great an emphasis on the expected importance of too small a selection of species when many more would make up the potential food supply. When considering this point in Argyll, it was found that using the same selective sampling as used in other studies reduced food availability to a level below the apparent point of viability in years in which two eaglets were fledged.

There is yet another factor that is commonly overlooked by the standard methodology: food source depletion by other species. The possible make-up of the requirement suggested by Brown and Watson (1964) and repeated by Watson (2010) assumes, in particular, that only golden eagles eat carrion and that nothing else kills hares, rabbits and grouse. Because of this factor, food availability has to be much higher than is implied for an eagle territory to be viable and if the estimated food requirement is almost doubled, it might be easier to see reasons to link low productivity to food supply.

Walker *et al* (2014) considered these points, and others, and after experimenting with carrion carcasses concluded that no more than about 20% of a carcass would actually be available to the eagles in the study territory. This was mostly because the speed at which carcasses were depleted greatly exceeded any realistic feeding capabilities of the eagles. For a carcass to have been entirely depleted by the resident eagles in the recorded time, their intake would have been roughly one kilogram per bird per day on every day the carcass was available. The carcasses were clearly heavily depleted by other species, in this case by at least fox, buzzard, raven and hooded crow. The situation will be different in other territories and it is also likely that some carcasses will be depleted more or less quickly than others.

To assess overall food availability in the Argyll territory, Walker *et al* (2014) used a fundamentally different approach to that used in other studies. In particular, all of the potential food sources were assessed, rather than only those with preconceived importance (this effectively increased the estimated availability when compared to other studies); the ongoing availability of live prey was considered (not all of the counted resident live prey animals are truly available because some had to survive to form the next year's breeding population, which would reduce the comparable estimates); and carrion availability was adjusted for depletion by other species (decreasing apparent availability). The recorded diet was also excluded because of all the biases that are relevant to that subject.

In this way the resultant biomass figures (Table 4) were minimum estimates, they could not be further reduced without excluding food sources known to be used by the eagles and, in practical terms, there must have been more food available than was estimated. In fact, the unadjusted annual mean estimate was in excess of 2,000 kilograms. The overall effect of the methodology was to reduce the apparent food availability in a territory with few of the so-called important food sources and which also had a very poor breeding history (0.05 young per year during 1989-2007 inclusive).

Table 4: Estimated minimum available annual biomass (kg) in an Argyll golden eagle territory, 2005-2012

Food Source	2005	2006	2007	2008	2009	2010	2011*	2012*
1: Major resident	216.36	207.52	182.16	190.48	186.32	187.36	195.49	196.49
2: Other resident	101.12	101.12	101.12	101.12	101.12	101.12	101.12	101.12
3: Summer increase	126.60	126.60	129.26	131.82	131.82	131.82	131.82	131.82
4: Small additional	5.25	5.25	5.25	5.25	5.25	5.25	5.25	5.25
Total	449.33	440.49	417.79	428.67	424.51	425.55	433.68	434.68
Eggs laid	+	+	0	+	0	+	0	+
Young fledged	0	0	0	2	0	2	0	1

Note: * because of changing methodology, there were fewer accurate counts in 2011 and 2012.

FOOD SOURCES

1: Sheep carrion, red grouse (*Lagopus lagopus*)
2: Rabbit (*Oryctolagus cuniculus*), fox (*Vulpes vulpes*), grey heron (*Ardea cinerea*),

pheasant *(Phasianus colchicus)*, common buzzard *(Buteo buteo)*, kestrel *(Falco tinnunculus)*, black grouse *(Tetrao tetrix)*, raven *(Corvus corax)*, crow *(C. cornix)* etc.
3: Sheep lambs, common gull (Larus canus), curlew (Numenius arquata), etc.
4: Small mammals, small passerines, passage spp, etc.

The main findings of this assessment were that by year, season, month, week or day food availability was always in excess of the estimated requirements for a pair of eagles rearing two young. More interestingly, and more importantly, there was little difference in availability between years in which no eggs were laid, years in which eggs did not hatch, years that produced one chick and years that produced two chicks. In fact, there was apparently less food available in 2010 when two young were fledged than in 2011 when no eggs were laid by the same pair of adult eagles. Put simply, breeding performance could not be explained by food availability and, in particular, breeding failure could not be linked to food supply.

This situation would not be recognised by a standard approach or methodology that expects food and certain species to be influential. An observer visiting this site would not perceive the amount of food available because, at most, they would probably only record one sheep carcass, rabbits on the low-lying farmland and forestry, and few red grouse; and they would not see red deer, mountain or brown hares or ptarmigan. They would see a territory in which apparent food availability and habitat quality would not support successful breeding in the long term; they would see reasons that explain the poor breeding performance prior to 2008; they would not see a territory in which there was sufficient food to support successful breeding.

The results of the Argyll assessment seem to contradict everything that is thought to be known on this matter but as they come from a single site study, their lesson is unlikely to be heeded. However, this is the only assessment which has considered all of the potential food sources during a long-term year-round study.

The Argyll results also show that the territory must have been fully viable during the period of extremely low productivity prior to 2008 and that the breeding failures must have resulted from causes other than food. In fact, since 1997 there have been at least five causes of failure or non-breeding, some of which applied in more than one year and none of which can be linked to food or habitat. This has major implications for species management because it implies that many site assessments will have reached unreliable conclusions about viability and their suitability for change.

SEASONAL CONSIDERATIONS

It might seem likely that food will be most commonly in short supply during the winter months, but while there may be fewer species available (those such as curlew and golden plover having left the hills) the resident species that remain will be more numerous and at higher densities than during the spring. The individual animals that will not be part of the following spring population do not simply die *en masse* in the autumn; some will survive throughout the winter but, in terms of biomass as well as numerical availability, a territory can hold more food during December and January than it does in March and April and the breeding activity of the prey species can initially make them less available in practical terms as the spring progresses. The opposite is true of carrion; there will be more in March and April than in December and January because mortality does not generally peak in the winter.

This has implications for breeding performance if eagles have to attain breeding condition during the pre-laying period. It can be seen that, rather than being most important during the summer months, live prey may be most important during the autumn and winter, when it is usually not assessed. However, this requirement has already been questioned and the combination of available food sources must not be overlooked with ideas of this type. It is total availability that is important, not the availability of certain sources.

Food availability during the incubation period is probably of least importance to golden eagle ecology, as the eggs will either be fertile or not, and there is little activity on which to expend energy. Even apparently poorly provisioned territories will be able to provide survival levels of food (or they would not be occupied) and the idea of both eagles having to leave the eggs unattended to obtain food is extremely improbable.

The nestling period obviously places a greater demand on the territory but it is not immediately greatly different to what has gone before. Hatchling eaglets are very small and do not require large amounts of food. A different impression might be gained because the breeding birds do not vary the size of the food item in line with the size of the chick, but simply provide what they retrieve. In this way, there is often more food on the nest when the chick is small than when it is large, and nests are often empty of food when chicks are ringed at six to seven weeks of age. This is not because small chicks require more food than do larger ones, or because there may be food shortages; food items on the nest are simply depleted more quickly by larger chicks.

The act of sibling aggression has long been closely associated with food but the evidence to support this contention is extremely tenuous. Most of the fatal aggression occurs during the first three weeks of life, when there is little likelihood of food being in short supply and fatal aggression occurs where there is clearly ample food on the nest; some apparently poorly provisioned territories are also capable of producing two chick broods and sibling aggression is not always fatal. Good quality observations also suggest that most aggression takes place during and immediately after feeding (Walker 2009) and while there may be some direct competition when begging for food, the nestlings do not fight for food at this time and it is not a lack of food that causes the aggression. The death of one chick may result from poor feeding as a result of weakness brought on by the aggression but early season chick deaths should not be directly linked to food supply.

The nestlings most likely to die as a result of food shortage are those that are much closer to fledging. Food requirements are greatly increased by chicks that are both growing physically and acquiring their full plumage. It is not at all unusual for older nestlings (those more than six weeks of age) to die before fledging, regardless of whether or not they have a nest mate.

Food availability is equally important during the post-fledging period, not least because the territory may have to sustain four full-sized golden eagles at this time. This period does, of course, coincide with a period of great food abundance. Resident species, such as hare and grouse, are at their most numerous, and probably at their most available in practical terms, and at least some of the summer visitors will still be present during August and into September. That the situation gradually changes is evidenced by the juveniles' dependency period commonly ending about six weeks after fledging, at which point they all appear to develop a broader diet and no longer rely extensively on freshly killed food provided by the adults.

There are obvious seasonal differences in food and food source availability and there will be more discrete variations within the seasons. There will also be much variation between individual territories, given that each will offer different levels of source availability. With territories of such great size and variable habitat it is not realistically possible for two to have the same level of food availability so direct comparisons should not be made between sites; one territory should not be said to be better than another because both may permit successful breeding.

To summarise, golden eagle food requirements are probably greater than is widely believed but territories also almost certainly provide a greater biomass than is required or is suggested when using the standard approach to assessments. Food has become, if it has not always been, a very convenient means of explaining territory occupancy and breeding performance without there actually being any robust evidence to support the conclusion.

FORAGING TECHNIQUES

It is safe to say that, as hunter-gatherers, golden eagles are probably always looking for foraging opportunities unless they have eaten very recently, are flying to the nest or are flying to the evening roost. Although they do have specific foraging techniques much of an eagle's food seems to be obtained, and prey items identified, in a very casual manner. Prey will be targeted by a bird incubating the eggs (Walker 1991), from a perch, from high circling, during transitional (point to point) or casual flights and while walking about on the ground, as well as food being located as a result of watching the activity of corvids around a carcass, and that makes it more difficult to separate foraging activity from general behaviour than is often implied. It is not simply a case that an eagle is either foraging or not foraging.

When trying to interpret golden eagle behaviour correctly, and separating the different elements of a single flight, it becomes clear that such an exercise is fairly meaningless as the eagle's overall intention is not always easily recognisable and the stimulus can change with great rapidity. For example, a bird found perched on a hillside in Argyll then took flight; during the course of the next ten minutes or so it travelled slowly and at low level across ground that was known to hold red grouse ('quartering the ground', as it might be called); after travelling for about two kilometres it began to circle and gain height (having apparently ceased foraging); having gained height it then reversed its route to circle more or less above its starting point (transitional flight), where it was joined by its mate (social interaction); after a while both birds began to flight-display (pair bonding) but part way through a display dip they turned on two ravens (foraging) but then broke away, landed and mated.

While there were obviously different elements to the flight, and different flight styles and techniques deployed, the divisions suggested in parenthesis are fairly arbitrary and based on an interpretation of the observed activity. Because eagles have been seen on other occasions to make kills or locate food from most of the described elements, it could be argued that the first eagle was continuously foraging until the pair dropped to the ground and mated. And when the interpretation of events is considered, some changes in the observed activity may have been influenced by the second bird being visible to the first before its presence was known to the observer. The correct interpretation cannot be made without all the facts.

Two (perhaps) more straightforward examples of the difficulties of determining an eagle's intentions would be an eagle that flight-rolled and caught a crow that was mobbing it (was the eagle foraging even though it was actually flying away from the prey item?) and an eagle that appeared to be in a transitional flight that suddenly stalled and drop-turned to kill on the ground (was it searching for prey throughout, even though its speed and elevation suggested that it was going somewhere rather than looking for something?).

The latter example also raises the question of at what point during the flight the eagle changed its behaviour to foraging. This might appear to be an easily answered question (its intention changed at the point that prey was spotted) but what is unknown to the observer is whether or not the eagle had actually identified the food source earlier in the flight, possibly even before the flight began, and had taken a deliberately selected flight line and attitude to carry it into the correct position to make the kill without forewarning the target animal. This would be the deployment of subterfuge and, while a fairly simple foraging technique, it is one that cannot be easily identified in the field. This also raises the problem of using food source distribution to define foraging areas, as foraging effort might begin before the eagle enters the specified area and therefore over ground which may be considered to have little importance.

For these reasons and because the interpretation of eagle behaviour is littered with difficulties, ambiguities and groundless assumptions, it is probably best to say that golden eagles have a continuous awareness of foraging opportunities, the intensity of which varies with the bird's requirements.

Watson (2010) describes the various hunting techniques but, while this is useful and informative, these may in fact be, as suggested above, the final element of a much longer approach or the attack may be incidental to the previous activity. Again, it becomes a matter of interpretation. For example, if 'high soaring with glide attack' is a foraging technique (Watson 2010), is 'high soaring' without an attack unsuccessful foraging? How does the observer separate non-foraging high soaring from that which is foraging, given that high soaring is also described as a territorial display? Also, for example, as most attacks on live prey involve a chase, is chasing prey a foraging technique (Watson 2010) or is it simply what happens when the prey tries to escape?

Another point to consider is that the different techniques can be used to capture a wide range of species. They are not designed to capture one type of prey; both the eagles and their foraging techniques are adaptable. The techniques employed to catch birds and mammals may seem to have obvious differences but birds on the ground are caught in the same way as mammals. Whether a prey species has a solitary or a flocking nature, the animals that become prey items are individuals and are singled out as such. An eagle does not simply batter into a flock to see if it hits anything, but instead targets its prey.

Not all attacks are successful, of course, and the various prey species have different ways in which they attempt to avoid capture; these are typically trying to out-fly, out-run, out-manoeuvre and hiding from the predator. However, the golden eagle can be a very formidable opponent, capable of out-pacing most other species, it has been seen to kill peregrines in flight (Walker 2009), it shows surprising manoeuvrability when pursuing and catching birds in flight and its ability to see 'hidden' targets is evidenced by the number of occasions on which eagles have been seen to descend into dense ground cover and emerge with a victim. Diving for cover in vegetation is an inappropriate means of escape and species including stoat, red grouse, common snipe and short-eared owl have all been seen to be caught in dense heather, with deer calves and rabbits commonly captured in bracken patches.

For birds, the best form of escape appears to be staying above the eagle, as one of the eagle's two main failings is its poor ability to gain height quickly (the second is acceleration) and crows and ravens typically escape in this way. For mammals, the best avoidance technique is to go underground but this really only applies to rabbits and foxes. Some other species might go underground temporarily, but whether or not an eagle can differentiate between a species that has a subterranean side to its life and one that does not is not known. However, golden eagles can certainly be seen to wait on perches above burrows and holes when an animal has escaped into one and be seen to wait in trees for rabbits to emerge from cover.

Given what may be called the patience that can accompany some foraging, it can be surprising to see just how quickly an eagle will give up the pursuit of a potential prey item and it often seems that if the prey is not caught quickly, then it is not worth chasing. This suggests that the element of surprise may be important or that eagles generally do not direct a great deal of effort towards pursuing live prey. This is somewhat contradicted by the number of long pursuit flights that are recorded, the occasions on which both members of a pair are engaged in chasing the same target and the fact that eagles are often present in a location for some time before they manage to make a kill. Again, the need to feed may determine the amount of energy expended but, even so, it is curious to see a foraging effort simply fizzle out.

In June 1992 a pair of eagles without an active nest was encountered in a Perthshire glen as they closed in on a red deer calf. The male attacked first and hit and rolled the calf but lost its grip. It flew and repeated the action and then the female attacked and did likewise. In total the calf was hit and rolled seven times, between each attack staggering across the hill. Although the calf was clearly small enough to be killed, the eagles, rather than pressing home their advantage, stayed on the ground after their next attacks. The situation then became more curious, with the eagles jumping to attack when the calf moved but ignoring it when it stood still. The calf was able to move a short distance each time and it eventually pressed itself against a large boulder and stayed there. The three protagonists had reached an impasse, with the calf not moving, the female eagle perched on top of the rock and the male perched on the ground. The encounter eventually ended with the eagles simply flying away as if unable to kill. This leaves the possibility that it was the lack of movement that saved the calf's life, as very few animals remain stationary when attacked by golden eagles. Something similar might even be seen with fresh carrion, as carcasses are commonly viewed and seemingly appraised before they are cautiously visited for the first time, as if the lack of movement is initially a deterrent.

This incident is of further interest as hunting on foot is often considered to be unusual (Watson 2010). In reality, hunting on foot is a very common occurrence, even if it is most usually associated with the hunting of small prey such as voles and the finding of pipit nests. Golden eagles are not uncommonly to be seen wandering about and making small pounces and snatches in both grass and heather and scratching with their talons before reaching down to collect prey items, which have been seen to include entire pipit nests. Although value should not be implied, this is another reason why small prey items must be considered in assessments of food availability, because they are a common source of food.

Ground-based foraging can be advantageous in other ways, as another of the eagle's problems when foraging is its size and therefore the silhouette it shows when crossing a ridge or when flying out from the hillside. This is actually used to its advantage on some occasions, as the eagle's sudden appearance can cause alarm among corvids, leading to calling and a flush of activity that betrays both their location and the possible location of carrion.

However, to avoid causing this type of disturbance, eagles often land below the top of a ridge or knoll and then walk over the rise to stand among heather or rocks and view the scene. They can remain in such positions for lengthy periods, walk into a better position or just walk about the site. This is different to when eagles perch on the summits of hills, often on top of cairns, as these birds are almost certainly not actively foraging. That said, foraging eagles often settle beside these permanent markers, possibly in the understanding that they disguise their presence even if they are very obvious from certain angles. No matter how obvious, a motionless object is easily overlooked and this could allow an eagle's presence to be missed, by both potential prey and by an observer. When a target has been identified from such a perch the approach is then made downhill or across the slope and close to the ground without breaking the skyline.

Eagles will also use other perches as they work their way across the site in a stop-and-go, perch-hopping approach; they do not always simply appear and quarter the ground or appear and chase prey but often arrive, wait and move then settle, wait and move in a sequence that can see them travel the length of a ridge. They will do something similar in flight by holding position over a point before moving to repeat the action. In a similar way, eagles will often drift towards a potential target, especially corvids at carrion, and then drift away as if uninterested before either attacking or taking control of the carcass.

This latter situation can be seen most obviously when two eagles forage in tandem. Although cooperative hunting has been little described, it is not unusual to see the members of a pair working together. In these situations the pair deliberately disturbs corvids (giving the appearance of trying to drive the scavengers from the area) before one turns away or gains more elevation while the other deals more actively with the corvids. This can take several minutes as the corvids gradually lose interest in the more distant bird but, once this is completed, the second returns with the advantage of speed and surprise and a better chance of capturing the target. Its return also causes panic among the corvids, improving the hunting chances of the first eagle when the scatter, and there have been such occasions on which both eagles were seen to make a kill. Corvids do pose a particular problem for hunting eagles, however, and it is more usual for only one bird to be successful and not at all unusual for neither to make a kill at these times.

There is a more typical corvid chase in which one or both eagles stoop at the target until it is eventually caught. Such pursuits may continue over distances of more than two kilometres with both eagles stooping, twisting and striking four or five times. As one attack fails the eagle pulls out upwards and the second stoops in to attack before the first stoops in again. When one eventually catches the prey, the other might accompany it to perch above and watch over its feeding mate or circle in flight above or beside its mate. Given that a crow is insufficient to satisfy an eagle, it can seem strange that an actively hunting eagle will stop all foraging effort when its mate makes a kill, not least because eagles are perfectly capable of successfully hunting by themselves. It may simply be that one requires less food at that time than the other.

This type of cooperative hunting can also be seen when targeting species such as red grouse and hare. In both cases, eagles will not approach side by side, but one ahead of and at a lower elevation than the other. The first bird flushes the prey and the second has both the advantage of speed (coming from a higher elevation) and surprise, as the target has reacted to, and may only have seen, the first. As the first bird gains speed it joins the attack and the same type of stooping in turn can be seen until the kill is made. These types of situation always seem unfair on the second eagle which then has to hunt alone, as a sated eagle may be disinclined to assist its mate. It may be that cooperative hunting (rather than foraging for carrion) is most common when there is a greater need for food, such as when provisioning large nestlings or during the winter months, when foraging may be more difficult.

Foraging for carrion is a great deal more straightforward than hunting live prey. Eagles find carcasses by searching or during general flights, by reacting to corvids that are already at the carcass and by deliberately checking known locations that provide multiple carcasses over the course of a year; the regularly-used flight corridors might encompass these locations.

Carrion is typically not considered as having spatial associations but detailed searches in different territories have found sheep carrion hotspots on an indistinct section of scree slope, in a discrete section of peat hags and, perhaps most surprisingly, on a fairly nondescript area of grass moor. Deer carrion hotspots have included a different section of scree in the same territory as that with the sheep spot, a chasm gulley, the foot of one crag but no others and a gentle grassy slope. Some of the locations in question appear to pose no risk of death and yet they have produced multiple carcasses in several if not many consecutive years. When known about, they can be as useful as checking known perches to an observer looking for eagles.

That such important spots are generally not recognised or thought not to exist, and so are not viewed as being important definable locations, means that they are the foraging opportunities most likely to be lost to changes of land use. As carrion can be an important source of food for golden eagles the consequences of this happening could be as great as destroying a source of grouse.

Although foraging as a pair may appear to be the most efficient form of foraging, golden eagles are fully capable of successfully foraging and hunting on their own. All of the above techniques are used by single birds and it is probable that most foraging is performed singly. During a successful breeding attempt the male performs most of the active foraging from the onset of incubation to the end of the juvenile's confinement period, potentially a total of 25 weeks. The female might forage for its own needs during incubation but may only play a full role in provisioning during the second half of the nestling period. Even then the female will feed from food delivered to the nest by the male, while the latter seldom feeds on food collected by the female. It is probably only during the juvenile's confinement period that females literally have to depend on their own foraging ability, as when there is no active breeding attempt the members of a pair are often seen together and will share carrion and the larger kills.

PROBLEMS

While the golden eagle is a hugely efficient hunter-gatherer, live prey items typically do not wait to be killed and there are situations in which eagles have obvious difficulties in foraging successfully. These do not relate simply to weather conditions or habitat. If a single eagle fully commits to a chase, an immediate failure will almost certainly mean that there is no second chance. This suggests that carrion feeding could be of great importance to non-territorial and young immature eagles because they are mostly operating as single birds and may lack the hunting efficiency of older birds.

Golden eagles are generally considered to be an open-habitat species that can rely heavily on such prey species as mountain hare, red grouse and ptarmigan and yet, as already noted, the eagle's size and its obvious silhouette when seen from below (from the position of most prey items) hardly disguises its presence. Prey species will have evolved predator avoidance techniques and many have explosive escape speed and usually greater manoeuvrability than the eagle, so an eagle in open country can be relatively easily avoided. This will be one reason why cooperative flush-and-chase hunting is deployed but it poses an obvious problem when one member of a pair does most of the foraging, such as during the bulk of the nesting season.

The problems associated with predator avoidance are most easily seen when crows and ravens are present in open habitat. Corvids do not simply flee from golden eagles because, while they lack the eagle's overall speed, they can gain height more quickly and once they are above the eagle there is little danger to them, unless attacked by a second eagle arriving from overhead. While members of the grouse species lack this manoeuvrability, they have an initial burst of speed that can initially outpace and out-distance the eagle because, while overall a faster species, the eagle's acceleration is slower because of its size. Because the ground can be to the eagle's advantage and a hindrance to escape, it is also not unusual for red grouse and, more commonly, ptarmigan to fly out over valleys or depressions rather than stay close to a hill or ridge as this reduces the problems caused by their lack of manoeuvrability. Ptarmigan pursuits often cease or lose their impetus almost as soon as the birds reach the void of a glen.

Something similar applies to hares; in broad terms, the more uniform the habitat, the easier it is to escape, as they can turn and reverse their direction more easily than can the eagle. If the eagle makes a failed strike and is grounded, the hunt is effectively over. Although peat hags may appear to offer a complexity that would favour the hare, they can become confined blind channels along which manoeuvrability is no longer an advantage.

An associated problem in open habitat is that any alarm calls and the sight of other animals in predator avoidance mode can act as a warning to others. One animal or species does not ignore the alarmed behaviour of another and so an entire community can be made unavailable simply by an eagle's obvious arrival.

There is another potential hindrance to successful hunting that is seldom considered: noise. The rush of air when a golden eagle is in a steep dive, or even in a rapid, almost level pursuit, is quite remarkable to hear. On one occasion the observer's attention was drawn to activity behind him by the sound of rushing air as an eagle pursued a cormorant over heather moorland. Given this sound, there seems to be little likelihood of an eagle successfully making a high-speed surprise attack on an alert animal in open country, which may be why most active foraging is performed at relatively slow speeds.

The reality is that, while it is seen as an open habitat species, the golden eagle's hunting efficiency is probably much greater in more broken habitats when the same target species are involved; a greater element of surprise can be achieved where there is potential cover for the target to use. This is why open scrub areas are so valuable to eagles and why more foraging than is probably expected can be seen in mature woodland. Golden eagles will obviously forage above mature plantation forest but they are principally interested in the rides and roads where prey animals can be channelled and where the forest edge can prevent an easy escape. As is the case with other types of cover, an eagle will not be deterred if the prey is visible and even a red squirrel has been seen to be killed below the canopy of a pine tree (Walker 2009).

Corvids provide a more interesting situation because they do not avoid eagles by flying into trees or bushes in which the eagle may become entangled. Their avoidance response remains one of gaining height and they will take flight on an eagle's approach even though they would appear to be safer in the tree. While numerous crows and ravens have been seen to be killed in open country, the comparative ease with which eagles catch corvids in wooded glens or in and above plantation forest is quite remarkable. The open habitat avoidance technique does not work as well in such situations because the eagle almost always begins at a higher elevation.

However, it is still much easier for eagles to kill larger prey items in open country and lambs, deer calves and foxes all typically fall prey in these areas, though foxes and calves will also be taken in forest rides. Lambs and calves lack experience and generally appear not to recognise a source of danger unless attacked and if the former is not close to the ewe (which is almost a prerequisite for an eagle attack) they demonstrate no predator avoidance behaviour whatsoever. Sheep have been seen to butt and otherwise cause perched eagles to fly and it is not at all unusual for lambs to inquisitively wander close to an eagle.

Red deer calves should be less vulnerable as they are typically hidden, when small, in dense vegetation such as bracken, but they also rely on remaining motionless and on cryptic colouration to avoid predators when there is little cover and, as a result, are not as well protected by the adult animal. In the above Perthshire example, the calf's mother was more than a kilometre away and seemed unaware of the attack until it was almost over, galloping in almost three minutes after the eagles had departed.

While they are highly effective hunter-gatherers, there are times when it is clear that golden eagles simply do not have to try very hard to obtain their food. Carrion is easily located and its location remembered and live prey often seems simply to surrender to its fate. Eagles often fly directly to carrion from the roost, showing that the location is remembered and not found anew but, interestingly, it has also been noticed that fresh carrion in the same location is not always immediately accessed, as if the birds 'believe' that food in that location has been depleted; conversely, of course, eagles do often return to old carcasses.

Because of all of these variables, the eagle's foraging success rate is probably impossible to calculate; they might not appear to be hunting when they are, and vice versa, and they might judge the possibilities and not follow through with an attack if success is unlikely.

FEEDING AND FIELD SIGNS

To a field observer, the amount of food ingested will not be apparent, or of any real importance, and the length of a feed may only be relevant if it disrupts their plans and they are to avoid causing disturbance. Given the comments made elsewhere about the low number of kills seen by observers, it would seem that few feeds, from either kills or on carrion, will have been watched from beginning to end. One of the main benefits of undertaking long-term, year-round intensive studies, rather than monitoring, is that kills are commonly seen and feeding is seen even more frequently.

As noted above, after preparation is completed and if there is sufficient meat on the item, a typical full feed will last for about 25 minutes. There is, of course, huge variation in the length of feeds because of the speed at which the eagle eats: a vole or pipit may be swallowed in one gulp while an eagle may feed continuously and voraciously from carrion for more than an hour. An eagle may also be at a carcass for a lengthy period but feed quite slowly and they often pause during feeds, both to look around and to chase or dissuade other species from approaching too closely, so a feed can be very disjointed rather than continuous. Because of this it can be difficult to determine the amount eaten but, when watched from a close hide, an eagle was seen to eat 280 pieces of meat, estimated to be c.500 gm in weight, during a 25-minute feed (Walker 2004). Perhaps most surprisingly, and of relevance to intake, the eagle's crop was not noticeably distended at the end of this feed so an eagle with an obviously distended crop has probably eaten a great deal more than might be expected.

While many feeds from carrion are taken from carcasses that have already been opened, most feeds will include the ingesting of some hair or feather and this will begin with the initial plucking. The amount of plucking undertaken varies considerably; while the smallest items might be swallowed whole, some intact small items, such as ring ouzel, have been seen to be almost entirely plucked of feathers (Walker 1987). On another occasion a kestrel was seen to be killed in flight and plucked on the ground, it was then carried to a rock on the opposite side of the valley and left there. When it was later examined it was found to be almost completely plucked clean of feathers but only the brain had been eaten, the back of the skull having been bitten out (Walker 2009). Larger prey items and carrion will always be at least partly plucked to allow access to the flesh but even grouse and crows are not always plucked clean.

Walker (2009) records the sequence from kill, through plucking and feeding to transportation to the nest of a lamb, beginning with the removal of 347 pieces of wool in seven minutes. In total 759 pieces of wool were removed, along with what was eaten (by both adult eagles) in 43 minutes of feeding before the lamb arrived at the nest. That one of the eagles was seen to feed from the internal organs during this episode shows why pellet analysis is not reliable and also how the value of a carcass can be underestimated: the number, duration and efficiency of feeds could not be determined by looking at the carcass. This episode is also an example of both adult eagles plucking and feeding from a kill made by one of them, the female, and of the carcass being left unattended overnight.

A fieldworker is most likely to see only the aftermath of foraging, such as the scattered pluckings left at the kill site, and will not always be able to separate a kill site from carrion. Prey is also not always fully plucked where the kill is made and small to medium-sized items are commonly carried to more than one location, even outside the breeding season and when there are no young in the nest. Even larger carrion carcasses might be moved and eagles have been seen to pull dead sheep out of ditches and (deliberately or not) cause deer carcasses to roll down slopes. This can make it difficult to read the field signs that are available as there might be too little evidence from which to reach a firm conclusion about the hunter involved, how many individuals (or even species) have used the carcass or the number and size of any feeds taken.

Identifying the predator or scavenger from the evidence at a carcass can be extremely subjective and not at all conclusive. In broad terms, because of their size and power, golden eagles usually leave very neat plucking piles with few stray items; the piles also tend to be on one side of the carcass remains as the bird is looking to access a single feeding point. When not preparing to carry food, eagles also tend to work from one position by turning smaller carcasses and they tend not to move parts of a carcass, so (if they are not eaten) legs and wings will usually remain at the site rather than being found some distance away. By contrast, crows, ravens and buzzards will change their position when plucking and feeding and, with corvids, more than one bird is likely to be working at the same time, usually resulting in a messier site. Foxes will usually tear at carcasses and remove larger pieces and, like corvids, will also move these away so that they can feed without interference from others using the carcass.

An obvious problem with carrion is that all the local scavengers may have used the carcass before it is examined (and crows in particular may visit a kill site and move the remains) but there are usually other signs of this having happened. Both foxes and corvids are likely to defecate on and about a carcass while an eagle is more likely to have stepped away before defecating, leaving a streak of faeces on nearby vegetation. If an eagle has been at a carcass, even a fresh kill site, for any length of time they are also likely to have left at least one piece of white down to be found, especially if they have had to defend the food against other species.

However, great care must be taken when interpreting field signs as they, at best, only reveal the past presence of an eagle and do not denote the eagle's status or that the location is part of a territory. As eagles commonly wander into territories with which they have no permanent association they are very likely to leave field signs that might be misinterpreted. For example, on Lewis in 1993 an immature eagle was found with a freshly-killed lamb near the heart of occupied territory in which the resident adults were rearing a brood of two chicks. If the lamb remains had been found without the culprit being seen, it would be easy to assume that the residents had made the kill.

This type of situation is not at all unusual. In 2013, for example, a farmer complained about lamb losses to breeding eagles but his description of the bird he had seen, and the subsequent observations, proved this to be the work of an intruder rather than a resident, even though the location was roughly at the geographic centre of the territory. Coincidentally, an intruder was watched feeding on carrion in exactly the same location in 2007 and if the bird had not been seen, the signs may have been taken to indicate the activity of a resident.

As it has been reported in other sources and appears to be expected behaviour, it is perhaps surprising that during 37 years of intensive fieldwork in this study, during which hundreds of kills and many, many more observations of feeding have been made, two free-flying eagles were only once seen feeding from the same carcass at the same time, and that was very brief and involved a recently-fledged juvenile with a deformed beak (Walker 1987; 2009). Even during or at the onset of deteriorating weather conditions the second bird always waited for the first to finish its feed before moving in and beginning its own feed. Eagles sometimes stand quite close to their feeding partner and may walk around them as they feed but only once has one partner been seen to displace the other.

That was also in the Lake District and resulted in both birds taking the heraldic 'spread eagle' pose, wings raised, before the first gave way to the second (Walker 2009).

It is perhaps even more surprising, given the care and attention eagles show to their young in the nest, that this one-at-a-time rule also applies to the juvenile of the year. While the adult may sometimes defer to the juvenile, adult eagles have been seen to physically defend food items from their own young, even jumping to talon-grapple the youngster away as it arrived in flight. If this was seen as a casual observation, such a situation could easily be interpreted as aggressive behaviour, with one eagle attacking and trying to drive the other from the food. It might also be interpreted as a sign of desperation, as evidence of food shortage or even used as an indication of the quality and suitability of the location for golden eagles. As with so many situations, if taken out of context an isolated observation can easily produce the wrong conclusion, especially if what is happening is unexpected or thought to be easily explained.

The timing of feeds also has some relevance to fieldwork as the idea that golden eagles tend to, or generally, feed in the early morning continues to persist. In reality, and even if carrion is known to be available, most feeds take place later in the day. Foraging activity may be seen in the early hours of daylight but feeding can be seen at any time.

That said, it is not unusual for golden eagles to roost close to a carrion carcass during severe weather conditions (presumably to have easy access to it the next morning if the poor weather persists) so early feeds do occur but, as with the idea that eagles are more active in the morning, it should not be taken as a rule. In the same way, and providing additional evidence, intensive studies show that the timing of prey delivery to the nest is more likely to be random than regular or predictable and that most items are not delivered in the early morning. A feed later in the day is also likely to reduce the need to feed early the next day.

While a golden eagle may curtail a feeding bout if weather conditions drastically deteriorate, they will often continue to feed regardless of the conditions and, in the same way, strength of daylight may not be entirely limiting. There have been numerous occasions on which eagles have been watched feeding until long after sunset and when too dark for them to be seen with ordinary optical equipment at even relatively close range. Although they are classed as a diurnal species, this activity not only means that the eagles were effectively feeding at night, but implies that they must also have flown to their roosts in the dark.

The number of feeds per day also varies considerably; an eagle is as likely to feed on three occasions as it is to feed only once. Kill feeds are not uncommonly followed by feeding on carrion (or vice versa) and additional kills may be seen on the same day. With food items varying in size from a field vole to a red deer stag, the number of feeds is very much a question of opportunity and an eagle will feed as often as it wants to feed.

A matter that has to be included in a section on food (and which has wider implications) is the question of whether or not golden eagles drink in the wild. Watson

(2010) only notes records of eagles drinking in arid regions, with the implication that it would be unnecessary for them to do so in such places as Scotland, and yet a reference cited elsewhere in that work (Walker 1987), reports drinking and bathing in Britain.

This raises further questions about the reliability of the received wisdom and how that knowledge has been obtained. More than twenty different British (and mostly Scottish) golden eagles were seen drinking in the wild during this study. That is not a huge number but none of the incidents (and with some of these birds there are multiple examples) was a casual observation, the drinking was only recorded during intensive studies of eagle behaviour and not while monitoring breeding performance, and it is not the type of activity that is likely to be seen by chance. While eagles may well obtain most of their moisture from the food they eat (and this must be true of nestlings) drinking is probably much commoner than thought.

It can be seen that too many of the ideas and too much of the discussion about the golden eagle's feeding habits suffer from subjectivity and the failure to recognise or accept the limitations of the available evidence and the way in which that evidence has been collected. As already noted, the fact that a red grouse is seen to be killed does not make red grouse the, or even one of the, most important food sources in that location; and the true importance of any food source cannot be determined by counting remains in nests or pellets, or its relevance be transferred to other locations. An observer can only get a subjective idea of the importance and influence of food sources or of the overall influence of food on breeding performance.

Much greater effort is required to fully understand the relationships between food, breeding performance and territory occupancy. The question of the species' overall low productivity has been almost conclusively linked to food in some sources of information and yet there is no investigative study that has proved this point. With most, if not all, occupied and established territories holding a sufficient food supply any problems with productivity are almost certainly the result of factors that are being overlooked.

BREEDING

More effort has been directed towards monitoring and recording breeding season activity than any other aspect of golden eagle ecology. This does not mean that there is little more or nothing much new to be said on the subject, because much of that effort has been a simplistic tick-box exercise focused on breeding performance and successful breeding attempts. Little effort has been directed towards investigating the other scenarios and, as always, observers tend to see what they expect to see and not necessarily what is actually happening. It is widely being missed that most of the available information is the result of nest watching rather than eagle watching and that there is little objectivity involved.

This means that much of the received wisdom is the simple repetition of casual observations in the belief that they must be correct and reliable because they represent what most observers already believe, even though those beliefs did not originate with and are not supported by robust evidence. Furthermore, it is not only many fieldworkers who still believe that nests have to be visited for a person to be knowledgeable and experienced: this also appears to be the attitude of many professional and influential conservationists.

The monitoring of breeding attempts with a few additional observations or records (such as what food is on the nest on the day the chick is ringed) does not provide an insight into golden eagle ecology, an explanation of what is being seen or sufficient information on which to base conclusions, guidance or advice. Unfortunately, because this type of recording and expectation has always dominated observer effort, it is almost impossible to have contrary evidence accepted, even when it is demonstrably more reliable than earlier ideas. There are numerous 'certainties' about the golden eagle's breeding ecology that are of dubious reliability because of this. One simple example is that while the 'breeding season' is under consideration, what is usually being discussed are successful nestling periods because as soon as an attempt fails, almost all observer effort stops at that site that year; failure is as much a part of the breeding season as success (if not more so) and yet it is very rarely thought of in those terms and even less frequently studied. There is a simple assumption in species management that failed breeding attempts are less important than successes and that what causes and what happens after the moment of failure has no relevance to the species or its conservation, unless it involves persecution.

NESTS

The most pertinent points to make about nests are that, firstly, and contrary to the impression given in other sources, nest building, refurbishment and adornment can take place at any time of year and do not have to be evidence of a breeding attempt or even the presence of a pair of eagles; secondly, nest sites do not have to be in what may appear to be the most suitable locations and, given the variety of locations that are used, the idea that nest sites may limit distribution is unrealistic; thirdly, the nests in a territory do not have to form an easily definable group; fourthly, breeding attempts do not have to be made in what would be called a full-sized nest; fifthly, a nest does not have to be used, as some nests are built and annually freshened over a period of many years without ever being used; sixthly, the standard idea that golden eagles have traditional nest sites does not prevent them from building new nests or using ones that are unknown to the observer; and seventhly, single and non-breeding eagles build and refresh nests.

Most nest building and refurbishment occurs during the pre-laying period (essentially February and March) and eagles will not unusually build entirely new nests at this time. They will also often build or refresh more than one nest simultaneously and may not select the one to be used until very close to the laying date; these refurbished nests might also not be close together or even in the same valley. However, nest building can happen at any time of year and material will even be taken to an alternative nest when there is a live chick in the active one; the potential for misinterpretation with this situation is clear if the observer does not know of the active nest. In addition, a breeding failure usually results in nest-building activity that is often outside the usual nest group.

There are surges in nest building activity which coincide with each of the major stages of the eagles' year, with the possible exception of the fledging time, and these can be seen with failed as well as successful pairs. Nest material is also added to the active nest throughout the breeding season. Material is delivered at many changeovers but also when nest visits are made without relief; breeding females, in particular, will also undertake bouts of collection while awaiting the delivery of food. Male golden eagles also appear to use the delivery of nest material as a means of checking on the nest contents or the female's willingness to be relieved.

As well as building new nests, eagles commonly carry sticks to previously unused locations that do not immediately (or sometimes ever) become nests, but which may be further enlarged in subsequent years and often after a break of several years; in the Argyll study a new nest was constructed in 2007 (by a single bird) but not touched again until it was used in 2014. This type of building seems to happen most frequently after a breeding failure and following the independence of the juvenile. Many of these nests do not progress beyond the collection of a few sticks or heather branches and are not unusually found on roost ledges. Put simply, the collection of nest material is not a definitive indication of any situation.

The idea of suggesting an average number of nests per pair is also therefore somewhat pointless as it is usually only the average of the numbers known about and will undoubtedly exclude many of the locations in which nests have been built. The number of nests known per pair varies considerably; there are established territories in which only one nest has been found while as many as 23 nests have been found in other territories. These points have clear implications when using the so-called territory-centre in species management, as this location will almost certainly not be the mean location of all the nests in a territory, and the smaller the number of nests known about, the more likely it is to be unrepresentative.

The idea that eagles rotate their nest use, and especially that they alternate nests after a breeding success or failure, is not supported by what has been seen. There is so much variation in patterns of use as to suggest that what happens is more to do with the individual eagles than with the species. While some pairs will use the same nest year after year, others change nest every year, in both cases regardless of breeding performance. The Argyll study saw 11 different nests used during a 12-year period, followed by the same nest being used in each of the next six years, then a previously unused one and then what had again become the most favoured one.

At Haweswater, over the space of 32 years, the different pairings at first alternated every year, brought in a new nest (and abandoned another) and then only moved after a failure; they then moved every year and stayed regardless of results. There were at least 11 full-sized nests constructed while the site held a pair of eagles (with material taken to at least six other locations) but only four were used for breeding, with one used only once and one used on 17 occasions. This also provides an indication of how the mean nest location can change over time without there being any real changes to the territory and how its location can vary depending on the information used; the mean locations of all the known nests, all the nests that have been used and all of the nests used per 10-year period were all in different places.

Golden eagles are not limited to nesting on large cliffs or crags and old pine trees. Nests can be on quite insignificant looking small rocky outcrops, on what is little more than broken ground and among peat hags. Featureless slopes and flat ground are the least likely locations to be used but it can take only a minor deviation for a location to become suitable for an eagle nest. A peat hag nest on Lewis was on virtually flat ground at low elevation in fairly featureless terrain but that did not prevent the eagles from using it to breed successfully.

Golden eagle nests can be found in other apparently unexpected locations, they are known from an oak tree in a glen bottom close to a well-used farm track; on the side of drainage ditches/water courses in a forest plantation; and beside a very small stream that flowed down an otherwise even slope. No location should be dismissed until it is proven not to be in use, but that does not prevent mistakes from being made because of over-confidence; as there are so many examples of breeding attempts almost being missed because a location was deemed to be unsuitable without it being checked, many more must have been missed.

As well as the idea of traditional nest sites (which are often not used) there are a number of other ideas about golden eagle nests that have probably been given too much importance. Watson and Dennis (1992) and Watson (1997) provide good examples of this, not least because the analysis was based only on nests that were active during the 1982 national survey. The choice of nest to be used in any given year will be determined by a number of external factors and comparing results can show how the selection of evidence can influence what appears to be known. For example, Watson and Dennis (1992) helps to perpetuate a myth about tree nests by reporting that only one of 18 used in 1982 was in the west of Scotland. That may well have been the case but there are many tree nests in the west (and south) of Scotland and the reasons for more not being used in that year will not be linked to their geographic distribution.

Watson and Dennis (1992) also report on the orientation of 407 nests and Watson (2010), comparing these results to the orientation of hill slopes, shows that most nests face between north and east. But that does not mean that this is a preferential choice as nest location is often the result of opportunity. There are many sites which only have south- or west-facing nests, there are pairs with nests on opposite sides of the same glen (so they have north and south or east and west facing nests) and pairs with nests facing all four of the cardinal points. There is nothing to suggest that breeding attempts are more successful in nests with a particular orientation. Furthermore, the analysis is again based on data collected in only one year.

To consider some of the other points and ideas, 568 nests in 142 territories were taken into consideration for this study. Of these nests, roughly 34% were under overhangs, roughly 31% were supported by a tree at their base, roughly 9% were in gorges and roughly 26% could not be described in any of these ways. Most pairs had more than one 'type' of nest and one pair had nests facing north, south, east and west, two in a gorge, one supported by a tree and one in a tree. It can be seen that there really is no such thing as a typical eagle nest site and setting out with or applying such an expectation is often why results are less than reliable.

While the nests of any territory are usually said to be in, and discussed as, a group this can actually equate to quite a large area and include more than one valley; it does not mean that all the nests in a territory are close together and an area of more than six square kilometres spread over three valleys is known from one site. As a result, a pair's nests are not regularly spaced, they may be metres or kilometres apart, and they may not create a neat and concise pattern. The distribution pattern formed by incorporating only the nests that are known to have been used will also be different from the pattern formed when using all of the nests in the territory.

A golden eagle nest is as deliberately constructed as the nest of any species and is more likely to have a neat and tidy appearance than appear rough and ready. Different types of material are used for different reasons and may be grouped as brown and green or hard and soft as the type of vegetation collected is influenced by what is needed. Hard material of various sizes, such as sticks and heather stalks, are collected at first and these may be broken from trees, collected from the ground and sometimes even transferred between nests; even clods of earth with vegetation attached may be collected. This forms the bulk and solidity of the nest which can be seen to grow quite rapidly. The annual additions can often add 50 centimetres to the height of an existing nest and the new material can be seen as a looser layer than those below it, which are often quite grey in appearance. This cannot be used as a sort of annual record, of course, as the nest may not have been in annual use.

'Softer' material such as dead bracken and heather sprigs may be added quite early in the process but is mostly used to construct the nest platform. The amounts collected can vary considerably, with some nests overflowing with softer material while it is barely visible in others. The nest lining is generally formed of even softer material, such as grasses and woodrush (although the material used varies between sites) and is usually not added until the final two weeks before egg-laying. That said, pairs which do not lay eggs (and some single birds) will line their nests. The female performs most of the nest lining tasks after the collection of material by both birds and, while males may breast the nest in readiness for the eggs, females dominate formation of the cup. Interestingly, the nest cup is usually not positioned centrally and, even when the same nest is used in consecutive years by the same birds, it is not always positioned in the same place on the nest platform, although it is usually set back from the front edge of the nest.

Nests vary greatly in size and while new ones are generally quite low in height, even long- established and well-used ones are not always as huge as may be expected, or contain a cartload of sticks, because the ledge may not support a large structure. Nests on long narrow ledges may spread out but be little more than a few sticks thick and might only consist of the soft lining regardless of their age. These nests are easily overlooked, even when in use, and especially when approaching with the idea that big birds build big nests.

A common discussion point about nests concerns the addition of green material and various theories have been put forward about this (Watson 2010). Most of these seem to be more fanciful than sound, and forget that, in countries such as Scotland, what was brown in February and March is usually green during May to July. The idea that green material is added as an indication of territory occupancy is particularly odd because if the nest is in use, it will have either an adult or a nestling on it and if it is not active, both adults are available to perform territorial defence. It must also be remembered that territoriality does not prevent intrusions by other members of the same species: it is a reaction to their presence.

To summarise, given the variations that are likely to be found in different territories, observers cannot afford to visit a territory with preconceived ideas about where to look, what to look for, what will be found or how to interpret what is seen.

THE PRE-LAYING PERIOD

Sometimes referred to as pre-breeding, the term 'pre-laying' is preferable because there is a tendency amongst non-specialists to think that the breeding season does not begin until the eggs are laid: with the golden eagle, the breeding season begins several weeks before the eggs are laid.

This might even be called the nest preparation period because all resident pairs (not just those which subsequently make a breeding attempt), single territory-holding eagles and at least some non-territorial eagles build, partly build or refurbish nests at this time of year. This is also why the idea that a recently repaired, newly built-up or lined nest is a sign of occupancy by a pair of golden eagles (Eaton *et al* 2007) is not at all reliable and is definitely not evidence of a breeding attempt. Pre-laying is also a part of the breeding season because human disturbance at this time can result in breeding failures.

The period is best defined as that between the onset of nest refurbishment or building in preparation for a breeding attempt and egg-laying. This may seem to be a fairly arbitrary period, as laying dates are so variable and are unlikely to be known, but it is a specific period that has obvious importance and a reasonably definable length of roughly seven weeks. Although first-egg laying dates vary considerably between pairs, and can vary between years at the same site, the majority of breeding attempts appear to begin during a fairly short window of time and so, for convenience, the pre-laying period can be said to begin on 1 February.

As already noted, golden eagles will collect, carry and position nest material at any time of year, will do so in bouts of activity regardless of the status of a breeding attempt (numerically, and even during the nestling period, eagles make more nest visits with material than with food) and will do so in previously unused locations. As a result, there may be little apparent difference in the significance of a stick added on 15 January and one added a month later but the later effort is invariably linked to an even greater association with the nest site than is seen at the other time. Non-specific nest additions, even in mid- January, can have a random or casual appearance.

Nest refurbishment is not simply a gradually increasing process with effort peaking close to the laying date. In fact, effort declines towards the laying date from an earlier peak as structural repairs will have been completed and the eagles are reduced to titivating the lining; as egg-laying approaches there may even be days on which the nest to be used is not visited. Refurbishment often involves relatively short intensive periods of activity followed by many hours without additions. It may also appear as little more than casual interest with only one or two items being added per day. Refurbishment bouts may last from the time it takes to collect and deliver a single item to two or more hours during which 40 or 50 items may be added. The male eagle appears to collect the most items, with a ratio of about 5:1 having been recorded (Walker 1991) while the female undertakes most of the adjustment work. The members of a pair will work together when building or refreshing a nest but they will also work independently and often when the other is absent from the nesting area.

Bouts of refurbishment may take place at any time during the period, at any point during daylight and seemingly in any conditions. A Lake District nest which later collapsed during incubation appeared to have been almost completely refurbished during the worst spell of weather that year (Walker 2009); eagles have built on top of snow that would later melt and have been watched building and repairing during heavy rain and snow in numerous locations. The timing of nest building activity also does not appear to be influenced by other considerations, with bouts being seen both before and after the first feeding of the day.

As nest preparation takes place at a time of short daylight periods and often uninviting weather conditions, it is not surprising that most of the recorded eagle activity at this time is seen inside the nest glen. However, while the eagles can spend an increasing amount of time in the vicinity of the nest as egg laying approaches, most pairs will spend time away from here throughout the period. In the Lake District and at some of the Scottish sites under observation, it was not at all unusual for the resident pair to be absent from the nest valley for much of the day before egg laying began.

This somewhat contradicts the idea of pre-laying lethargy which is further contradicted as, even on the laying day, females have been seen actively refreshing the nest, making determined foraging attempts and engaging in nest area defence against other eagles and other species. The idea of pre-laying lethargy may have come about simply because females naturally spend more time in the nesting area than do their mates.

Food is, of course, of vital importance as, if nothing else, the female needs to attain bodily condition if it is to produce fertile eggs (Newton 1979) and it is the main reason why the pair may spend much of their time away from the nesting area during February and March. As a result, the greater territory area is of specific importance at this time of year as live prey availability is declining and carrion availability may still be low, scattered and further made difficult to obtain by heavy rain, snow cover and freezing conditions. In many territories, foraging over a greater than usual area is an almost unavoidable necessity at this time of year as weather conditions affect food source availability. Prolonged snow cover can force resident pairs on to lower ground, including low-lying farmland, just as it does immature birds.

A resident pair of eagles will often travel and hunt cooperatively at this time and it provides a good opportunity to see eagles waiting their turn at a carcass. While one of the pair appears to be standing guard when the other feeds (and may be seen to chase away foxes, crows and ravens) it is probably merely waiting to feed. If the second to feed does so only late in the day, not only might it have to rush its feed because of failing light, but it might also suffer the attentions of other species more than did its mate, which may already have flown to the roost. This one-at-a- time rule means that if the eagles arrive at their evening roost 20–25 minutes apart, it is almost certainly because they have been feeding from the same food source. On other occasions, in decent weather conditions and after feeding, the pair may be seen to loafing in almost any part of the territory rather than only in the nesting area. This is, in fact, when the pair is most likely to be together most frequently and for the greatest amount of time.

Watson (2010) considers the absence of food provisioning of the female by the male prior to egg laying (supplementary feeding) to be the norm with golden eagles but this simply reflects the lack of detailed records and it is undoubtedly more common than is appreciated. When engaged in intensive studies, this behaviour has been recorded at four sites (admittedly not many, but then few sites are watched intensively) and in the Lake District quite a few observers have seen this type of provisioning (Walker 2009). Observers there were able to watch the male make the kill and then carry the prepared prey to the female, waiting on a perch which appeared to have been adopted for this specific purpose.

These perches had not been seen to be used prior to the onset of this behaviour, and were seemingly only used when the female was waiting to be fed. Similar actions were noted at Scottish sites and in all cases both carrion and freshly killed prey were seen to be delivered to the female. In fact, the very first record of this behaviour, on 10 March 1988, involved the hind leg of a red deer, and the female (on its favourite rather than a feeding perch) appeared not to know why the male was carrying food at that time of year and apparently had to be coaxed into accepting it (Walker 2009).

Territorial activity is one of the most frequently reported types of behaviour at this time of year and, by implication, is often considered to be most in evidence at this time. Flight displays such as the sky dance and high soaring are particularly associated with this period and numerous sources have reported or suggested its prevalence at this time of year (including Newton 1979; Watson 1997 and 2010; and Hardey *et al* 2009). However, this is a prime example of how an idea is accepted, believed and repeated by the majority without there being any reliable supporting evidence; this is discussed in more detail in the section on general activity. It must also be remembered that territorial activity can be very different to territorial display. That is not to say that flight displays are not performed at this time of year, only to stress that the influence of observer effort and expectation needs to be recognised in the interpretation of events.

Numerous observers have reported seeing several pairs of eagles simultaneously soaring above their nest sites during the pre-laying period and this is usually interpreted as a display of their presence, but with such a long-lived, largely monogamous, site-faithful species it seems unlikely that pairs would need exhaustively to display in this way to neighbours they may have 'known' for ten or more years. Given the distances involved, it is also usually only assumed that all of the birds are in their pairs but most intrusions happen at this time of year and a common response to this is a resident and an intruder circling above the nesting area.

Courtship and mating is an important part of pre-laying behaviour and both the sky-dance and soaring displays are used primarily in courtship and pair-bonding rather than for territorial purposes. This can be seen as displays are actually mostly, though not exclusively, performed below the ridge tops and within the box confines of the nesting glen where they are not easily seen by their neighbours. There are other types of flight displays and these and the relevant points are more fully discussed in the section on general activity.

Gordon (1955) reports on the 'game' of dropping an object that is re-caught, or caught by the partner, as a part of courtship behaviour but, in reality, this type of behaviour can be seen at any time of year and it does not appear to be a display or a game. More often than not the dropping is entirely accidental and the frequency with which such mishaps occur might surprise many observers. Golden eagles commonly drop food items and nest material when in flight and these might be caught by the bird involved, by the partner or by neither.

While mating is principally about the fertilisation of eggs, it is clearly performed when this is not necessary. Although Gordon (1955) and Watson (2010) only record mating at around the beginning of the breeding season, Walker (1991) notes that it can be seen at any time of year and intensive studies at more than one site have even recorded mating during successful nestling periods. On many occasions, mating obviously has no relevance to the production of fertile eggs and the actions might be more stylised in nature. That said, mating immediately before the laying date can be very stylised: the pair may perch side by side, either on the ground or in a tree with their heads closer together than the tails, before both bow with partly open wings until their beaks almost touch the ground, pause in that position and the male then mounts its mate. However, more often than not, there is little ceremony involved and calling may or may not be heard. Most mountings take only about 15 seconds and appear to take place at fairly random locations, although Walker (1991) notes two occurring in the same place almost exactly one hour apart and without the female having left the perch between times.

All of these actions and activities can be as easily seen at pairs which fail to lay eggs as at those which do lay eggs and there appears to be no obvious means of predicting whether or not a pair will make a breeding attempt. The idea that non-breeders show less interest in the nests or may not go through the motions of nest preparation and mating is simply incorrect; the actions have all been seen at sites where no breeding attempts have been made in several successive years. It is perhaps not realised that the amount of activity, including nest refurbishment, can vary greatly between years and between pairs regardless of their status or future events and that certain activities are easily missed during casual observation time.

Adverse weather conditions can also influence the recorded results and expectations, not only because few observations are made in poor weather, but because it can have unexpected and difficult to recognise consequences. If a nest becomes snowbound at the point of egg laying, production of the first egg may be delayed or it may be laid away from the nest. Alternatively, as happened in the Lake District in 1986, the first egg may be deserted but the second still laid in the same nest (Walker 2009). How often this happens is not known but it is clear that such events might result in misleading conclusions, such as a failure being reported because the expected hatching date had passed without any evidence of hatching being recorded.

The idea of eagles keeping their nests free from snow at this time of year may be relevant but, as needs to be stressed, observers tend not to know when the eggs are going to be laid so, even when the evidence appears to be conclusive, it may only be coincidental with the site visit. There are clear examples of when it does not happen and in which the eagles have had to wait for snow on the nest to melt before the first egg is laid.

NON-BREEDING

The reasons for non-breeding by established pairs are many and varied and cannot always be knowingly determined. Human activity might be suspected but this would have to be almost constant for breeding not to be attempted. The influence of food supply is usually assumed rather than proven and the evidence for its influence is weak. Weather conditions are more likely to cause a breeding failure than a failure to breed. As a result, although the national surveys indicate that non-breeding is a common event, it rarely has a clear explanation and so is rarely unambiguously proven, simply because most fieldworkers do not have the opportunity to undertake the necessarily intensive recording that is required to confirm that a resident pair has been seen and that no

[ABOVE] SOME TERRITORIES CLEARLY FAIL TO MEET THE EXPECTED QUALITY CRITERIA BUT CONTINUE TO BE OCCUPIED BY EAGLES WHICH BREED SUCCESSFULLY

[BELOW] AS A TRULY RESIDENT SPECIES, THE GOLDEN EAGLE COMMONLY HAS TO SURVIVE UNDER EXTREME AND LIMITING CONDITIONS BUT SITES ARE STILL OCCUPIED THROUGHOUT THE YEAR

[LEFT] SOME BREEDING SITES ALSO FAIL TO MEET THE EAGLE'S POPULAR IMAGE AS A BIRD OF REMOTE MOUNTAINS AND MOORLAND

[MIDDLE] EAGLE NESTS ARE NOT ALWAYS IN REMOTE LOCATIONS AND MANY ARE EASILY VISIBLE FROM PUBLIC ROADS; IN THIS CASE FROM A DISTANCE OF LESS THAN 1.5 KILOMETRES

[BOTTOM] EVEN SUCCESSFUL NESTS CAN BE MISSED IF OBSERVERS HAVE RIGID IDEAS ABOUT SUITABILITY; THE ABSENCE OF CRAGS OR LARGE TREES IS NOT THE SAME AS A LACK OF POTENTIAL

[ABOVE] Eagles will often perch and roost close to food sources rather than in their more favoured locations during harsh conditions

[BELOW] Eagle activity can also be limited when dense mist shrouds the hills, and be caught off-guard (photo taken without a hide and through a standard 50mm lens)

[Left] The simultaneous availability of these two red deer stags on Jura (where there are no foxes to scavenge the remains) reduced their overall value to eagles and helps to show why food should not be assessed by using the number of items needed to meet the expected food requirement

[Middle] Red deer often hide their calves in bracken but foraging eagles will target these areas and 'soft cover' will not prevent an attack

[Bottom] Sickly deer often seek any shelter they can find and so carrion is often found in bracken patches

[RIGHT] THE RED GROUSE IS OFTEN CALLED A TYPICAL PREY SPECIES BUT THAT CAN ONLY BE THE CASE WHERE THEY ARE RELATIVELY COMMON

[MIDDLE] GOLDEN EAGLES USUALLY LEAVE A VERY NEAT PATTERN OF PLUCKINGS BECAUSE OF THEIR STRENGTH; NOTE ALSO THAT THE HEAD AND THIGH HAVE BEEN EATEN RATHER THAN THE FLESH

[BOTTOM] ALTHOUGH THERE IS A SURPLUS OF FOOD IN THIS NEST (MOUNTAIN HARE) AND NO EVIDENCE OF SIBLING AGGRESSION, ONLY ONE CHICK FLEDGED; ALSO NOTE THE LACK OF A SOFT NEST LINING

[Above] That this breeding attempt was reported as a failure to hatch eggs shows how easy it is to make mistakes when interpreting observations

[Below] (Nestling removed for photo) Fulmar and more especially mink might be thought of as unusual prey but eagles utilise what is available, not what is expected of them; an assessment of food supply in this territory would prove to be very interesting

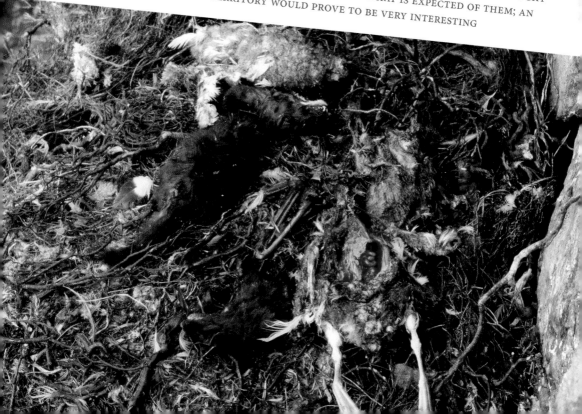

[ABOVE] ADULT FEMALE GOLDEN EAGLE INCUBATING INFERTILE EGGS IN JUNE

[BELOW] EGGS IN A SMALL WOODRUSH NEST LINING

[ABOVE] INFERTILE EGGS IN A LARGE GRASSY NEST PLATFORM AND CUP

[BELOW] SCAVENGED EGGS IN A ROUGH NEST CUP

[ABOVE] THE DAY AFTER THE
NEST WAS ROBBED (APRIL
5); NOTE EVIDENCE OF
INCUBATION-PERIOD FOOD
PROVISIONING (MOUNTAIN
HARE AND RED GROUSE)

[LEFT] TREE NESTS ARE NOT
ALWAYS IN NATIVE PINE OR
BLOCKS OF WOODLAND

[RIGHT] A PINE TREE
NEST BALANCED ON A
BRANCH RATHER THAN
CLOSE TO THE TRUNK;
IN SPITE OF THIS THE
NEST WAS USABLE FOR
ABOUT 20 YEARS AND
PRODUCED SEVERAL
TWO-CHICK BROODS

[MIDDLE] NEST AFTER
ITS COLLAPSE

[BOTTOM] OLD
EAGLE NESTS CAN
DISAPPEAR INTO
THEIR SURROUNDINGS
SURPRISINGLY
QUICKLY; THIS ONE
WAS PHOTOGRAPHED
ONLY TEN YEARS
AFTER IT WAS USED
SUCCESSFULLY

[ABOVE] RATHER THAN FIGHTING WHEN THE ADULTS ARE ABSENT FROM THE NEST, SMALL CHICKS USUALLY HUDDLE TOGETHER AND LIE STILL FOR MUTUAL PROTECTION

[BELOW] TWO CHICKS SHOWING NO SIGNS OF SIBLING AGGRESSION; AT ABOUT THREE WEEKS OLD, THE SOFT PARTS ARE NOW YELLOWISH IN COLOUR AFTER BEING FLESH-TONED AT FIRST AFTER HATCHING

[ABOVE] NESTLINGS AT ABOUT SEVEN WEEKS OLD;
THE SOFT PARTS ARE NOW BRIGHTLY YELLOW

[BELOW] AN ALMOST-FLEDGED NESTLING AT ABOUT ELEVEN WEEKS OLD; JUST DISCERNIBLE IS
THE JUVENILE'S LEGS-TOGETHER STANCE, OLDER EAGLES HAVE A MORE LEGS-APART STANCE

[ABOVE] ONE OF THE PLATE 39 NESTLINGS AFTER FLEDGING; NEITHER JUVENILE COULD FLY COMPETENTLY AT FIRST BECAUSE THE TAIL FEATHERS HAD NOT EMERGED FROM THE SHEATH

[BELOW] RECENTLY-FLEDGED JUVENILES SPEND LENGTHY PERIODS PERCHED ON THE GROUND OR ON LOW PERCHES WAITING FOR FOOD TO BE DELIVERED

breeding attempts have been missed. In fact, most non-breeding records are probably better described as failures to prove breeding; and of course, on some occasions, the observed birds will not even be a pair.

There is one potentially major cause of non-breeding that has probably been under-recorded and which justifies some consideration: the interference caused by other eagles. Pairs within dense populations may be limited by direct competition with other eagles rather than by being in competition for food sources, but with paired activity being mostly focused in the nesting area prior to egg laying, even this is unlikely to be a major problem. Potentially greater is the interference from eagles without mates or territories. It is generally accepted that immature-plumaged birds are more tolerated by residents than birds in adult plumage but they are still encountered with what can be time-consuming confrontations and the majority of intrusions appear to happen during the pre-laying period when their presence could be most disruptive (the number of intrusions declines over the year with very few occurring during the post-fledging period). This was highlighted at the Argyll study site with young fledged there the previous year disrupting the following pre-laying period by visiting the nest during February and roosting on the nest crag in February and March, and even into April in one case.

It seems too great a coincidence for non-breeding not to be linked to the presence of these juveniles and the same might be happening quite commonly within the population. The chances of seeing an intruder on or even close to a nest at this time of year are very small, given the type of observation sessions performed, and the chances of such an encounter being interpreted as anything more than a fleeting event are even smaller. That said, just as is the case with birds in flight, intruders might be being seen on nests or in nesting areas with some frequency without their actually being recognised as intruders.

One final point to be made here is that, while it is often said or implied that most breeding failures occur during the incubation period (Watson 2010), the laying of infertile eggs is actually a pre-laying failure.

THE INCUBATION PERIOD

This is quite easily defined as the period between the laying of the first egg and the hatching of the last to hatch. The problem here becomes immediately apparent because the laying date is rarely known for the first egg, never mind the last, which also might not hatch. Watson (2010) notes that incubation began between 16 March and 4 April in two-thirds of the population in 1982 but too much should not be read into these dates. While they support the idea that most eggs are laid during the second half of March, it is unlikely that precise dates were really obtained for two-thirds of the population that year. The national survey methodology on which the statement is based was not designed to record this moment and most dates were probably estimated on a count-back based on the apparent age of chicks, even though less than half the paired population reared young.

There is a wide spread in the known laying dates of eagle eggs but the accuracy of most records has to be seriously questioned as the chances of an observer actually being present when incubation begins are very slim, away from the very few projects with intensive monitoring. And, as already implied, the idea of estimating the laying date of an egg from the plumage development of a nestling is fraught with problems and uncertainties, not least of which is the identity of the egg from which the chick hatched. It is a common assumption that when there is only one chick in the nest it must have come from the first egg to be laid (as must the larger of two chicks) but this is not necessarily the case. In 1986 a Lake District nestling in a one-chick brood definitely hatched from the second egg to be laid but there would be no way of knowing this from its plumage development.

The earliest confirmed laying date in this work is 9 March (at an inland deer forest site in Argyll) and the latest definite first egg laying witnessed was 13 April (in the Lake District). The former was during a highly successful period, the pair's breeding attempts rarely failed when using a tree nest in the west of Scotland and two chick broods were quite common. The latter date was the last breeding attempt in a territory (2000) and followed a non-breeding year (1999) and a one-egg clutch laid on 12 April (1998). It is possible that the latest laying dates were linked to the age and condition of one or other of the eagles; in 2000 the Lake District male was at least 28 years old and its mate at least 24 years old. Factors other than age must also be involved as there is too much stability in the laying dates of established females and too much variation across the population for it to have a straightforward explanation.

Although established females can have a quite small spread of laying dates, there can still be unpredictable anomalies, as with the two April dates in the Lake District. These also gave that female a 24-day spread of laying dates rather than the four-day spread if they are excluded. Clutches laid by an Argyll female that ultimately produced broods of two chicks saw incubation begin on 25 March in one year and on 16 March two years later. Neighbouring pairs also do not have synchronous laying dates. Again in the Lake District, where absolute accuracy could be achieved, there was up to seven days between the two pairs' usual laying dates and similar situations are obvious and common in Scotland.

There appears to be no particular association between the female's age and its laying dates apart from the suggestion that laying may get later once the eagle enters old age. From what is definitely known, young females do not always breed earlier (or later) than older ones and there is no conclusive evidence to suggest that their dates become earlier (or later) as they age into their 'prime'. How food influences the laying date is also not known with any certainty as there are too many anomalies simply to state that pairs in rich territories will breed earlier than those in what are perceived to be poorer ones, which is anyway not always the case. The deer forest Argyll pair mentioned above undoubtedly began incubation earlier than many of the pairs in supposedly better territories and eagles in the Argyll study site, reasonably described as low quality under the usual terms, laid eggs at the very beginning of Watson's typical period. As also discussed earlier, the laying dates of each female would surely be more variable if food was a major determining factor. In conclusion, the laying date is not predictable from the eagles' behaviour and not easily calculated or explained retrospectively.

There is no need to count eagle eggs and too much disturbance has resulted from people, including eagle workers, who want to see and count eggs. It does not need to be confirmed that most breeding attempts involve two eggs, that some involve only one egg and that fewer again involve three eggs. In real terms it is only the number of young fledged that is of any importance to the species.

Watson (2010) notes the records of replacement clutches being laid with the clear implication of its rarity, and how most records were not truly confirmed. He suggests that replacement clutches might be uncommon because there would be insufficient time in which to rear young unless the original failure was early in the attempt and further links this to food availability in the late summer. Unfortunately, this implies that the prospects of juvenile survival determine whether or not breeding is attempted. In fact, food availability is usually greatest in the late summer and it would be perfectly feasible for eagles to lay their eggs in mid-May, breed successfully and fledge their young before food availability is greatly reduced. The nestling from an egg laid on 16 May would fledge on about 14 September, at a time when the numerical and biomass availability of species such as mountain hare, red grouse and ptarmigan are close to their greatest point in the annual cycle. This clearly does not preclude relaying on the grounds of food supply in the way suggested. However, what is reduced at most sites is practical food availability during April, the potential pre-relay period, so relays may be unusual because eagles simply cannot regain breeding condition when practical food availability is at or towards its lowest point in the year.

The situation is clearly not straightforward and relaying may or may not be more common than is thought. There is always the problem of observer effort: the observer might not be available or may not be making daily visits throughout the relevant period; failed sites tend not to be revisited that season and such are rarely subjected to intense searching and scrutiny; the relay might not be in the same valley as the known failure and so might easily be missed; and a suspected relay away from the usual nests might actually involve different eagles. That said, relaying appears to be very unusual and apparently ideal situations have been seen not to produce a second clutch of eggs. A Lake District breeding attempt failed on the day or the day after the second egg was laid (roughly 20 March) but there was no suggestion of the adults laying again that year.

While its onset cannot be predicted, it is pretty obvious when incubation has begun. A nest that had previously only been visited by the pair of eagles now has almost continuous occupancy. The time that incubation begins is very variable and has been reliably recorded from about an hour after sunrise to about two hours before sunset.

To witness the onset of incubation is probably rarer than witnessing the first flight of a juvenile, and waiting for either to happen can be frustrating and time consuming. When seen in both England and Scotland the eagles' behaviour was similar in all cases, with both members of the pair making a series of nest visits, usually with but at times without nest material; both might stay on the nest for several minutes; they might adjust the nest and both might breast the cup into shape. There might be nearby perching and mating might be attempted (though this is by no means a regular observation at this time) and some display flights might be flown below the ridge tops, often while the bird is carrying nest material.

When on the nest the eagles sit and stand and sit again and it can appear as if the female has laid the first egg only for it to then breast the cup in a way that no egg could survive unbroken. With a fairly rapid series of nest visits by both eagles, it is not at all obvious during which the egg is laid but incubation suddenly begins, often after a shorter rather than a longer visit by the female, and on four occasions it can be said with absolute certainty that it was the male which took the first stint of incubation. It may seem logical for the female to lay and then sit but this is clearly not always the case. There is no obvious behaviour that reveals the laying of the second or subsequent eggs. The second's date was only definitely known on one occasion in the Lake District, when the first egg was deserted because of snow and the second laid in the same nest three days later.

It is often said that the golden eagle's incubation period is about 43–44 days but this is the time taken to hatch each egg and so, with a laying interval of three to five days between each egg, the incubation period is better said to be about 48 days. This may seem to be pedantic but it has important management implications, not least when the progress of land management operations may depend on whether or not eggs are laid or on the eggs hatching or not. There are numerous examples of failures being wrongly reported because of observers getting the dates and timing wrong (as well as the interpretation of behaviour) and so it is possible that management operations might be allowed before non-laying or failure has actually happened. If there is any uncertainty about laying dates, sufficient time must be given to allow for the possibility of late laying or the second egg hatching before a failure is confirmed.

The division of incubation duties between the members of the pair seems to have long been of some interest. This is extremely difficult to determine during normal fieldwork as it clearly requires a continuous observation effort that would often have to begin in mid-March and some estimates are clearly not based on such intensive observations.

The RSPB wardens at Haweswater in the Lake District were better placed than most to achieve this and during1980–1985 it was found that the male's share varied considerably between years, from 9% to 33% of the daylight period, averaging, for what it is worth, about 20% per year. Everett (1981) summarising information from the same site, but with the involvement of different eagles, produced a figure suggesting that the male took about 6% of the total incubation period, with only the female incubating overnight. By comparison, studies referred to by Watson (2010) give the average male a share of 10–14%, although daylight is not specified and it is probably only an assumption that the female sat overnight.

As well as varying between years, the male's share can vary depending on the experience of the individual birds involved. The Lake District observations suggest that the less experienced the female, the smaller the male's share of incubation. A settled, established bird was more likely to share the duties than a younger, less experienced eagle. This might seem to be counter-intuitive (inexperienced birds might be expected to be more prone to disruption than older ones) but the statement can be made with clarity because it was known that the same birds were involved in different years and the male's share was seen to increase from year to year. While it is correct to say that female eagles take the greater share of the incubation duties, this does not mean that it is unusual for males to incubate, for them to take more than four stints per day or for their stints to be in excess of two hours in length.

Nest relief – the exchange of incubating duties between the members of the pair – appears to follow no pattern; the first changeover of the day is as likely to take place in the late morning as it is shortly after first light and the last of the day may take place several hours before sunset. It may be thought that nest relief is simply associated with the sitting bird's bodily functions, especially the female's need to feed or defecate after a long, cold night on the nest, but this is not always the case; even after the first changeover of the day and when fresh food is available close to the nest, the female does not always fly straight to food in the morning and often does not feed during its first break from the nest.

Females often spend their entire off-duty period preening on a perch inside the nesting area. Both feeding and drinking can occur during these breaks but a necessity to feed can appear to be an almost unusual reason for nest relief. As it can be inferred that females may have reduced food requirements during the incubation period (when they are largely inactive and usually quite well protected from the worst of the weather) and the male has a greater freedom to feed at any time and a willingness to incubate, the idea that breeding failures may result from both eagles having to leave the eggs unattended in order to feed (Watson 2010) is fanciful. There seems to be no proven examples of this happening and the notion seems to be based on ingrained assumptions about food availability rather than on evidence.

There also appears to be no evidence to suggest the length of time it takes for eggs to die through lack of attention and breeding success has been seen to follow several absences of about 20 minutes plus additional shorter periods throughout incubation. Female eagles often leave the eggs unattended to defecate and while they might defecate in flight during a quick off-and-on manoeuvre, they are just as likely to perch for a few minutes before returning.

It is, in fact, not at all unusual to see both members of the pair in flight during the incubation period as some changeovers result from the female leaving the nest before the male arrives, and these not unusually begin when the male is out of sight of the nest. By contrast, during the intensive Lake District and Argyll studies, it proved incredibly unusual for a male to leave the eggs before the female had returned to the nest, it being recorded only twice during this study.

Flight relief also raises the possibility of mistaken interpretations of behaviour, such as the idea of both birds being off at the same time to feed. Not only is flight relief perfectly natural, though rarely reported, but it sometimes follows a performance of the pursuit-flight display. With its speed, twisting nature, the use of flight rolls and talon touching, and it usually ending with one bird leaving the area and the other flying to the nest, it is remarkably similar to how territorial defence behaviour is expected to be performed.

Flight relief also suggests that most changeovers are initiated by the female as these are effectively never initiated by the male. Equally, at other times, males will make a series of nest visits, with and without material, and may spend several minutes arranging material around the female without the latter standing. Conversely, females often stand as soon as, or even before, the male arrives whereas males almost always wait for the female to indicate its intentions by lowering its head or stepping in and almost pushing the male.

After the sharing of incubation, what seems to have most fascinated eagle watchers is the question of nest provisioning during the incubation period, the delivery of food to the nest before the eggs have hatched. Gordon (1955) considered this to be unusual behaviour and Watson (2010) considered his example of provisioning to be exceptional. In fact, food provisioning is much more common than is generally believed; it is not commonly seen because of the type of fieldwork being undertaken.

Again, the detailed observations made in the Lake District provide the best and most complete information on this issue from Britain. Here one pair habitually, and possibly daily, carried food to the nest (both carrion and freshly-killed prey) while for much of their history it was extremely rare for the pairings at the other site to do so. When provisioning was seen at the second site it involved the same birds that had previously not been seen to do it under apparently similar conditions of food availability. Observations in Scotland also showed sites where the degree of effort varied between pairs and years.

There is clearly no obvious pattern to this behaviour; it varies from pair to pair, within pairs, between individuals and between years and is not determined by the available food sources or food's overall availability in a territory.

It should also be stressed that while this type of behaviour is usually described as the male delivering food for the female (Watson 2010) it is actually provisioning the nest. At more than one site, both members of the pair have been seen to carry food to the nest and both were seen to feed from this (food delivered by themselves and by their mate) while incubating. Females have also been seen to immediately fly off with food delivered by the male and, of course, both members of the pair remove prey remains on which they often nibble before dumping, just as they do during the nestling period.

The general behaviour of the off-duty bird during the incubation period has been little reported. Nest watching tends to exaggerate the amount of time that both eagles are believed to spend in that vicinity, although it does have to be said that it is not unusual for neither to leave this area during the course of a day at this time. The nesting terrain plays a part in this as, during the normal course of events, it is easier for a bird to remain in a large open glen all day than in a small one, a heavily afforested one or where the terrain is more moorland in nature.

As the male spends less time on the nest than its mate, it is likely to be seen in flight more often than the female and more likely to be seen in outlying parts of the territory. That the incubating female has few enemies is perhaps evidenced by the length of time males sometimes spend away from the nesting area. Not only might a male's absence extend for four or five hours, but there may be more than one such absence on any given day.

Males can appear to be hunting or simply drifting around, they may spend long periods perched as if standing sentinel over their territory or they might be seen interacting with corvids that neither pose a threat nor are needed for food. More often than not, all four types of behaviour will be seen and it may not be easily possible to determine which is most closely associated with the location in question or which provided the initial impetus for the bird's presence.

Male eagles generally have time on their hands, especially if they are not provisioning the nest, so it is not surprising that much of their time is spent perched. Their territorial duties are typically low key in nature, with presence rather than activity usually appearing to be sufficient to maintain dominance even though intrusions into outlying parts of the territory by immature-plumaged and unmated birds appear to be very frequent at this time of year, possibly because the pair is less in evidence. With one bird on the nest for most of the time, the incidence of flight displays is relatively low and, as carrion is used, foraging is typically not time-consuming.

As a result, there can be little flight activity during the incubation period although amounts can vary greatly between sites and birds. One Lake District female made, almost daily, long flights away from the nesting area while its successor rarely did so. The latter would appear to be more typical behaviour with females usually finding most of their food close to the nest site and, during their longer absences from the nest, usually spending most of their time perched somewhere within the nesting area.

Presumably because of the time they spend on the nest with closed wings and folded legs, females seem to more commonly stretch and 'exercise' than do their mates. They seem to fold and refold their wings more often than males, they seem to ruffle their feathers more often (often doing so in flight) and, when perched, often stretch each in turn while simultaneously stretching the associated leg. They often perch with loose wings and on one foot, with the other hanging limply below a branch. Males do these things as well, of course, but they appear to be more obviously used by the female when relieved from the nest duties. In a similar way, females seem to bathe more often than males. Given the often wet and cold weather it might seem unlikely that eagles would bathe during March and April but it has been seen.

Other elements of the incubation period include egg turning (which at times appears to follow a pattern but at others does not), the collection of nest material (which may be thought of as nest adornment but which can also appear as little more than habit) and nest area defence against other species. Crows and ravens are an almost constant irritation to golden eagles at some sites and are dealt with because, presumably, they pose a threat to the eggs when the nest is left unattended.

All in all, while golden eagle activity during the incubation period is by no means limited to the nest or the nesting area, the birds are typically less active than at any other time of year. The entire territory area is still used, mostly by the male, and both members of a breeding pair will forage, perform territorial duties and undertake general flights when they are not on the nest. Females appear to want to spend more time on the nest and will usually return to replace their mate at the onset of poor weather conditions. Females will also return to allow their mate to deal with other species (and will call to draw the male's attention to buzzards, crows and ravens) although the records suggest that females are more likely to confront other eagles, even leaving the eggs unattended to do so on some occasions (Walker 2004). Both members of a pair spend long periods perched when off the nest and the routine of this seven-week period can appear to be tedious, with both the sitter and the off-duty bird not unusually appearing to fall asleep during the daylight hours when there is no stimulus for other activity.

NON-BREEDING AND FAILURES

It needs to be accepted that there are many more potential causes of non-breeding and failure than can simply be linked to perceived problems with the food supply and that most of these causes are unlikely to be seen when they have effect. It must also be noted that most non-breeding records are probably better described as sites at which breeding has not been confirmed.

While almost every pair of eagles will go through the motions of preparing for a breeding attempt, a proportion of the population do not lay eggs in any given year. Non-breeding can be extremely difficult and time-consuming to prove as the possibility of there being an unknown nest or an early failure has to be ruled out of the equation. In fact, it is likely that many of the non-breeding records, including some of those recorded by the national surveys, are actually very early failures that have not been found or recognised.

The possible reasons for breeding failures are many and varied and are not always easily recognisable, and most failures probably cannot be categorically explained. The most likely causes of incubation period failure are desertions due to weather conditions and human activity, along with interference from other eagles that can result in the eggs chilling or being broken. It is not unusual to find broken eggs in eagle nests, or even eggshell on the ground close to nests, but the reasons for the breakages are seldom apparent and they may have been broken during a scuffle or the eggs may have been deserted and scavenged. Interference by other eagles is commonly not given sufficient consideration with regards to breeding failures, even though the majority of intrusions into the nesting area by other eagles occur during pre-laying and the incubation period.

Territory holding non-breeding singles and pairs also show an attachment to the nest site and often to a particular nest. They are as likely to be seen in the nest vicinity as a breeding pair and will carry fresh material to a nest long after the expected laying date. They make nest visits and will spend time standing on a nest, sometimes together but often alone, in a way that can suggest the nest to be in use. It would appear that there is an instinct to be about the nests at this time of year and this can be slow to wane. Indeed, with females typically spending more time in the nesting area than males, the patterns of behaviour within the pair can be little different from those seen during a breeding attempt, excepting the lack of an active nest.

It is more difficult to be certain of how unattached singles behave at this time of year. As already suggested, with breeding pairs usually tied closely to the nesting area, it is not unusual to encounter intruders inside occupied territories during the incubation period. These birds are less likely to be confronted by resident eagles and probably spend a great deal of time travelling between territories in a way that could suggest that they were searching for vacancies. It is not at all unusual to see young eagles in this way and at one site, where a resident was lost from the pair in early April, a succession of visits by different eagles began almost immediately. They would, presumably, not have been as obvious had the territory still held a pair of residents.

There are other scenarios but it is clear that young birds spend a great deal of their time inside the occupied territories of other eagles. One long-standing idea is that the previous year's juvenile will return to visit the natal area. This has always been difficult to prove and may seem to be a romantic notion but, thanks to the visible satellite transmitter backpacks, it is now known that juveniles fledged the previous year revisit the natal site and, in Argyll, this may actually have caused non-breeding because of their disruptive presence. The visitors are not always returning young, of course, and visits are known to have been made by young birds that could not have been fledged at the site.

The other, though quite small, group of eagles involves unmated territory-holding adults. Contrary to some expectations, these birds perform all of the expected patterns of behaviour; they perform attraction flight displays at the expected times, refurbish old and construct new nests, kill and carry prey, generally stay within the territory rather than make extensive excursions in search of mates or vacancies, perform territorial defence behaviour and use their territories as if they were the member of a pair. It can be seen with this summary why the assumption that a simple sighting of one bird or a built-up nest can be counted as a pair is entirely without foundation.

The behaviour of failed pairs is very similar to that of the non-breeders, can be surprisingly similar to that of successful breeders and can result in mistaken conclusions being reached. How the failed birds respond is directly linked to the time of failure.

Pairs failing during the incubation period are typically very active, are usually to be found close to the nests in the immediate aftermath of the failure, will continue to visit and add material to the used nest and will usually carry nest material to other locations. They may make nest visits that have the appearance of nest relief and, when watched from a distance, it can be easy to believe that the eggs have hatched when they have actually been abandoned or removed. However, at other times the pair may almost disappear into the territory, abandon the nesting area altogether and occasionally be found behaving as if at a nest site in some other part of their area. It is also not unusual for failed eagles to construct or begin to construct a new nest some distance from the usual group at this time.

An additional, but possibly often overlooked, problem for the observer trying to determine an outcome after the event is that of eagles burying their eggs beneath fresh material. There have been numerous occasions on which a fully lined nest (with flecks of down attached) has been viewed and thought to be empty, only for a close inspection to reveal two unbroken eggs beneath what would appear to be the nest cup.

THE NESTLING PERIOD

More time, effort and resources have been directed towards this phase of the eagle's year than any other. In fact, most of the received wisdom, including what is thought to be known about food, diet, territory and habitat use, is the result of recording during the nestling period. Most fieldwork is directed towards monitoring breeding performance and most of the conservation management is based on successful breeding. To worsen the situation even further, this actually means that most of what is thought to be known is the result of what has been seen or found in successful nests.

Watson (2010) states that it is essential for observers to make 'frequent visits to nests' and make long watches from hides (that is, from hides close to the nest) for the gathering of information at this time. It is never essential to visit an active eagle nest and doing so or watching from close hides simply interferes with behaviour, limits the field of view and reduces the value of the record. As is noted in other sections, information collected at the nest is also heavily biased. As a simple example, the food remains found at the nest primarily indicate the nestling's diet and not that of the adult, nor food availability within the territory.

No specific length can be ascribed to the nestling period and it cannot be accurately predicted at what age a nestling will make its first flight. This is not helped by the habit in some eaglets of walking or scrambling (or branching in trees) from the nest before they can fly. Watson (2010) states that young eagles spend about 70 days in the nest while, incredibly, Holden and Housden (2009) state that eaglets will fledge after 65 days.

The correct length of the nestling period can only be known if the hatching and fledging dates are both known. As with the onset of incubation, the correct hatching date cannot be determined by countback based on the nestling's appearance. This is because there are variations in growth rates, there may be gender-related development and while sources such as Watson (2010) provide apparently detailed descriptions of plumage development, they are not precise to a day. Where laying, hatching and fledging dates have been known with absolute certainty, such as in the Lake District and Argyll, the range of fledging ages was 72–85 days. The most likely fledging age has proved to be 78 days.

The nestling's gender appears to have no relevance to this and neither does brood size. While it might be thought that females may take longer to fledge than males, the above-mentioned nestling taking only 72 days to fledge was believed to be a female, while that taking 85 days was thought to be a male. The nestlings from two-chick broods where gender was determined by DNA analysis fledged no more than one day apart whether they were of the same or different gender. Multiple broods may take longer to fledge but there can still be variation between years. There are a number of possible reasons for these variations but there is little robust evidence to suggest that food influences the length of this period.

After a seven-week period, during which most of the activity on the nest involved little more than standing up and sitting down or occasionally rearranging the nest material, notable changes in behaviour begin even before the chick finally emerges from the egg. Chicks obviously call before breaking free of the egg and their chipping the shell must be obvious to the incubating adult. Long observation sessions can reveal that the sitting bird appears uncomfortable, standing and sitting more frequently than before and staring into the nest cup. They do the same when incubating, of course, but not as frequently or as inquisitively.

As the brooding and incubation postures are almost indistinguishable, with a two-egg clutch and a laying interval of more than one day the sitting adult is both incubating and brooding for the first few days. This is often overlooked and breeding failures have been wrongly reported because the adults were still sitting after the expected hatching date of the first egg.

It is not possible to determine whether or not a second egg has hatched from distant observations of adult behaviour at this point, but that is not an excuse to go close to the nest. The adult can sometimes appear to be offering food to different parts of the nest, as if two eggs had hatched, but the chicks are usually close together and, settled in the nest cup at this young age, they are unlikely to require the adult obviously to change its position to feed each in turn. In fact, two chicks are often fed with alternating pieces rather than one being fed until sated before the other is fed. As the adult tends to keep its head low when feeding small chicks, it also feeds with delicate rather than obvious movements.

This type of activity can be seen from a distance at all but the most obscure of nests but the adults' behaviour can imply the hatch even when they are not on the nest. Even though males will incubate the eggs and brood small chicks, the female appears to be present at the time of hatch and so will be taking longer stints on the nest. This can make it appear as if the male is failing to elicit nest relief when it visits but it is actually determining the point at which to deliver food for the nestling. Interestingly, in a number of years and at different sites, including those at which incubation period provisioning had been recorded, the male delivered the first food for the chick to a nearby point rather than directly to the nest. It was then retrieved by the female which then, technically, delivered the first food rather than the male.

Food delivery then continues in the expected manner throughout the period and it is probably only restrictive weather conditions that prevent it from being daily exercise. The number of deliveries per day can vary greatly, as any delay or difficulty in securing a sizeable food item is often addressed by the collection of several smaller items. It is by no means unusual to find meadow pipits and field voles on eagle nests but this is not evidence of food shortage, should not be taken as proof that these are important food sources and it often does not even indicate an inability to obtain larger items. Their delivery, and the delivery of nest material at this time, is what might be called displacement behaviour, almost an excuse to visit the nest.

The amount of food or the number of food items delivered to the nest is of interest as it does not appear to be a simple reflection of the nestling's requirements. The adults do not increase the amount delivered, or the size of the items collected, as the nestling grows, but typically deliver similarly-sized items throughout the period. A nest is therefore as likely to contain a red grouse or half a hare on the day after hatching as it is 60 days into the period when more food is required. Some nests can be seen to contain a great surplus of food at an early stage and one checked in north Argyll only a week after hatching contained two red grouse and the remains of three lambs.

Surplus food is seldom wasted during a successful period as, certainly during the first half of the period, the adult female often almost exclusively feeds while on the nest rather than when elsewhere. The female will consume the remnants of prey items but also feed fully from larger items, usually after the chicks are sated, although it will also eat pieces offered to but rejected by the nestling. While adult males will brood and feed the chicks, it is extremely unusual for them to feed themselves on the nest during the nestling period and their doing so is a sure sign of food shortage: the survival of the adults is more important than the survival of the nestling, and as the male is the primary provider, to see it feeding fully while on the nest is a bad sign. This mostly happens during June when live prey has a low practical availability.

Food remains are regularly removed from the nest by both adults and dropped from flight or taken to a perch where they may be nibbled on before being rejected. As little food would be found in the nest because of this, it can give the impression of there being a limited food supply when, in fact, there is a more than adequate supply. Although it would appear to be extremely rare, golden eagles have also been recorded caching food and retrieving it for later delivery to the nest. This might be taken to suggest a restricted food supply but it was seen where this situation was not apparent (Walker 2004; 2009).

It is generally accepted that the male undertakes most of the foraging to provision the nestling but it should not be thought that this is almost exclusively the case. While the male will be the principal provider during the close brooding period (about the first three weeks) this does not preclude the female from foraging, especially if food is available close to the nest. The female's involvement increases as the season progresses and during the second half it can play a very active part in foraging to feed the nestling. However, the male does still appear to dominate the foraging effort and would certainly do so numerically, as females, overall, tend to take larger prey than males at this time of year. Not all prey is delivered whole and males usually feed from their kills before carrying them to the nestling. It should be noted that, contrary to what is often suspected, eagles will take carrion to their nestlings and there is no evidence to suggest that this is in any way linked to food shortages, as carrion is a part of the normal food supply.

An interesting feature of note is that, probably contrary to expectations, eagles do not always make direct flights to the nest once they have obtained and prepared food for the nestling. As noted elsewhere, eagles typically have regular access and departure routes around the nesting area, to ensure that the partner is aware of the other's location or intentions, and these continue to be used regardless of circumstances. They are often given preferential use even when a more direct route would seem to be more appropriate. During panoramic observation sessions, eagles have on many occasions been seen to approach the nesting area, cross to the opposite side of the glen to travel closer and then cross back to the nest. An artefact of this is that when attempting to determine the location of foraging areas by considering flight lines, the eagle might actually arrive from the opposite direction to the food source.

Perhaps surprisingly, it is by no means unusual for the adults to leave even very young chicks alone in the nest, although this does usually only happen during the mildest and driest of conditions and the adults will not or will only very briefly be out of sight of the nest. Breeding females at this time usually develop or adopt a perch, close to the nest, from which they can monitor their surroundings and the nest. As the season progresses the nestlings are left alone more frequently and for longer periods and the female will often abandon the close perch in favour of one of their more usual locations. This seems to be the result of the almost constant pestering to which the adults are subjected by the nestlings; even if they are simply in sight of the nest, the adults will elicit calling from the nestlings that have not recently eaten.

It might be thought that this habit is to reduce the likelihood of the nest being found by a predator but this seems unlikely, not least because eaglets will call almost incessantly if they require food, even if the adults are absent from the nest area. This calling also somewhat cancels the idea that green material is added to nests in order to demonstrate site occupancy.

The adults will forage together and independently during the second half of the period and may cover large tracts of the territory, leaving the nestlings unprotected for quite long periods, but they also make frequent return visits to the nesting area and females in particular can often be seen sailing at high elevation above the site. Not surprisingly, females also take the lead in nest area defence and often deal with intruders and potential threats alone, especially if they are inside rather than above the glen. On occasions, males can be seen arriving at speed after the event, as if having had to cover some distance, and their response can as a result be disproportionate to the threat, with corvids energetically harried from an area they were already leaving.

Males will also spend long periods perched in the nesting area, often alongside the female (giving the impression of a lack of interest and possibly suggesting that there is no active nest), but will often leave immediately after delivering food or when no food is required. While males will feed from kills made for the nestling, which will also be partly eaten by the female, they also have to forage for their own needs and the greater territory area becomes their main domain, with them commonly feeding away from the nest area. Male eagles can also often be found perching for long periods away from the nesting area at this stage. As the season progresses, even the pair can often be found perched away from the nesting area and, if stumbled across, can again give the impression of having no current attachment to a nest. A successful pair can behave very similarly to what is expected of a failed or non-breeding pair.

The nestling's development has been well documented with the rate and patterns of plumage change well known. As they increase in body size they become more active and usually begin feeding themselves at about six weeks of age, although the female will continue to visit the nest and can be enticed into presenting food to the begging nestling almost up to the fledging date. Although nestlings are often to be seen standing on the front of the nest, they also spend an increasing amount of time exercising their wings, eventually gaining some lift, and running about the nest top and on to adjoining ledges if any are available. They jump and pounce, pull at nest material and throw it around as if plucking food and snatch at food with their talons as if killing. They also spend an increasing amount time preening and stripping the sheath from their long feathers.

SIBLING AGGRESSION

The act of sibling aggression, or Cainism, and the killing of one chick by another, has been much described and discussed (Gordon 1927 and 1955; Newton 1979; Watson 2010) but its reasons and purpose (if it has a definitive explanation) remain unclear and the subject of much speculation; that some chicks survive the aggression also makes finding a suitable explanation extremely difficult. That it is aggression rather than fighting is shown by the unusual nature of records describing retaliatory action. This is seen occasionally but, more often than not, the subordinate chick, if it does anything more than lying still, tries to escape.

Although the aggression can appear to be incessant, it is not continuous and death is by no means inevitable; small chicks are often to be seen in close proximity to each other without any aggression taking place. It is generally accepted that if both chicks survive to about three weeks of age, then both are likely to survive and any later death is unlikely to be the result of aggression.

As would be expected, fatal sibling aggression has been closely associated with food supply (Newton 1979) but if a pair of eagles is capable of producing two fertile eggs it seems unlikely that they would be incapable of finding sufficient food to satisfy chicks that may only weigh one kilogram by the end of the first three weeks of life. It should be noted that the adults do not simply fail to feed both chicks or give preferential treatment to one over the other unless one is incapable of begging. There is direct competition between the chicks in the form of begging (which can involve barging, and this is when most attacks begin, as the more demanding chick is likely to be fed first. Even so, that chick is not always fed to its satisfaction before the second is fed, and if it is, it is not usually interested in what is happening afterwards. The smaller chick has also been seen to be fed in advance of the larger one.

It is also implied that fatal sibling aggression may result from the nestlings being left unattended when the adults hunt but at this stage it is unusual for the nest to be left unattended for any length of time. The chicks are also much more likely to settle into the nest cup when there is no adult present, both for comfort and protection from the weather, than to continue any protracted aggression.

It has also been suggested, using the lesser spotted eagle as an example, that the association between sibling aggression and food is a response to overall food availability, rather than being linked to availability at the time it takes place (Watson 2010). This would appear to put the *Aquila* eagles in something of a novel position as most other animals seem to rear as many young as possible to take advantage of possibly good conditions rather than rearing as few as possible because conditions might not be beneficial to their future survival.

In fact, there is very little robust evidence to link the act and outcome of sibling aggression to food. As well as it being unlikely that the adults would be unable to obtain sufficient food to sustain two very small chicks, many of the nests in which one chick has succumbed can be seen to contain a surplus of food, and to contain a surplus at the time of sibling aggression. Food is probably delivered to the nest on at least a daily basis at this time and the first items to be delivered after hatching will almost always be unavoidably sufficient to sustain both chicks for several days. That the adults will regularly remove food remains from the nest also argues against any suggestion of food shortage at this time, as they are unlikely to ignore a begging chick when food is available.

There are two more interesting facets of sibling aggression that add to its curiosity. First, all of the attacks appear to be performed with the beak but golden eagles kill with the talons and only pick things up with their beaks. Second, given that very small chicks are often thought of as being weak and feeble (with little leg strength and at times finding it difficult to support the weight of their own head) the viciousness of the attacks and the chicks' mobility as they chase or avoid is somewhat out of character. If only a single egg hatches, the small chick is typically very inactive and spends most of its time sitting in the nest cup, and the same is true of the survivor of sibling aggression. Once it has lost its nest mate, the survivor becomes inactive and a chick that was seen to run across the nest on one day will, a couple of days later, simply sit as if incapable of such movement. This may suggest that movement is the stimulus for sibling aggression.

It is possible that the outcome of aggression may well be determined by the hatching (and so the laying) interval. Chicks emerging after a shorter interval may simply have better survival prospects than those emerging after a longer interval. If the eggs hatch five days apart the first chick will have a much greater advantage than if they hatch only three days apart.

It is also possible that the outcome of sibling aggression may be determined or influenced by the chicks' gender. Correctly sexing nestling eagles, especially during the period when one may die, is probably impossible in the field but gender considerations must be taken into account. It is possible that two chicks of the same gender might only survive if the hatching interval is short, and two chicks of different genders might only survive if the hatching interval is longer and/or if the first to hatch is a male and the second a female. This is pure speculation, of course, but it raises another issue that appears to be common within the idea of sibling aggression. It is almost invariably only an assumption, however logical, that the survivor of sibling aggression was the first to hatch. Given gender considerations and a varying hatching interval, it must be possible for a healthy second chick to defeat the first.

Similarly, it should also be remembered that, really at any point during the nestling period, the larger of two nestlings need not be a female. Although the growth curve for female eagles apparently moves above that of a male (Watson 2010) there is size variation within the genders and the presence of two chicks in the nest may bring their growth rates closer together. A good example of the difficulties involved with this type of idea occurred in 2012: measurements were taken of a singleton nestling at about seven weeks of age and, with experienced eagle ringers involved, it was decided on site that these indicated the bird to be a male. This contradicted the opinion of the experienced observer involved and, when seen in flight after fledging, the juvenile appeared to be at least as big as the adult female: its gender could not even be proven with accurate measurements.

As well as with the outcome of sibling aggression, food has also been connected to the survival of two-chick broods and it has been noted that most two-chick broods are found in areas that are believed to be better supplied with live prey (Watson 2010). However, this does not preclude the fledging of two chicks in other areas and, as noted elsewhere, determining territory quality and food availability without intensive study is extremely subjective. The Argyll site again provides a good example of this. With relatively few rabbits and red grouse and no red deer, hares or ptarmigan, the territory does not match the image of a high quality site and yet it produced two young in both 2008 and 2010. It is also the case that pairs in the 'good' areas do not always rear two young. Again, it has proved too easy for expectations rather than evidence to be used to explain complex situations.

OTHER DEATHS

Brood depletion and the death of nestlings can also occur at other times and in the absence of nest mates. It is not unusual to find dead singleton chicks of less than a week or a fortnight old, and to find them in nests that were overflowing with food and where neither adult was missing. Larger nestlings, both singles and one of a two-chick brood, may also die and this appears to be often overlooked. The assumption that a large nestling equals breeding success (Hardey et al 2009) is not at all reliable.

It is probably easier to link the deaths of large chicks to food than it is the deaths of smaller chicks, given the problems that can arise with food supply in mid-summer. As overall food availability and the availability of different food sources vary across the nestling period, it is not surprising that there can be shortages from time to time and these become most apparent during the month of June. At this time carrion availability is probably at its lowest point on the annual cycle, prey such as sheep lambs and deer calves are mostly fit, healthy and capable of defending themselves and species such as red grouse and rabbits are often not at all obvious or easily caught. As the eaglets are by then increasing in body size, exercising and expending energy in the promotion of feather growth, food requirements probably increase when supply is most stretched and becomes a plausible reason why deaths may occur at this time.

Nestlings of all ages also die as a result of accidents. An unbalanced nest may collapse at any time and it is known that some large eaglets have died when falling out of nests. It cannot be said how often this happens because so few sites are checked after a large chick has been seen and, because of this, it is no surprise that the skeletal remains of nestlings have been found at sites that, apparently, had bred successfully.

Nestlings may also die as a result of general weakness, illness or disease, succumbing to cold or heat, or even as a result of rainfall. As well as soaking and chilling the nestlings, rainfall can influence foraging success and, in 2013, both members of a brood of two died during a period when there was heavy rain on a long succession of days which must have affected the adults' ability to obtain food as well as soaking the chicks.

There are many potential causes of death and it cannot be assumed that any eaglet will survive to fledging if it reaches a certain age, or simply because it appeared big enough to survive when it was last seen or that one of a two-chick brood will die or has lower life expectancy. It should also not be assumed that a missing nestling has been illegally removed, not least because eagles have been seen to remove and dump dead chicks away from the nest.

FLEDGING

Events around the moment of fledging are more open to interpretation than at other times and are the cause of some speculation. Although it has often been suggested, and is sometimes believed, that eagles 'starve' their young from the nest, there is no reliable evidence of this, as food deliveries are easily missed unless there is a round-the-clock watch and it would make no sense for a bird to weaken its young at such a dangerous time. During detailed studies, records of food being delivered to the nest on the fledging day are not at all unusual and this would act to delay the first flight rather than encourage it. Along with this, the fact that some very recently vacated nests are found still to hold fresh and little-used prey suggests that provisioning continues at the normal rate, rather than being changed, and the juvenile leaves when it is ready to do so.

It is very easy to take isolated observations out of context or to give them too much importance, not least when there are expectations involved and a suitable date appears to have been reached. Perching, hunting on foot, circling and making slow passes in full view of the nest may all be taken to be types of enticement if seen in mid-July but they are all seen too often and too early in the period for them to be specifically influential. In fact, the adults appear to have no involvement with the act of fledging; it is not unusual for the adults to be perched some distance away, or even to be out of the nesting area, when fledging happens. They can also appear to be unaware of the event even when present and may take food to the empty nest even when the fledgling is close by and calling loudly.

With all the legends that surround the golden eagle, perhaps the most disappointing reality is that of the juvenile's first flight. Although it is difficult to be absolutely certain, because there are very few reliable first-hand accounts of first flights, the idea that the young eagle spreads its wings and instantly becomes a magnificent master of the skies is a long way from the truth. Of the ten first flights witnessed for this study, not one covered more than 100 metres and most covered no more than 50 metres. And when the first flight is known to have only recently taken place, the juveniles have always been found to be very close to the nest.

This is not surprising because, whether fledging 72 or 85 days after hatching, juvenile eagles simply cannot fly very well; they lack full flight-feather development, wing strength and, almost certainly, a true sense of the perspective of their new surroundings. Most first flights are short because the juvenile almost invariably loses height as soon as it leaves the nest, they are made close to the ridge or cliff face (very few, if any, natural first flights are made straight out over the glen) and they usually end with an undignified crash landing. Some juveniles have been seen to skid off rocks and crash into bushes on landing and it seems that no proper first flight ever ends with a safe landing in a tree.

It might seem logical for juveniles fledging from beetling sea cliffs or inland rock walls to make longer first flights, but these birds face even greater dangers and, not surprisingly, are often to be found clinging on to very small ledges or clumps of vegetation on the near-vertical face. Any great loss of elevation in these situations, even without the juvenile reaching the sea, could make it almost impossible to be tended by the adults or recovered to a place of safety. The fledgling eagle rarely appears to have much control over its actions and flaps its wings to limit rather than increase its progress and so it is not surprising that many walk or jump when they first leave the nest.

BREEDING FAILURES

Failures during the nestling period may not be as common as earlier failures but many things can go wrong during an 11-week period of time. With the standard methodology suggesting that a large nestling equals a breeding success, it is likely that many failures will be missed.

Very early failures – those within the first two weeks of hatching – usually produce an adult response similar to an incubation period failure, with the pair refreshing nests and being very active. Mid-period failures often result in the apparent near-disappearance of the pair from the nesting area which, coupled with their inactivity, can make the confirmation of territory occupancy at this time of year very difficult. Most nest building activity under these conditions typically takes place outside the usual nest group and often in very isolated locations. Late nestling-period failures can also result in the usual nest group being vacated but generally does not produce much nest building activity. While all failed eagles do eventually – and sometimes comparatively quickly – become less active, some of the nest building activity can result in the construction of entirely new and sizeable nests.

With the loss of interest in the nests, resident eagles, not surprisingly, also commonly roost outside the core area during failed seasons. Coupled with the general difficulty of obtaining food during June, this can make even long-established occupied territories appear abandoned when observer effort is concentrated in the nesting area. It must not be forgotten that, although the core area of a territory is of paramount importance, the other parts of the territory do not have negligible importance and should not be ignored.

As noted, unlike eggs, dead nestlings do not appear to be buried beneath fresh material but they are also not always left in the nest. Failures involving both small and large nestlings have been recorded with the corpse left in the nest but there are also examples of nestlings being removed and dumped some distance from it. While the breeding attempt has obviously failed, as is the case at other times of year, the type of failure cannot be determined from an empty nest viewed from a distance. However, a close inspection can reveal the approximate timing of failure; the loss of small chicks may be marked by the presence of faecal splash, larger nestlings can also leave feather sheath and nestlings that are larger again may have left pellets, although these are sometimes eaten or removed by the adults (nestling and young juvenile pellets are generally larger and looser than those produced by adults). There may also, of course, be no available evidence to be found.

A failure during the nestling period ultimately means that very little flight activity is likely to be seen. As well as not always using their main roosts (which can also be the case with successful breeders) the members of a pair might be absent from the core area and spend most of their time perched elsewhere. While there is some evidence to suggest that such birds wander further afield than do those with young, some of the latter group make long foraging expeditions and there are obvious problems associated with confirming this in general fieldwork.

Confirming the breeding failure is relatively easy, especially if the active nest has been previously identified, but there are a surprising number of examples of successes being reported as failures and vice versa. Such situations are invariably due to over-confidence on the part of the observer and the failure to recognise the limitations of the available evidence. Laying dates are seldom known so there can be no expected hatching date and looking for a certain type of behaviour at a certain point in time can be incredibly misleading. As noted earlier, with a breeding attempt being known in which the single chick came from the second egg to be laid, the expected date may be nowhere near the actual date of hatching.

THE POST-FLEDGING PERIOD

It is astonishing but not at all surprising that so little effort has been directed towards studying the post-fledging period. There is an embarrassing lack of detailed information available, given how important the period is to the species' conservation. It is also astonishing because there are more free-flying eagles at this time of year than at any other, but not at all surprising given the general attitude that if something does not happen at the nest, it can be neither interesting nor relevant.

This situation is exacerbated by ideas that the first flight equates to a freedom that makes the birds more difficult to find, as the family party disappears into the vastness of the territory so that the adults can teach their young to hunt. This, though, has not been proven nor in any way recorded. The paucity of the available information culminates in the presumption that at some point the adults turn against their young and drive them from the territory.

The need to have a greater knowledge of this time is becoming increasingly important and there should be a real concern that the full development of juvenile eagles could be hampered by the established ideas considered in respect of changes of land use such as windfarms. While attempts to moderate the impact of intrusive changes of land use are centred on what could be called interference with breeding attempts and protection of the core area, what might appear to be sympathetic management when allowing changes to take place elsewhere in a territory could result in greater competition between adults and young, shorter post-fledging periods and the greater immaturity of independent juveniles. Because there is so little information available about the post-fledging period, species managers are guessing at how major issues will impact on eagles outside the nesting period and area.

Radio and satellite technology is being employed in the study of young eagles but these only reveal the, at times, almost random locations used by eagles, and what is proving to be of greatest interest to science and research are the movements of such birds after they have left the natal territory, in other words after the post-fledging period has ended. It is what happens during the initial development phase within the natal territory that is of probably greatest relevance to juvenile survival and eagle conservation; the birds have to survive this phase of their development without it being disrupted or curtailed. This is, in fact, as important as not disrupting the incubation period but it has seldom been given any consideration, even though disruptive habitat change can be rapid and decisive with, for example, one juvenile seeing no windfarm in its territory but the next seeing a field of windmills that removes land utilised by the first. The second might leave the area at an earlier age as a result and so could have lower survival chances.

The post-fledging period is the time between the abandonment of the nest and the juvenile's full independence. Astonishingly, the most detailed study of this period remains work undertaken in the English Lake District during the 1980s and 1990s (Walker 1987; 1988; 2004; 2009). This has been supplemented in recent years by work in Argyll but most other information is still in the form of casual and isolated observations.

Rather than it resulting in the juvenile sailing across the sky and exploring its surroundings, the juvenile's first flight is invariably followed by a period of virtual inactivity. As recent fledglings are not strong fliers, and are therefore vulnerable to predation or attack by other species, they can be surprisingly difficult to find if the landing site was not seen, as they are adept at hiding in lush vegetation and amongst rocks. It is this habit which may have led to the idea that they disappear into the territory and some very experienced people have walked past juveniles without seeing them, in the belief that they must have travelled further than they did.

However, fledglings are not all immediately inactive and their initial levels of activity are to some extent governed by the security of the nest site or landing site, with young from exposed nests (those in very open situations) being enticed to a less conspicuous and safer location. The adults achieve this by perching close by, to attract the juvenile, and then moving in the direction to be followed before again perching in an enticing fashion. Food is also delivered along the route rather than to the juvenile, as further encouragement for it to move, until it arrives at the chosen location. Juveniles from more cryptic nest sites tend not to be moved from the vicinity of their first landing site, unless that is in an exposed position. Once in a safe place, the juvenile becomes very inactive and may not move more than a few metres over the next few days as food is delivered direct to its location.

The juvenile's behaviour during this time is very similar to that during the final days on the nest. They pull, strip and throw vegetation as if preparing food, exercise their wings and will call almost incessantly if the adults are in view. As they become stronger, the juveniles begin to make short, hopping flights away from the safe perch, which gradually become longer as they begin to explore the area, although they typically return to roost on the safe perch for some time afterwards.

Juveniles are still not competent fliers at this point, typically staying close to the ridge, and have been seen to make ridge-hugging flights all the way around the head of the valley to reach a perch directly opposite their starting point. Flights away from the ridge, out over the valley, do not usually begin until about 25 days off the nest. Height is at first gained on foot or by means of tiring, flapping flights and truly competent circling to gain height is not usually seen until about five weeks after fledging. There are exceptions, and some birds do develop more quickly than others, but the study of a succession of different juveniles showed the shorter sequences to be exceptional. The same pattern of development was seen in the Lake District and in Argyll.

As a result of their weaknesses, juveniles can spend a surprising amount of time exploring on foot and commonly travel in this way rather than in flight, both when covering distance and when gaining height. They explore gullies, run about on open ground and pull and strike at plants and dead branches as if it were prey. It is not unusual for them to become so engrossed in this that they fail to see the adult with food. If the adult cannot locate the juvenile quite quickly, which may seem unlikely, they will normally eat the item rather than waste it. This presumably happens because, if the juvenile is not calling, the adult will assume it to have left the valley or not to require food. As their flight skills improve it is also not unusual for juveniles to find and visit nests, both the one from which they fledged and others in the valley. In October 2014 the Argyll study added more new information when a juvenile was seen to feed on a nest from which it did not fledge, and on food delivered by the male before the juvenile arrived.

Great similarity can be seen in juveniles' development both between years and between locations. Juveniles from different years have even been seen to bathe in the same place at about the same age and without being led there by an adult. Juveniles in different years also used the same safe perches, perched and roosted in the same places as they developed and their flying ability developed at the same pace.

One of the points of greatest interest revealed by the Lake District study was that, in spite of the idea of them roaming freely over the territory, the juveniles of three consecutive years (1982–1984) did not leave the nesting valley until about six weeks after fledging. This was entirely unexpected but direct observation and satellite tracking results showed the same to have happened at the Argyll site in 2008 and 2010.

The Lake District young fledged after 1984 made their first excursions at a slightly, but obviously, earlier age, after five to six weeks off the nest, as did the 2012 Argyll juvenile. In the former location the change was undoubtedly due to the loss of some important post-fledging period food sources. These included the loss of the nearest red grouse population and losses resulting from the felling of woodland in areas never visited by the eagles but which supported rookeries which, in turn, allowed flocks of several hundred corvids to be present and available to the male as prey on the hills on most days during August and into September. This helps to illustrate how events outside a territory can impact on eagles and it raises the danger of reaching simplistic conclusions about land value and importance within a territory. When coupled with adverse weather conditions, the 1986 juvenile was that most affected by the noted changes, left the territory at the youngest age and died before its first winter.

What was perhaps most surprising of all the Lake District findings was that the adult male provided virtually all of the juveniles' food during the first six weeks after fledging; the adult female played virtually no part in this (Walker 1987). This situation was repeated in Argyll and, even with broods of two to be sustained at that site, only the male was seen to deliver food. In both locations the males delivered freshly-killed prey and, on occasion, were seen to obtain this at more than ten kilometres from the nest. This changed from 1986 in the Lake District because of the above-mentioned losses and the later juveniles fed on carrion at a much earlier age than those fledged before 1986.

The adults clearly have separate roles during the post-fledging period and these are not dissimilar to their pre-fledging roles. The male hunts for, and provided almost all of, a juvenile's food while the female mostly stays on guard in the juvenile's vicinity to defend it and, if necessary, encourage it away from potential dangers. The female generally keeps its distance from the juvenile, to avoid or lessen the incessant calling, and when approached by the juvenile usually changes perch or uses its greater flying skills to gain height away from the juvenile. One obvious difference was that the study females generally left the area when their mate returned, whereas during the nestling period the male would seldom be alone with the nest.

This period of confinement or total dependency ended with the juveniles leaving the nesting area for the first time. In 1982 this was seen to correspond with an aerial food pass between the male and the juvenile which seemed to mark the culmination in the development of its flying ability. It followed a development sequence beginning with the male delivering prey directly to the juvenile, continuing with the youngster gradually becoming more adept at meeting (at first on foot), chasing and intercepting the male, through flight rolls at some distance from the male and on to the successful food pass. Although no food passes were seen in the following years the development of the other juveniles, including those in Argyll, so closely matched that of 1982 that it seems likely to have occurred during all years in which the male provided freshly- killed prey. It is less likely to happen where the juveniles utilise carrion at an early age.

From this moment the juveniles became more independent, began to explore the greater territory area and eventually began to spend nights away from the nesting area. The first flights away from the nesting area were usually quite short in distance, although the duration of absence could be great because the juveniles continued to spend a great deal of time perched. The distance travelled increased quite quickly after this and, presumably because they had no knowledge of the territory, appeared to be in random directions from the nest and little more than a continuation of the initial direction travelled. In this way apparently little-used parts of a territory, where there were no specific food sources, increased in importance in a way that is unlikely to be seen during normal fieldwork or recorded during environmental impact assessments.

The adult male continued to play a more active role than its mate but now stopped providing the juvenile with freshly-killed prey. As live prey still has high availability at this time of year (effectively September) it seems likely that the change resulted from the juvenile's unpredictable movements, making it impractical for the male to obtain prey and then find the juvenile, rather than it being a deliberate choice. The male accompanied rather than led the juvenile once it was wandering, usually following behind and taking perches from which to watch the youngster. The juveniles themselves appeared uninterested in the adults unless they were required for protection.

The juveniles at all the studied sites relied heavily on carrion they found for themselves at this time. As a result, the idea of the adults teaching the young to hunt was in no way confirmed or even implied by the observations made on the 16 juveniles closely watched. Although the food pass might be interpreted as a simulated kill, its successful completion did not make the juveniles adept killers. In fact, they were barely able to defend themselves against crows at this time. The juveniles were not even taught by example, as they would have witnessed more kills while still on the nest than they did during the confinement period immediately after fledging.

The juveniles did attempt to kill prey during the confinement period but had little success. A part of this development process was the habit of swooping and striking at sheep and deer, and while this might be taken to be the result of starvation or desperation, it is actually the honing of skills and not a serious attempt to kill. Juveniles can also be seen flashing their talons in this way at trees, at rocks and even at the perched adults.

From about nine weeks after fledging, the juveniles explored a much larger area and as time progressed they clearly began to leave the territory. The frequency with which they roost in the nesting area reduces until it becomes an exceptional event. Once the juveniles' movements are regularly beyond the usual territory area, the adult male effectively deserts them and returns to its mate. The pair can then be seen together more often; they move around the territory together but also seemingly limit their movements as if trying to avoid the juvenile. The juveniles' movements appear to be random and unpredictable rather than determined by a clear purpose and their movements return them to the nesting area from time to time, so they could be said to be still using the territory as a home base.

Juveniles typically become fully independent at about 12–13 weeks after fledging. By that time they have long since stopped relying on the adults for food or protection and the territory holds little further attraction to them. As noted by Gordon (1955), a resurgence of nest building activity coincides with this and provides an indication of the juvenile's full independence, although this autumn activity can also be seen after failed breeding attempts. At this point, and without identifying marks, it is difficult to be certain that an observed juvenile is the bird from the site and not a visitor. However, one indication is that a local bird will be familiar with and will use the favourite perches while these will be unknown to, and unlikely to be used by, outsiders.

In this way, the post-fledging period can be divided into three sections: a roughly six-week confinement period of total dependency on the adults, about three weeks of semi-independence (when accompanied by the male) and about three weeks of total independence but while still using the territory. There is clearly some variation between years but different juveniles in different years and at different locations have followed this basic pattern.

The post-fledging period also ends without any suggestion of the adults driving the youngsters away from the territory. In fact, at around the time of full independence the adults appear to be avoiding their young. Having devoted so much of its time to the juveniles up to this point, the male can seem uncertain of how to respond when the juvenile reappears and may make short following flights and ones that appear to allow it to watch the juvenile once it had left the immediate vicinity. By contrast, the female almost invariably drops to land when the juvenile approaches, giving every impression of wishing to have no involvement whatsoever. This response may also assist in separating young returning to the natal territory from strangers.

However, some more physical interactions can be seen, including flight rolls and talon grappling, which could easily be mistaken for aggression. These are always initiated by the juvenile, often do not elicit a response and commonly result in the adult dropping to a perch. In all aspects of the post-fledging period the learning process seems more about the juvenile developing its abilities than being shown how to survive.

But the interpretation of events still requires a definitive knowledge of the birds under observation. For example, on 16 October 1999 an adult pair was seen talon grappling and chasing a juvenile-looking eagle with extensive white markings in what could easily be taken (84 days after a reasonable fledging date) as the adults driving away their youngster as per the expectations, but it was known with certainty that the pair had reared no young in either 1999 or 1998. The immature-plumaged bird was not their juvenile, but an intruder.

It has proved difficult for some of the above findings to be accepted. Watson (2010) suggests that the Lake District juveniles were 'largely independent of their parents for food by 75–85 days after fledging' when Walker (1987) actually says that they were independent in terms of food at about 42 days. Watson (2010) also suggests that the earlier departure of some juveniles may have been because feeding on carrion might have 'enhanced the condition of the chick'. This fails to recognise that carrion was available to all the juveniles and contradicts the idea that carrion is of less calorific and overall value than live prey (Watson 2010), the reason why live prey is presumed to be more important than carrion for the nestling.

It is only during the Argyll study that fledged broods of two juveniles have been closely followed and this also produced some unexpected results. While the pattern of development described above was repeated, one of each brood of two did not gain full independence at the expected time, and at the same time as its sibling, but remained in or about the territory for all of its first winter, a finding confirmed by satellite tracking.

The behaviour and movements of the stay-at-home juveniles was difficult to confirm after the first six weeks (during which they rarely, if ever, strayed more than one kilometre from the nest) but the satellite tagging retrospectively provided a daily location for each. The observed behaviour varied between similarities with the semi-dependent and full independent stages of a normal post-fledging period, with the juveniles exploring away and returning, sometimes utilising food sources and roosting in the territory and sometimes not doing so. There were still some variations and the 2010 juvenile appeared to be much more closely bonded to the territory (making fewer excursions) than that from 2008, even though the latter would ultimately remain about the site for longer than the former. Interestingly, singletons fledged at this site in 2012 and 2014 also stayed on site until at least the end of their birth year.

The adults' response to these juveniles was also interesting. They behaved with and treated the 2008 bird as if it were simply a regularly returning independent juvenile until into the following spring (see below). With the 2010 bird being present on a much more regular basis, the observed behaviour was more similar to that seen during the semi-independent phase. Here, the male was often seen with the juvenile (even perching beside it in January 2011 as it fed from carrion) while the female seemed, at times, almost confined to the nesting area but also making the typical departure flights when the juvenile returned.

Something very similar was seen with the 2012 and 2014 singletons, with the former, after beginning as the most adventurous, becoming the least so of these six. The male was also seen to deliver food to both of these juveniles during October, the latest this has been seen. What makes the second of these records even more curious is that the male took food to the 2012 nest (not used in 2014) and the juvenile arrived to feed there for 19 minutes before leaving for ten minutes and then returning to spend another 45 minutes on the nest. The incident would be easier to explain had the juvenile been waiting on the nest, but it had only been seen in flight that day before the male's arrival.

The delayed independence periods of 2008(9) and 2010(11) also produced some interesting records with the former seen on the nest in February 2009 with the adults delivering and arranging nest material around it. This bird remained about the site until mid-April (confirmed by satellite tracking). This bird and those of 2010 and 2012 were also known to roost on the nest crag even as the pre-laying period progressed. In each case the adults eventually turned on their young and did force them out of the territory, although it seemed too late to allow a breeding attempt to be made in either 2009 or 2011 and, as the behaviour was not seen before the February after fledging, it did not match the traditional idea of driving the young away.

While the 2008 juvenile was on the nest in February 2009, the adults ignored and tried to work around it, but when it was on the ground shortly afterwards the male stooped at it in an apparently aggressive fashion. Both adults later pursued it in flight and this continued with increasing vigour during the following weeks until it finally left the area. The last sighting of this juvenile involved the adults aggressively chasing it out of the nesting glen in April 2009 even though they had not laid any eggs.

There is no easy or obvious explanation as to why the siblings in a two-chick brood should develop in such different ways. It is possible that all four stay-at-home birds were females, DNA analysis confirmed both the 2008 juveniles to be female, but it seems unlikely that none of the other observed birds were males, especially given the comparative size of some of them. There was no apparent problem with food supply in any year and no evidence that the adults encouraged or tended one juvenile more than another.

FAILURES

Just as with large nestlings, there is little likelihood of a juvenile's death being recorded and many juveniles might even die before they reach independence. Even the point of fledging has its risks. As juveniles are not strong fliers and are even worse at landing, they can easily damage wings or legs in a way that precludes their survival. Even uninjured birds can find themselves in difficult situations and those fledging into forest might not be able to extricate themselves. Juveniles might become waterlogged, one has been seen to be washed over a waterfall while bathing (Walker 2004) and they are also at risk from other species. Lake District juveniles were seen to lose aggressive encounters with foxes, peregrines and ravens, any one of which could have inflicted a fatal wound.

That so many of these situations arose during a single study suggests that they must be common events, some of which are likely to have worse outcomes. In addition, and in this same study, juveniles were fledged with deformed beaks from different sites in the same year and these probably had very low survival chances. On Lewis, the members of a two-chick brood both fledged with their tail feathers still encased in the sheath. While the blades did eventually emerge after the birds had been in heather, they could not fly properly, were easily caught and could have been injured or killed as a result. How many young eagles fledge with similar problems is simply not known.

POST-INDEPENDENCE

Whether remaining in or leaving the natal territory is more beneficial to the species or to the individual remains open to question and arguments can be made in favour of both; a juvenile that remains in the natal territory throughout its first winter may improve its survival chances at that time (via familiarity with the foraging areas) but its lack of independence or self- sufficiency may be detrimental to its survival in the long term; by contrast, a juvenile that leaves before its first winter may risk an early death but alternatively may become better equipped to deal with the challenges it has to face.

Satellite tracking may be helpful in answering this question. One of the Argyll tracking systems failed almost immediately but direct observations, and tracking, showed that at least five of six juveniles survived their first winter and that at least four of the six would have survived their second winter had a 2010 bird not been poisoned early in 2012 (RSPB *pers. comm.*); both of the 2008 juveniles survived to make breeding attempts and were alive in 2015. This is interesting in itself, given the expected high pre-adult mortality in this species, and the general belief that juveniles are the most vulnerable of eagles.

The results suggest the post-independence period to be the most variable of any in the golden eagle's year. It cannot be predicted that a juvenile will stay or leave and in the studies there was no observed aggression to suggest that one of a brood of two dominated the other in a way that would force it to leave the area. As the adults were not provisioning the young at this time, there was also no suggestion of one juvenile receiving preferential treatment.

The recorded aggression eventually shown towards the lingering juveniles also some-what contradicts the idea that immature-plumaged eagles are more readily tolerated by territory-holding adults. This idea generally holds true, especially with what are clearly the youngest birds, as young eagles commonly elicit little response from adults. A more robust response is elicited when the young are clearly older, or lacking much white feathering, probably because such birds pose a greater threat to the pairing and the individual's status as a breeding bird.

In the absence of unambiguously-marked birds, the recording of young eagles has provided little more information than the location in which they were seen. In many cases it will not even be known if the same or a succession of different birds is being seen. The satellite tracking of juveniles should increase our knowledge of these birds although it must be remembered and recognised that the tags only produce locations and not explanations for the bird's presence. That still has to be investigated in the field and the effort to produce this information has to be greatly increased if it is to have real value.

The tags have shown that the movements of young eagles are unpredictable and so show that too much should not be read into simple sightings. They also show that visits can be very brief and that some of the locations visited are not suitable golden eagle habitat; a location cannot be assumed to be suitable or important simply because it is visited by a satellite-tagged eagle. That said, the tags have confirmed the existing field evidence which shows certain areas, the safe havens, to attract a succession of different birds. The tags have also confirmed that young eagles will roam widely and often, will make return visits to the natal area and may eventually settle close to where they were born.

This age group moves freely around Scotland, making it difficult to track individuals in an investigative fashion. However, with a greater period of observation than that provided by tags it can also be said that such birds can occupy certain locations for lengthy periods of time (in both summer and winter), will utilise more than one such location (possibly taking advantage of variable food availability or responding to competition) and will sometimes establish these as temporary territories. These areas are larger than breeding territories, probably because they do not always have the attributes of a territory (they may provide a well-dispersed survival level of food availability rather than a fairly concentrated surplus) but, once settled, these birds utilise them in a way that is similar to use of a territory, they exploit seasonal food sources and availability and develop favourite roosts and even nest sites.

On most occasions an observer's experience of unpaired eagles in this age group will consist of encounters with birds visiting the established territories that are being monitored. It is by no means unusual for territories to be visited by young eagles during the breeding season as well as at other times of year. That said, most of these intrusions occur during the first quarter of the year with fewer occurring during the nestling period and very few indeed made during successful post-fledging periods. While some of the birds involved may well be youngsters from that site, they are just as likely to be unrelated to the site or the occupying eagles and immature-plumaged eagles are often seen in territories from which they could not have originated. For example, many such eagles were recorded in the Argyll territory in each of the 11 years between the breeding successes of 1997 and 2008.

Much more work and more evidence is required to confirm the detail of what this age group requires and how it operates, and observers and knowledge should not be distracted by technology that only records locations. It is important to undertake a field investigation of all aspects of a location that is known to be used by immature eagles, either in a succession of years or by a succession of eagles, for its true value to be understood. Failure to do so could mean that locations valuable to eagle survival, along with possible breeding sites, will be made unavailable and unusable, while some unsuitable areas will be taken to be suitable.

SURVIVAL

What becomes of the individual young eagle after it gains its independence is largely unknown and little value appears to be placed on non-breeding locations that are known to be used by young eagles. Unsurprisingly, one of the most difficult things for conservationists to achieve is the protection of areas that are not breeding sites. Because of this, while conservationists would generally like to see the golden eagle increase its range, many suitable areas have already been or are being lost to windfarms and forestry because there is no current reason to object to the changes and no understanding of the areas' value to eagles. Such changes must affect the survival chances of young eagles in a way that will probably impact on the existing population as the remaining suitable areas become more congested. Breeding performance and even lifespans may be reduced as a result.

There are many ways in which eagles of any age may die or be fatally weakened or injured. While persecution is the most commonly discussed, it is probably not the most widespread artificial threat to be faced by golden eagles. The increasing number of windfarms poses an obvious threat of collision but overhead cables of any type present a difficult obstacle to avoid and it is likely that many more eagles than we realise die as a result of collisions with them. At the very least, a Lake District juvenile died from electrocution or collision, an older immature died from collision in Argyll, an adult died from electrocution elsewhere in Argyll and an adult died from collision on Lewis; and these are only those cases known to one person. The problem of expanding the plantation forest in areas used by golden eagles must also not be underestimated as it will affect both breeding performance and survival by reducing foraging opportunity and juvenile development areas.

Even though the breeding season is probably the most straightforward aspect of eagle ecology to study, it can be seen that there are still a great many gaps, assumptions and ambiguities in our knowledge. While some of these may not appear to be particularly important, most will almost certainly have important consequences that are being overlooked.

GENERAL ACTIVITY

The routine activities of the golden eagle are commonly taken for granted and presumed to be easily understood and of only minor importance, but the differences that can be seen in different locations show that reaching easy conclusions, or basing observer effort on what is expected, can produce misleading results. It is not always safe to apply in one location what has been seen in another, no matter how mundane the activity may appear to be.

Activity levels vary across the year and depending on an eagle's status and the stage of a breeding attempt. It is very easy to believe that successful breeding requires a greater level of activity than does non-breeding but it can be seen that birds with a nestling to support can be surprisingly inactive, can spend more time perched than in flight and can be more difficult to see than those without an active nest; during the incubation period a pair with eggs might not even leave the nesting valley on some days, while those without eggs might cover the greater part of their territory on most days. Eagle activity is not simply about finding food or performing nest duties, and how eagles use their territory and the observable situations this produces can vary considerably, depending on other requirements.

It is therefore worth considering the various aspects of the golden eagle's ecology in relation to both day-to-day activity and how that may be interpreted during fieldwork and recording. It must be remembered, though, that variations in topography and food resources make generalisations dangerous, and even where there are basic patterns of activity, there can be tremendous differences in how these apply and are seen in different locations.

PRESENCE

For such a large bird, the golden eagle can be surprisingly difficult to see; when in flight, its cryptic colouration can blend beautifully with a complex background of mountain and moorland vegetation and, if it is not seen to land, a perched bird can be incredibly difficult to find. If the viewing conditions are not ideal, if the habitat is a mixture of open ground, trees, shrubs, boulder fields, nooks and crannies and lengthy distances (which should be the norm if the birds are not to be disturbed) and if the weather or time of day is affecting visibility, it can be extremely difficult to confirm the presence of eagles in an occupied territory. If the goal is to confirm the presence of resident eagles rather than simply the presence of eagles, the task becomes even greater (that this difference is generally not given due consideration does not help the quality of recording). There will also be many occasions on which no eagle is seen when at least one is present within the viewing area throughout the observation session. A record of no eagles does not always mean that no eagles were present.

Golden eagles can also spend an inordinate amount of time simply perched and showing no apparent interest in anything. They do not have to fly and the popular image of the golden eagle soaring majestically over its territory is, while not a complete fallacy, by no means typical behaviour. Observer attention is also too often focussed on the sky or skyline when an active eagle is more likely to be flying at lower elevation.

Something similar applies to the idea of eagles 'performing well' in the best weather conditions, those winter days with clear skies or hot summer ones that produce thermals; in other words the days when observers are most likely to be in the field. An observer only has to try to find a high-flying eagle against a clear blue sky to realise the near pointlessness of that task, as they are often beyond easy viewing with the naked eye. Observers are typically looking for flying eagles most of the time but an eagle is actually more likely to be perched than flying. When subjected to heat, eagles will usually take shelter in deep shadows, in the canopies of trees or may even prostrate themselves on a high ledge (Walker 2009) and on cold days they are less likely to expend their energy unnecessarily.

With eagle territories covering many square kilometres of varied habitats and the birds themselves aiming to fulfil different goals (foraging and territorial duties, for example) proving the presence of resident eagles in a territory can be extremely time consuming when the nest is not in use. This is because, contrary to popular belief and in spite of the eagle being a territorial species, the observed presence of an eagle in a known territory is not proof that it is resident in that location. Confirming the status of the observed bird is not achieved by a simple sighting, and even its showing an interest in a nest or roost is insufficient evidence to confirm residency or the presence of a pair of eagles where the site is not under regular observation. When the nest is not in use, the confirmation of residency has to involve frequent repeat sightings of what is known to be the same bird or birds in the same location over a period of at least several weeks, because there is known to be quite a frequent turnover of birds in some locations and because some locations are only occupied on a casual basis. This is another reason why the sort of 'smash and grab' national survey approach is almost guaranteed to overestimate the size of the national population.

THE PAIRING

Pair formation has already been discussed but it is worth reiterating that the surviving bird in an established territory might not pair with the first visitor of the appropriate gender; the choice is probably made by the arriving bird and not the resident; the choice is probably also on the basis of the territory's attributes rather than the presence of another eagle; and the first bird that appears to have settled might not be present in the long term and might be replaced before a more permanent pairing is formed.

To confirm what is happening, the observer has to know that they are looking at the same eagles on different days and not a succession of different birds, and they must not assume that they are seeing the same birds. Most importantly, a pairing cannot be confirmed simply because two eagles are seen together where the observer expects to see a pair or because they are performing a flight display together. The importance of being able to recognise the birds as individuals, using plumage characteristics, cannot be overestimated, but neither can the difficulty of achieving this under normal observation conditions.

THE PAIR BOND

The golden eagle is usually described as a species which pairs for life and the few examples, such as from the Lake District, where the frequency of observation throughout the year was sufficient to confirm the presence of the same eagles for more than 20 years seem to support this idea. However, there are too few studies of this type for it to be taken as the norm and, as most pairings will involve eagles of different ages (something that does not appear to be readily recognised), long-term pairings might be exceptional rather than normal. Studies implying few changes of partner within a population over a lengthy period of time are probably mistaken. If there were to be few changes in the long term, it would indicate an ageing population that would ultimately see higher mortality in a shorter space of time and this does not appear to have been recorded.

The idea of pair stability or loyalty also begins with the idea that an eagle's long-term presence can be confirmed with casual, and often well-separated, observations; in other words by assuming that there has not been a change in partner. Although individual eagles can be quite distinctive in appearance, there is a general similarity of plumage that can make definite recognition difficult even under normal field conditions. As a result, changes of partner are probably not uncommonly missed.

As an aside, it is interesting to note that while some sources mention that the eagle's plumage will bleach during the summer months, this was never noted in the Lake District where it was known that the same two birds were being watched throughout the year and over a period of many years. The idea would further seem unlikely given that eagles moult during the summer months, meaning that the plumage should appear fresher with stronger colours, not paler or faded, in the late summer. Because the moults are incomplete, the remaining older feathers may well bleach to some extent, but they should not dominate the plumage in the way implied and it is possible that observers reporting bleaching are simply misidentifying the birds they see due to the imperfect nature of most sightings.

The pairing is often thought to be sacrosanct but, contrary to the pair-for-life idea, there are examples of paired eagles being replaced while still alive. This could happen more often than is suspected because it need not be an instantaneous change, with one bird arriving and ousting another. In an example from Argyll, it took several months for a male to oust the paired bird, so it did not happen in a way that would be seen during normal fieldwork. Possibly the most interesting aspect of this example was the apparent failure of the female to intervene on behalf of a mate with which it had made a breeding attempt. This does not appear to be the behaviour of a species which pairs for life but of one in which the individual has no choice of partner.

There have also been situations suggesting that one member of an established pair has simply chosen to move on without being ousted. This may seem particularly unlikely given the set ideas, but a pair that becomes a singleton need not be the result of death. This is probably most likely to happen near the beginning of a paired relationship, and perhaps most especially if one or both eagles show immature plumage, but it can happen with adults in a way that has no easy explanation. An associated problem is that, with the immature plumage being so variable, what might be thought to be the same bird in two or three years might actually be a succession of different birds. Even when an adult-looking eagle is eventually in the pair, it may also be different to the last-seen immature bird, rather than being a sign of that bird's plumage changing over time.

This has major implications for monitoring results, as these potentially commonly overlooked, misidentified or unconsidered situations can produce a false impression of events at a site, and not only over the make-up of a pair. Numerous assumptions can be seen in projects considering the longevity of pairings. For example, when discussing golden eagle mortality rates, Watson (2010) includes suspected changes of partner but, by implication, some changes of partner probably passed unrecognised, meaning that it would be more common than was considered. This has importance because longevity and productivity are linked to population stability: shorter life spans require higher productivity to maintain numbers.

As noted with the timing of fieldwork, if observations are made at the wrong time or in the wrong way the observed 'pair' might not even have existed in the first place. Given that there is evidence to suggest that the strongest bond is with the site rather than with the partner, it becomes even more likely that pairings will be broken and change in a way that probably would not be noticed.

However, some pairings clearly do persist in the long term and so, even if the main attachment is with the location (as suggested by single birds, both those which have lost a mate and those which have never paired, generally, and often in the long term, staying within their usual ranging areas) there must be more to a pairing than two eagles simply being present in the same location on a number of different occasions. This is especially so given that the number of breeding failures and non-breeding years mean that most pairs have little reason to remain together in most years. It is easy to suggest that there must be a strong bond when breeding is attempted or is successful but there can apparently be a lack of interest at times during the incubation period, and after hatching the bond may be with the nestling rather than with the mate.

While there must be pair-bonding activity for a pair to form and for there to be breeding attempts, such behaviour has been poorly recorded and it is easy to gain the impression that, once paired, golden eagles simply exist together without making any great effort to maintain the relationship. Flight displays are typically treated as territorial activity (Watson 2010) even though many, and probably most, display flights cannot possibly be for that purpose. For example, most sky dancing is performed below the ridge tops and an eagle sky dancing to the nest while carrying food or nest material is performing a display not for the benefit of its neighbours, but for its mate. As will be discussed, as many simplistic conclusions have been reached about flight displays as have been reached about other aspects of golden eagle ecology: expectations often overrule the available evidence.

The members of a pair sharing roosts and perches, hunting co-operatively and patrolling the territory together will probably help to maintain the bond but there will also be more subtle behaviour that is not easily recognised. Calling may be a part of this and Walker (2004) described how the arrival of a new female, in near-adult plumage, temporarily increased the vocalisations of the established male during the breeding season. It was suggested that this was to familiarise the new bird with the location of perches and the male's habits and that it continued, with diminishing frequency, until these were known to the new bird. This type of calling was not heard when the replacement was a male and when there was no breeding attempt, although such familiarisation is probably less important at that time.

Even long-established pairs probably need to perform pair-bonding activities but these may not be at all obvious during successful breeding attempts, when the active nest ensures the commitment. The bond may need to be most overtly demonstrated outside these periods, but also during the incubation period, when reluctance or a lack of impetus to take part could result in failure. With male eagles typically spending more time away from the nesting area than females, and often wandering quite widely during the autumn and early winter (often roosting away and potentially coming into contact with unpaired eagles), the association with the partner might, in reality, be quite fragile and need to be reaffirmed on a regular basis.

The female remaining on site and mostly in the nesting area may be part of this (it being the focal point of the territory) but this is also more likely to demonstrate a commitment to the location; observations suggest that the longer the male is absent, the greater the length of time the female spends closer to the nests. The male's return is then usually accompanied by the pair perching and flying together, and often performing the sky dance as if re-acquainting themselves with each other and re-establishing the bond. As there appears to be no simple acceptance that the two birds belong together, this may suggest that the bonding activity is actually what might be called showing a commitment to share the area.

NEW PAIRINGS

The activities associated with the formation of new pairs have been alluded to by Gordon (1955) but there still appears to be a hit-and-miss element to this. What appear to be immature-plumaged pairings clearly break down in some cases, pairs appear to settle in an area but only stay for a year or two (without there being any evidence of persecution) and single residents do not always form pairs with the first possible replacement that arrives. Confirming the presence of a new pair is not at all straightforward and the clear existence of transient pairs and occasional territories makes this even more difficult, and difficult to confirm the number of pairs in the population. Some of the pairs recorded during national surveys are probably no more than casual associations.

The level of secrecy that unavoidably surrounds the finding of a new pair means that their behaviour is little known. This is not helped by effort being concentrated on finding nests and roosts rather than considering the relationship between the birds. As most new pairs will have been in the location for some time before they are known about, and might be thought of as visitors, there is probably little hope of the attraction, bonding and pair formation being seen or recognised on a large scale.

An observer is more likely to witness a new pairing, the replacement of a lost bird from an established location, than a new pair but even these are not always easily recognised. Unless the new bird is in immature plumage, the typical monitoring effort coupled with the level of familiarity with the habits of the birds at the site is unlikely to reveal easily the presence of a new bird. A bird in immature plumage may also be taken to be a visitor rather than a resident if it is simply seen to pass through a glen or if it is seen in apparent conflict with an adult.

It is easy to believe that a new bird of the appropriate gender just has to arrive to be accepted and that it will then immediately fit into the routine of the territory holder, but that is not the case. A new bird in the Lake District gave the initial impression of being an individual within the territory rather than being a partner. It did not use the established roosts or perches and often hunted alone in locations not used by the previously established birds. Perhaps most interestingly, it also showed signs of nervousness or uncertainty when approached by the established bird and gave the impression of preparing to defend itself or flee if necessary (Walker 2009); this is hardly the behaviour of a bird that is a confirmed member of a pair, even though it was roosting in the nesting valley at the same time as the established resident.

In this case there were no great demonstrations of attraction in the form of flight displays or the other activities noted with an entirely new pair by Gordon (1955) to establish the partnership, and the new bird appeared to grow into its role as it became more confident. The formation of the pairing seemed to require a greater commitment from the newcomer than from the resident. This further suggests that the location is more important than the bird and it might be concluded that the resident holds a location that the newcomer wants to occupy, rather than wanting to be the member of a pair. This might also help to explain why some eagles remain unpaired and remain alone on territory for many years rather than leaving to search for a vacancy; at Haweswater in the Lake District, a male which has never made a breeding attempt has now (2015) occupied the site for 11 years without a mate.

This idea is further suggested by variations in the rapidity with which a lost bird is replaced. There are very few examples where the date of loss and replacement are known, or where the intervening behaviour and activity have been recorded in any detail. Again in the Lake District (where there were not thought to be many eagles) it may only have taken only about six weeks for a lost male to be replaced (Walker 2009). It would be expected that the speed of replacement in Scotland would be at least as quick as in England and yet in the Argyll study it took 18 months (April 2006–October 2007) for a lost male to be replaced. At least five other eagles were seen inside the territory and interacting with the established resident during this period and it seems unlikely that they would all be females. A selection process must have taken place and the observations again suggested that the newcomer chose to stay, rather than being chosen as a mate by the resident.

Changes of partner also often appear to have less impact on breeding performance than might be expected. While observers often hope that a new bird will improve performance, most sites seem to continue at the established rate of productivity after a change. For example, both members of a north Argyll pair changed in the space of three years during the 1990s but productivity was no different in the 2000s than in the 1980s. Contrary to this, a change of bird at the Argyll study site resulted in productivity greatly improving, changing from one chick in 19 years to five chicks in five years, although other factors, such as reduced disturbance, were involved and probably had greater importance. That said, some changes do not improve breeding performance and the last change of partner in the Lake District did not produce a return to successful breeding; in fact, despite being continuously occupied, there have been no breeding attempts in this territory since 2000.

Because the quality of eagle may also be an important factor (the quality of either the resident or the newcomer, neither of which can be determined in the field) it cannot be assumed that territory quality played any part in the resultant breeding performance in these examples. The Argyll experience shows that even very unproductive territories can be viable breeding sites, while the Lake District example shows that a potentially viable site might not be returned to productivity by a change of bird.

DAY-TO-DAY ACTIVITY

The members of a pair are commonly expected to be seen together when the nest is not in use and when there is not a juvenile to be tended and they do regularly leave the roost at the same time, perch together and travel on foraging and patrolling expeditions together. That is not to say, though, that they will not operate independently and, as already suggested, male eagles seem to act more independently than females. In fact, the members of an established pair spend much less daylight time together than is generally realised.

The pair is most likely to be seen together during the pre-laying period, much less so when the nest is in use (because one is usually on or close to the nest) and less so again when there is a juvenile to be attended. While the pair might be expected to be closely associated during a failed or non-breeding year, the patterns of behaviour are actually little different from what is seen during successful breeding attempts. The pair may be seen together during most visits to the nesting area but males continue to use a larger area than females and roam as if foraging for a nestling. Single birds occupying established territories also behave in a surprisingly similar way to those with mates and follow the patterns associated with their gender, with only the younger non-territory holding birds appearing to have less established or less predictable patterns of behaviour. A large part of the reason for this will be that established birds continue to respond to the variations in food source availability that occur at the same time every year; even if the available biomass does change annually, the distribution of food sources does not, unless there has been a major change of circumstance.

Other than for their indication flights prior to leaving the nesting area, golden eagles are not known to have simple means of informative communication so, when together, decision making probably results from dominance or necessity within the pair, when one may be more in need of food than the other. Even so, it becomes clear during intensive observations that the female generally takes the lead in most mutual activities, with the male usually only leading at an immediate moment; the male may, for example, be the first to see and react to an intruder. This dominance of decision making is commonly seen during general flights. Circling is usually a precursor to a travelling flight and it is not unusual to see the male break away first, travel some distance and then return to its mate, which then leads the pair on a line flight, often in a different direction. Males sometimes overtake females on these occasions but the initial direction of flight appears to be mostly decided by the female.

Something similar can be seen with flights from perches, with the male more likely to react to the female flying away than is the female to the male. This can be said to apply to nest relief as well, with males (unlike the female) very rarely leaving the eggs unattended and reacting to the female's early departure by flying to the nest. Male-on changeovers often also involve more than one visit before the female stands.

Either bird may lead in co-operative hunting or may claim a carrion carcass first but, in general terms, female eagles appear to dominate their mates in this way as well. While both will usually wait for the other to finish feeding before moving to a carcass, the one known example of one adult displacing the other from a carcass involved a female ousting a male. A female has also been seen forcibly to claim a kill made by a male (Walker 2009). It would seem that male eagles are subordinate to females, even when there is not a great size difference between the members of a pair.

Most day-to-day activity is of a fairly prosaic nature (feeding, resting and simply being present in the territory) and a great deal of it can appear to have little real purpose or great importance. Golden eagles rarely seem to be hurried or need to make a concerted effort to achieve their goals and give the impression that they are always in control of the situation. The eagle's physical dominance over most of the other species with which they have to contend will play a major role in this and it does result in what may be called spare time. Even the presence of intruding eagles does not always elicit a particularly active response and this is probably because most intruders will be known neighbours that do not pose a direct threat to the pairing. Some interactions with immature-plumaged eagles, and especially during the summer of failed and non-breeding years, can also seem to be prolonged by the casual nature of the resident birds rather than by the persistence of the intruder.

While foraging may seem to require an increased amount of effort, being a hunter-gatherer rather than a simple predator means that food is often easily located and eagles will readily curtail a hunt if fresh carrion is found. While the need to provide freshly-killed prey for the nestlings has been overstated, even this does not appear to be as difficult as may be inferred. Golden eagles are remarkably gifted hunters capable of taking a wide variety of prey that is, mostly, not at all difficult to catch. They are not engaged in an almost constant quest for food as often seems to be the case with smaller raptors.

Golden eagles will spend quite lengthy periods in flight but even this can appear to have little real purpose. Flights which encompass large parts of the territory may be seen but their correct interpretation is dependent on elements that might not be seen. Such activity is best described as a patrolling flight, as this allows for unknown and changing motivation. A flight might be interpreted as foraging activity but any attack may be opportunistic and the lack of an attack may be the result of a lack of interest rather than a lack of opportunity. More often than not the observer does not know if the eagle has recently eaten and foraging can only be confirmed if the flight results in an attack or feeding. In the same way, a territorial flight can only be recognised if the reason for territoriality is seen by the observer.

Soaring, or high circling, is often too quickly interpreted as a territorial display when it is mostly a simple non-specific flight. Eagles will often perform circling flights at low elevations, below the ridge tops, that can appear too lengthy to be meaningless but which simply end with the bird attaining a perch. These are probably more to inform the partner of security than anything more specific and, whether on the nest or a perch, the inactive bird can be seen to be relaxed and unengaged when it knows its partner is present in the area.

Another common habit is for eagles to make perch-to-perch flights. When performed in a foraging area, it is easy to interpret these as a foraging technique, which it can be, but the same actions can have little to do with foraging. Eagles often change perches for no apparent reason and will gain their final perch for a lengthy stay after briefly landing at a succession of different locations. As such activity commonly leads to the bird reaching its most commonly used perch, it would seem reasonable to wonder why it did not simply fly there in the first place. The bird may, of course, be checking, determining and dismissing the importance of numerous different situations on its way around the territory in advance of resting.

The day-to-day activity during the breeding season can be routine in nature. In fact, while fascinating, the incubation period can be quite dull to anyone expecting to see exciting behaviour; there will be days on which neither eagle leaves the nesting glen nor makes a kill and when the off-duty bird spends most of its time perched inconspicuously some distance from the nest. Even the female may do little more than defecate, perch and ruffle its feathers on being relieved from the nest and any feeding to be seen is most likely to be from carrion in many locations. With food not uncommonly being taken to and eaten on the nest during incubation, there might be very little flying to be seen. This pattern of routine behaviour does not simply develop with the passage of time, as might be expected, but can begin very early in the incubation period.

While the eagles will be more active during the nestling period their behaviour is still very repetitive. The female will spend most of the period within sight of the nest and, once the nestling no longer requires close brooding, will spend many hours simply perched and watching. The male performs most of the foraging duties, still working for itself, the female and the nestling, but will also spend hours on perches, especially after food has been delivered to the nest. There is still territorial behaviour to perform and flight displays can be very apparent but these are often missed or misinterpreted at this time of year.

Perhaps contrary to expectations, the late nestling period can be particularly lacking in activity. As the adults do not entice their young from the nest, and obviously do not know when the young are going to fledge, they spend a great deal of time waiting inconspicuously on perches that are often high and remote from the nest. If food is on the nest, the adults might neither leave the nesting area to forage nor visit the nest every day at this stage in the breeding cycle.

Activity away from the nesting area during a successful breeding attempt includes foraging by the male and, eventually, the female but this is not always as obvious as might be suspected. Most foraging is not performed with high elevation flights and a foraging eagle may spend most of its time perched and watching rather than flying and chasing. The time of day is not really relevant, either, as effort is mostly determined by what food is available on the nest, rather than the idea of trying to deliver food as early as possible every day.

Territorial duties will be performed, especially with near neighbours, but observations suggest that the number of intrusions by outsiders decreases from March to July and that their intensity also declines. Intrusions into the nesting area are quite common during February and March but are much more unusual during June and July, even at failed breeding sites. Similarly, while the early intrusions mostly involve eagles in obvious immature plumage and active close encounters, the later intrusions seem more typically to involve older birds which show little interest in the site itself. There are intrusions at all times of year, of course (and there must be a great many during October–December because of the newly independent juveniles) but it seems likely that the activity associated with a successful breeding attempt is largely sufficient to deter other eagles from being too intrusive when there are young to be tended.

The low-key nature of much of the activity associated with breeding and even breeding success can seem surprising. Observers might expect a nest with young to receive almost constant attention from the adults or that the adults would be intensely active when rearing young, but that is not the case. As a result, and contrary to expectations, it can be surprisingly easy to miss a successful breeding attempt if the observer is relying on flight activity and nest visits to provide an indication of what is happening.

The moment of fledging does not really change the eagles' activity and what changes there are may seem quite surprising. Just as behaviour at the time of hatching changes little from that seen during the incubation period, so the immediate post-fledging behaviour closely resembles that during the later stages of the nestling period. The female usually stands guard over, but some distance from, the juvenile while the male continues to dominate the foraging effort. Females play a minor and mostly passive role at this time of year and, with their only real need being to feed, breeding success or failure does not greatly vary their behaviour or their association with the nesting area, although they will often leave the area when the male is present after fledging. With the male taking the greater role after fledging, they are more active than their mates, but much of that activity is determined by the juvenile's behaviour. The males accompany their young almost until full independence is achieved and so can travel more widely than usual but, even then, much of their time is spent perched and watching over the youngster; they do not lead or teach the juveniles, not even by example.

Once the juvenile has become independent the adults' winter behaviour is mostly low key, involving the need to feed, shelter and perform territorial duties. Mating, nest building and flight displays (all of which can be seen at any time of year) continue at a low level and there is greater use of the entire territory, with many patrolling flights being undertaken. A pair will commonly perch together for many hours, often in outlying parts of the territory, and in doing so reveal the true value of the greater territory area. The behaviour of single birds, failed and non-breeding pairs can be remarkably similar to that of successful pairs, with matings, nest visits, the collection of nest material, a female remaining in the nesting area while a male forages more widely and a pair perching as if guarding a site.

Just as there is likely to be a resurgence of nest building at the point of juvenile independence (Gordon 1955) there is usually a surge in nest repairs (or material collection) at any time of failure which can make it appear as if there is still an active nest. In fact, whether involving success or failure, each of the major steps in the breeding cycle (other than for fledging) is marked by a resurgence of nest building or repair activity.

Eagles that have failed to make a successful breeding attempt do eventually fall into a quiet period that can often lead to them spending little time in, and even roosting away from, the nesting area for many consecutive days. As the distribution of food sources varies little from year to year, spatial use of the territory changes little, but the female may forage relatively more widely for itself at an earlier date after a failure. As a result, an occupied territory can appear to be deserted if observation effort is concentrated in the nesting area.

The eagles' use of the outlying parts of the territory and their temporary residence therein at different times of year is commonly overlooked and under-appreciated. This is problematical for interpretation and species management and is exacerbated by a common misunderstanding about the value of the different parts of a territory. This is not helped by the recent use of statistical models that produce shorthand interpretations of ecology, encouraging the use of simplistic distance constraints in management. While the core area is the most important part of the territory (because it holds the main nests, roosts and foraging area) no territory is only comprised of the core area; the other parts can provide equally important foraging and survival areas. The value of land does not simply decrease with distance from the nest.

Failed and non-breeding eagles use the non-core areas more than successful birds during the nesting season because, as well as there being no active nest, foraging to survive is less intensive than foraging to provision and they can devote more time but less effort to foraging. However, these other areas are of particular value during successful post-fledging periods. All pairs also use the greater territory area to a greater extent outside the breeding season because habitat and topography (linked with weather conditions) have a greater influence on food source availability at these times than during the summer months. There are fewer food sources outside the breeding season so obtaining sufficient food generally requires a more expansive, if not more intensive, effort.

VOICE

The adult golden eagle is commonly described as being a usually silent species but this is far from being an accurate generalisation; in reality it is not at all unusual to hear golden eagles calling. There are probably two reasons for the usual statement; firstly, a casual involvement is unlikely to be sufficient to hear much calling; and secondly, unlike most other species, the eagle does not have an alarm call for use when humans are causing disturbance. As most fieldwork usually involves a degree of disturbance, it is little wonder that the species is considered to be usually silent – most encounters are with disturbed eagles.

The usual adult call can be described as a yelp but there are numerous variations in tone and intensity. The yelp is a contact call and, while usually only heard singly or in short bursts, 'conversations' or exchanges between the members of a pair are not unusual. There is also a juvenile-type call used, apparently exclusively, by the female which is usually an indication of the need for food at the nest, but which has also once been heard during a failed breeding attempt (Walker 1988b). As this last event happened with the birds still incubating in June, it possibly suggests that the call was used because of its association with that time of year, even though the nest held eggs and not a chick. Calling also occurs during some copulation, when on perches and roosts, when being mobbed by other species and when in flight. Calling is also not limited to when inside the nesting area or to the breeding season, but can be heard in any part of the territory and at any time of year.

The nestlings' two-tone cry is probably the most commonly heard eagle call as it is used from hatching to at least the time of independence. It is useful to the observer as it can confirm a hatching or reveal the location of an unknown nest or juvenile. It is not known at what age the call changes from juvenile to adult and this probably varies between individuals and, as adult females use a very similar call, the change may also be gender-related. Unfortunately for anyone wanting to determine this timing, it appears to be the older immature-plumaged birds that are the least vocal eagles.

One additional feature of calling is that the adult female voice is of a deeper tone than the adult male voice. This cannot be used for confirming gender when dealing with unfamiliar eagles because of the variations that can be heard. However, the difference is quite distinctive when a pair is known to be under observation. It is not known if the distinction can be made between birds in immature plumage, not least because correctly determining the gender of such eagles in the field is even more difficult than it is with adults.

ROOSTS

At most times of year the confirmation of presence and occupancy is usually most easily obtained by undertaking evening roost watches. This is because eagles not uncommonly leave their roosts in the morning before it is light enough for them to be seen from a safe distance and, outside active breeding attempts, it is more by luck than good judgement that eagles are seen in the nesting valley at other times of day.

The golden eagle may be a diurnal species but flights in near-darkness are quite common. While early morning observation sessions are often encouraged, and are still believed by some to be the best sessions, they can be the least productive. If the bird is not seen, it is not known if it is still in the area, possibly very close by but out of sight, or if it has flown beyond the viewing area, and this cannot be confirmed unless the bird is seen to return, which may require a long wait. If the observer is not present before first light there is also little certainty that a resident is being seen when anywhere other than close to an active nest.

Evening roost watches are more efficient simply because there is the likelihood of the eagles returning at some point before darkness has fallen. However, just as an eagle may leave the roost unobtrusively in the morning, so it might also not enter the roosting area until it is too dark for it to be seen below the skyline. While eagles may make a checking flight above the chosen roost before landing, they may not even do this if they are already in the area and aware of what is happening. In the latter situation they may also either linger longer before going to roost or fly to the roost an hour or two before darkness, and in the summer months they may simply stay on the day perch on which they are settled and not use an established roost. Furthermore, the members of the pair might not roost together at any time or even both roost in the nesting glen when there is an active breeding attempt.

An ever-present problem with roost watching (as can also be said about nests) is that the total number and the location of all those used by the birds are unlikely to be known to the observer. Roost selection can appear to have little if any relevance to nest use, with both members of the pair often roosting closer to unused nests than to the active one. The male's roost can also be more than two kilometres from the active nest during the incubation period and neither member of a pair may roost close to any nest outside the breeding season. It is not simply a case of there being three or four roosts per territory and these always being close to nests. While there will be favoured and most-used roosts, many more than are easily found are likely to be used over the course of a year.

An associated problem is that even well-used roosts may be located in more than one glen so an observer roost-watching in a known location may still be in the wrong location and, of course, when the alternatives are watched, the eagles may be using the first ones to be viewed. In addition, many roosts and their approaches (such as roosts on the far side of an active nest from the observer's approach) cannot be easily viewed by a cautious observer and an observer's incautious presence can prevent a roost, or even roosting area, from being used.

The most frequently used roosts tend to be those established during the winter months; these might be used at any time of year and have almost daily use from October to May. They are typically protected from the prevailing or most common wind direction, are typically at low elevation above the glen bottom, not unusually on minor features such as small rocky outcrops, and many seem to be surprisingly exposed. Some are more discreet, such as those in gorges, but roosts seem to be situated to avoid wind rather than precipitation. It is probably safe to say that all eagles will have alternative roosts for use during severe weather from less regular directions and which may therefore be in a different valley system rather than just on the other side of the usual glen.

Perhaps the greatest cause for uncertainty when checking sites or when using roosts to collect more specific information involves coastal sites. The battering that such sites can suffer at the hands of the weather almost throughout the year means that all will probably have inland roosts and these are commonly in small gullies along minor watercourses or on insignificant outcrops that might easily be overlooked; woodland or forestry some distance from the cliff will also be used. It must be remembered that coastal sites are still inland territories so the sea cliff should not be targeted at the expense of other possibilities.

While the main winter roosts may be used throughout the year, the principal summer roosts tend not to be used in the winter as they are typically in more exposed and usually higher locations. Where a territory has a relatively low maximum elevation, there might be little difference between the locations of summer and winter roosts and, indeed, there may be little or no difference in their use, with the same spots being chosen throughout the year. Roost use during the summer months can also appear to be at the whim of the eagle and while regularly- used locations may be known, the eagles, especially the male, may simply not bother moving from the last day-perch when night falls.

However, long-term studies show that even some of these apparently random locations will show repeated use. At the Haweswater site, for example, roughly 25 multiple-use roosts were identified over the course of about 25 years, even though only two produced the vast majority of roosting records (Walker 2004). Some of the others were linked to breeding performance, not least in relation to the female roosting near the nest during the nestling period when it used roosts that are not known to have been used at any other time of year. These roosts were also nest-specific and not seen to be used by the male.

There were fewer regular roosts known about at the Argyll site (19) and these were divided almost equally between the two nesting glens. There were also none that were definitively male or female, although both birds used certain locations more than did their mate. It might also be said that all the roosts here were nest-specific, as the birds were not known to roost in one glen while there was an active nest in the other.

That said, the male of any pair might sometimes, and occasionally regularly, roost several kilometres away and outside the nesting valley during the nestling period and will roost even further afield during the post-fledging period when it is accompanying the juvenile. Paired females tend not to be so adventurous and, once established in the site, tend to have fewer roosts than their mates and are more likely to be found using the most-used roosts. As noted in the section on territory, the female is more likely than the male to be found in the nesting area and may be the only member of the pair seen to come in to roost.

The members of a pair will often roost together at any time of year but they will also be seen to have their own specific roosts on which the mate may never be seen. An interesting finding in relation to this from long-term studies is that, while it might seem logical that the best locations would be recognised and used by any eagle based at the site, roost use always seems to change when one member of the pair is replaced. Even the most-used locations can fall into disuse as well as those specific to the replaced bird. In the 23 years during which one Haweswater female was followed, it was never seen to use the most-used summer roost of its predecessor. Similarly, a replacement male at the same site ignored the most-used roost and developed two year-round roosts that had not been seen to be used during the previous 21 years by the bird it replaced. With the loss of the two long-established eagles from this site, even what had been the most-used winter roost, producing records over a minimum period of 25 years, ceased to be used.

It can be inferred from these examples that if there is not a concerted recording effort, and if observers only rely on what has gone before, it can be easy to misinterpret the available evidence. They also show that there is no situation that is ideal for every golden eagle. Because of this, if the most-used roost ceases to be used, with checks failing to find pellets, feathers or faecal splash, and there are no eagles on view, it would be easy to think that the territory has been abandoned when it has not. Even regular roosts, though, do not always produce much evidence of use simply because there will be unknown alternatives and the amount of time spent on the roost varies by time of year; observers are always more likely to find pellets at roosts during the late-winter period than during the high summer.

There is another problem closely related to resident birds not always roosting in the nesting valley during the breeding season, and their often having unknown roosts scattered in remote parts of the territory: roosting by intruding eagles. Although the golden eagle is a highly territorial species, just as a pair cannot prevent other eagles from entering their territory and exploiting their food supply, so the resident pair cannot prevent all other, especially immature-plumaged birds, from roosting in their territory. There has long been the idea that such eagles are squeezed into gaps between territories or into the most remote and least-used areas within populations but, in fact, there is reliable evidence to show that their generally larger ranging areas encompass several breeding territories rather than being discrete features within the population. As a result, immature-plumaged eagles will often roost well inside territories that are occupied by pairs of adult-plumaged birds.

For the observer, the real problem is in separating a resident's roost from one used by an itinerant eagle, and this is not at all straightforward. It is not simply a case of a younger bird's feathers being more boldly coloured or even the idea that a younger bird will leave more down at a roost. Unless the bird is seen and the residents are known to the observer, it can be impossible to reach a reliable conclusion about the roost user. Roosting spots are regularly found in unexpected locations, they are often some distance from an active or any known nest and where use by a resident bird might seem unlikely. However, they should not be assumed to be a visitor's roost simply on the grounds of location.

There seems to be little real preference about the actual roost, with choice probably only limited by weather conditions. Ledges and branches seem to be interchangeable selections, and the size of outcrop or tree also appears to have little if any relevance to the birds. It is not simply a case of an almost inaccessible ledge or the biggest tree being used because they provide the best security; many well-used roosts are very accessible both to humans and potential predators and it is difficult to describe some as being more than just a rock on a hillside. As well as impressive outcrops, the known favourite roosts in various territories have included a hazel bush, a broken, dead rowan branch in a bramble thicket and the root of a small rowan tree on a very open hillside. All were locations unlikely to be targeted by observers as being possible roost sites.

In spite of changes of roosts resulting from a change of bird, Walker (1987) noted that juveniles from different years used the same roosts, roosts that did not appear to be selected by the adults and roosts that were not used by the adults. It would seem more likely that the different juveniles would choose different locations but that was not the case, and the situation was repeated by later juveniles there and in Argyll. In a similar way, the same roosts have been used in long-vacant territories by a succession of immature-plumaged eagles that could not have been born there. This seems to support the idea that eagles will recognise and use the best locations but it might be the case that adult eagles are more individualistic in nature and less likely to select the most obvious place to roost.

Away from the safe havens, young and unmated eagles often just seem to make the most of what is available. A roost used on more than one occasion by an independent juvenile bird in its first winter was simply in a small, isolated, open group of pine trees that appeared to provide no shelter from the elements whatsoever. Such birds can sometimes also be found in low-lying areas outside the population and quite close to occupied buildings. It seems likely that this is often the result of the bird being benighted on a foraging trip; as young, non-territorial eagles wander widely they often, not unusually, seem to put food ahead of security.

PERCHES

Very similar points can be raised in relation to day perches as can be raised for roosts. The number of perches used will be greatly in excess of the number of roosts, even if simple landing sites are excluded but, as with roosts, territorial birds will have a number of preferred perches that are in regular use and often used on multiple occasions each day. While knowledge of these locations is hugely beneficial to the observer, they are unlikely to be known at most sites and their locations cannot be easily predicted; a favourite perch may simply be a ledge amongst a multitude of other ledges which provide almost identical overviews of the site.

Not only will there be more regular perches than roosts, but these will also be spread more widely across the territory and will include look-out posts in the nesting valley, overlooking the main foraging areas and the greater territory areas, and loafing perches that can be almost anywhere. The establishment of favourite perches is not limited to breeding territories or pairs, as following the movements of young independent eagles suggests that these have preferred perching places across the entire area they cover.

Eagles of all categories can often be seen travelling in a series of perch-to-perch flights rather than in longer flights. While many of the landing spots on such flights appear to be random locations, longer-term observations show many of these to be used with some frequency. It can be surprising just how often the same nondescript spot on a hillside is revisited when the next rock or patch of grass is never seen to be used. To the observer, such locations may appear no different from a spot five, 50 or 100 metres away, but it has clearly been learnt and has recognisable value for reuse by the eagle. This also shows that most landings are not hap-hazard events but are made for a purpose, possibly because regularity of use allows the other member of the pair to locate its mate more easily. In effect, an eagle entering any part of its territory does not have to search or scour the hillside for its mate, but just has to check a relatively small number of locations. When the first is not on a known spot, the second may circle, as if searching, and then fly to wait on a favoured perch, or travel to the next area.

Walker (2004) noted that, over a period of about 20 years, an established pair of eagles was seen to have about 60 regular perches and many more occasional ones. Given the time period involved, and the year-round whole-territory nature of the observations, this might seem to be a surprisingly small number (a mean of little more than one per square kilometre, with most in the core area) but it shows how eagles can have very regular habits.

Fewer regular perches were found in the Argyll study but the two territories were very different topographically, with the former being quite mountainous and with a larger and more open nesting valley giving a broader overview from both the nests and perches. The Argyll territory had smaller, more enclosed valleys and more rounded hills; the main nesting glen was also forested, with the nests on an abutment facing down the glen; the main perches were therefore mostly about and down valley of the abutment rather than simply being opposite and on either side. Similar variations have been seen elsewhere with, in the main, large open nesting glens having more and more widely spread perches. Regular perches outside the nesting glen can be in various positions and are not easily located, nor in predictable locations.

As with roosts, the favoured perches can change over time and with a change of partner. Some will also become unusable as trees die and landslips remove a rock or ledge. However, more perches than roosts retain their attraction regardless of the pairing and the most commonly used of all generally also becomes that most used by a replacement bird once it has settled into the site.

If perch location is known to the observer it can not only make finding the birds easier, but can also help to indicate whether the eagle in view is a resident or an intruder; the latter seldom, if ever, access the favoured perches in a territory because, as with roosts, they may not be the most obvious landing sites. For the same reason this can also help to separate returning juveniles and immature-plumaged birds from those with no previous attachment to the location.

The favoured most-used perches, those on which the greatest amount of time is spent, may be on branches, ledges, rocks or even simply on the ground. The location may be tucked into a sheltered nook or as open as the very summit of a hill. With general perches, eagles will take advantage of any and even the slightest promontory. They will use stone cairns, fence posts, vertical stumps and humps and bumps as well as small rocky outcrops; anything, in fact, that provides a broad overview of the area. Even if the buzzard on the telegraph pole is something of a cliché, wooden overhead-cable posts are used as perches in remote locations and have undoubtedly led to the deaths by electrocution of some eagles.

As with roosts, the most-used perches will often be marked by faecal splash, down, feathers and pellets. It is not, in fact, unusual for more pellets to be found at the favoured day-perches than at night roosts because, outside the winter period, it is not at all unusual for the eagles to spend more time on a perch than on a roost. However, because it is generally easier to find and access regular roosts than it is the favoured perches, this is often overlooked and is another reason why pellet analysis as part of an investigation into food is not fully reliable.

Finding perches without extensive observations is largely a matter of chance and under the typical fieldwork methodology an observer is probably more likely to see use of a lesser perch than a preferred one. One reason for this is that the observer is unlikely to see a perched eagle during their approach and a flying eagle is more likely to take a perch from which the intrusion can be watched than one on which it loafs.

The length of time spent on any perch can be very brief and even an arrival at what is known to be the most used perch is not a guaranteed precursor to a lengthy loafing session. Golden eagles have the irritating habit of flying when not being constantly watched and they will also walk away from the perch, often wandering for 20 or 30 metres, or might perch-hop in a way that leaves the observer struggling to keep track of events.

The main problem is that an eagle's location can become totally unknown within a few seconds of the last sighting. It may have left the perch horizontally to the left or right, have flown down the slope or straight out from the perch and in a few seconds may have turned and covered more than 100 metres. It may also have only moved ten or 20 metres to another perch while the observer is scanning the sky and slopes in the hope of relocating it in flight. That said, there are some helpful pointers and it is not unusual for an eagle to fly shortly after it has defecated. Whether this can be termed 'lightening the load' cannot be said, but it is a common event. It does not precede every flight but there is a likelihood of flight if it does happen.

The amount of perching can also vary considerably both during the course of a day and by time of year. Eagles that have recently eaten well tend not to do much flying, although they may choose to return to the nesting area via a very circuitous route before settling on a perch. By contrast, active territory defence activity may end with the resident birds quickly gaining a perch and standing alert. They often do not pursue an intruding eagle for any great distance but will also not always settle in a position from which they can watch the intruder, often preferring to return to a perch in the nesting area almost as if they had a great need to feel the security of their home patch.

While eagles might be expected to be most active during successful breeding attempts, the amount and extent of perching actually increases as the season progresses, with the adults eventually just waiting for the juvenile to fledge. Walker (1991) suggested that the adults could spend upwards of 50% of the daylight period perched while waiting for the juvenile to fledge.

The amount of time spent perched in the winter might be expected to be reduced given the need to obtain food and yet eagles are often to be seen perched for lengthy periods regardless of the time of day or the weather conditions. With this, Walker (1991) suggested perching for up to c.70% of the daylight period. On one occasion, in that location, and after failing to catch a crow, an eagle was seen to land and perch for four hours before going to roost about an hour before sunset. On another day, a cold

February one, the same bird landed on a sunny perch and remained there for about three hours during which it was engulfed by the shadow of the opposite ridge and sat through three heavy snow showers before eventually simply flying to its roost (Walker 2004). It is probably not difficult for most eagles to obtain food and while the required effort will vary over the weeks, there are clearly days on which they do not have to try very hard to survive.

Failed and non-breeding eagles (those without responsibilities) do not necessarily spend any more time perched than those breeding successfully. Non-territorial eagles, and especially those in immature plumage, seem to spend more time in flight than others but, as noted, even these develop preferred perches on which they can be relocated on subsequent occasions and are probably just as likely as paired adults to perch for lengthy periods.

As with the amount of flight activity, the amount of perching mostly varies as a result of necessity. If a golden eagle does not have an imperative, it is unlikely to make any effort and will remain perched for hours on end, with more than twelve hours of continuous daylight perching not at all unusual. If it is hungry or needs to defend its territory it will spend less time perched. There is no way in which the amount of time spent perched can be accurately quantified as a proportion that is relevant to the entire species, although there are typical days: the ones on which the eagle spends a lot of time perched.

FLIGHT DISPLAYS

Golden eagle flight displays are usually described and discussed as primarily territorial (Watson 2010) but this is far from correct. Flight displays are used in a variety of different situations and by eagles of different status, including those which are clearly not defending or advertising a territory; it must also be remembered that flight displays can be used as an attraction to other eagles, and are not simply about defending the territory. This means that there is a great potential for the misrecognition and misinterpretation of flight displays because of the expectations that have arisen over their meaning and purpose.

The most commonly noted flight displays are soaring and sky dancing , but there are also display chases performed between the members of a pair that are easily and often mistaken for aggressive behaviour. There is also the disturbance display most commonly associated with human intrusion. Golden eagles also assume poses and postures that can be called displays. That some of these are not commonly seen does not mean that they are unusual; the more obvious displays are always more likely to be seen, especially when they are performed above the skyline. That some are not recognised or are misinterpreted is probably mainly the result of expectation and the failure to recognise the complexity of eagle behaviour. In fact, flight displays provide the best examples of observers seeing what is expected to be happening rather than what might actually be happening.

The correct interpretation of behaviour is always problematical and Orton (1974) provides a good illustration of this. Two immature-plumaged golden eagles were seen talon grappling in September and this was interpreted as aggressive behaviour. It could also, though, have been an interaction between siblings, pair formation or pair-bonding activity. The original interpretation may well have been correct but there is insufficient evidence to allow the correct conclusion to be reached. This is a commonly overlooked problem when attempts are made to interpret isolated observations or casual encounters.

SOARING/HIGH CIRCLING

This is the most likely display to be reported but not all soaring is a flight display, which is why the terms 'high circling' and 'sailing' (holding position without circling) should be in wider use. It is better to describe the activity than assume its purpose and a circling or sailing bird may be said to be soaring, even though the two activities are entirely different. It then also becomes easier to see how confirming this type of activity as a display rather than as a performance for another reason is much more complicated than many observers believe.

Soaring or high circling as a display is widely reported as being associated with fine days during the late winter period (Watson 2010) and Hardey *et al* (2009) highlights such displays as being a feature of eagle activity at that time of year. Although widely accepted, this idea is actually largely an artefact of the monitoring effort and has never been confirmed by studies of flight activity. Put simply (though discussed in more detail below) observers are typically looking at that time of year for eagles in flight, while later in the year their attention is more focused on the nest (they also pay very little attention to failed and non-breeding birds); observers are therefore more likely to think they have seen a display in the late winter than during the summer. Watson (2010) also suggests that soaring will be of shorter duration during the summer months but this also an unsupported assumption and, in reality, soaring and high circling can be more common and of much longer duration during the summer months.

Even so, there are many records of several pairs of eagles being simultaneously in view above their nesting areas during the late winter period and these episodes are usually interpreted as being the neighbouring pairs advertising their presence. Whether or not they are all pairs remains largely unconfirmed. It is easy to assume that they are pairs but interactions between residents and intruders can involve little more than two birds circling above the nesting area and most intrusions take place during the first quarter of the year.

While it may seem logical (and it may be the case) that the eagles involved are performing in their individual pairings and above their own nesting areas, this has not been proven. The point is best emphasised by eagles that are known not to be inside an existing territory: these will perform identical soaring/circling flights but they are not said to be demonstrating occupancy of that location; the same two birds may then be seen to behave in the same way inside a known territory, but that does not make them the residents in that location either.

In fact it is very difficult to separate high circling/sailing as a display from the same actions being used for other reasons and many performances are for the benefit of the mate rather than for other eagles. Such flights are used to indicate an eagle's intention and as these can be prolonged and longer than needed simply in order to gain height above the ridge tops, they can be mistaken for an occupancy or territorial display. Because soaring and circling has many possible uses and explanations (and potentially more than one simultaneous purpose) the main problem for the observer is that the stimulus is not always apparent, not easily determined and often outside their field of view. An eagle soaring or circling and then travelling may be responding to an intruder or it may just be leaving for another part of the territory.

That said, soaring and circling flights are used as territorial displays but are most likely to involve fairly casual encounters with neighbouring birds during the breeding season, rather than before it begins. One or both members of the pair may circle in full view of a neighbour but on their own side of the divide (often in or above their respective nesting areas) and often for quite long periods of time without any real interaction being involved before they lose interest and move away. It is difficult to know whether or not the birds were really performing for the benefit of the neighbour, or if the performance had any real meaning, and the fact that the members of adjacent pairs will be familiar with each other suggests that it would be little more than a casual encounter.

High circling as a display cannot be said to be more associated with the nesting area than the territory boundaries because nesting areas are commonly close to the separation point between pairs. The display's use close to more remote separation points can often appear to be an uncomfortable experience with the birds staying some distance apart, often more than two kilometres from each other, and often drifting horizontally back and forth rather than remaining above a spot in a way that would suggest strength and confidence. The question of dominance within the population probably plays a role in this. The presence of genuine intruders or unfamiliar eagles can elicit more extensive circling but more commonly involves a challenging approach flight, the half-flight; circling, if it occurs, usually follows the intruder's departure from the area and often when it is out of sight, as if it is being used to watch for, rather than challenge, the intruder.

High circling as a display is most commonly performed by one eagle at a time and most frequently by the male of a pair. One of the most obvious examples involves the male indicating its intention to leave the nesting area during the breeding season. The bird circles in full view of the nest, and often for longer than is necessary to gain sufficient height to leave, before turning away on its trip. If it intends to be away for more than a few minutes, the bird will also usually leave the nesting area via an established familiar route, one of the flight corridors that cross the territory, rather than over a random point. This type of display has obvious importance during the incubation period when the sitting bird may have to respond to developing situations. During an advertised absence the incubating bird is less likely to take casual breaks from the nest than when the off-duty bird is known to be present. That females seldom perform this type of flight may be linked to their not usually venturing far from the active nest or because they will usually not be away for as long as a male might be absent from the area.

After its absence, the returning bird usually arrives less obviously but again generally via one of the established routes. In other words, not only does the sitting female know that its mate is about to leave, but it does not have to scour the skyline for its return: it more or less knows where to look. The off-duty bird will sometimes also perform this type of circling while still some distance from, but in full view of, the nest if it intends to prolong its absence.

Female eagles commonly high circle or sail (floating or remaining fairly stationary by facing into the wind) above the nesting area during the nestling period when watching for the male's return. Although it may have the appearance of a display, and may be recorded as such, the bird is not really displaying occupancy of the site, but is simply looking for its mate. This is further indicated, once the male is sighted, by the female becoming more active and then dropping to a perch or the nest in readiness for the male's arrival with food. Because of the male's greater use of the territory it is also not unusual to see this type of behaviour during the autumn and winter months, even though the male is unlikely to return with food.

The circling display most likely to be seen is the principal disturbance display that will be familiar to too many people, as it will be seen almost whenever a human visits or closely approaches an active nest. It typically begins with one member of the pair – either the bird disturbed from the nest or its mate – circling in the vicinity of the nest site and usually eventually sees both members of the pair circling. They may begin close to the nest site but may drift away if the disturbance persists or if the humans move closer to the nest. Although called a display, the birds are actually responding to a potential predator that they cannot dissuade. In a lengthy disturbance event, the birds may even stop circling and find a perch from which to watch.

The observed variations (such as reversing the direction of circling by flying in a figure of eight, the pair circling in opposite directions while together, or even the diameter of the circle and whether the circling is above a point or travelling across the hill) appear not to be determining factors as to whether or not the flight is a display. As is being implied, not only can it be difficult to recognise circling as a display: most of the time it probably is not a display at all.

It seems unlikely that non-territorial eagles, including immature-plumaged birds, would perform circling/sailing displays, but they circle and sail in ways that are virtually indistinguishable from those of paired birds, and they will circle with territorial birds both inside and around the fringe of occupied sites. Their high circling, when it is not simply about travelling, is more likely to be a case of looking for other eagles, either to avoid or to meet them, and this is another illustration of how the simple interpretation of events can be misleading; an adult-plumaged bird is said to be displaying while an immature-plumaged eagle performing in exactly the same way will not be said to be displaying.

THE SKY DANCE

The most obvious and recognisable flight display is the sky dance, the undulating, pendulum or dipping flight display in which an eagle gains height, closes its wings at the top of the climb to present a heart-shaped silhouette, tips over either head-first forwards or sideways over one wing and then plummets with tremendous speed before (without changing its wing position) pulling out of the dive, ascending and repeating the process, often for tens of dips. The direction of each dip may be reversed so that the entire performance is played out in a narrow vertical chimney of air, or the bird may dance its way across broad stretches of the territory in shallower undulations, and everything in between. The bird might flap its wings a few times as it reaches the top of the climb and it can usually be seen to turn its head and look around at the top of the climb. Very occasionally a bird might briefly level out one of the dives before continuing to fall, the 'pot hook' variation, and it is not unusual for a bird seemingly to change its mind and not bother to swing up from the bottom of the last dive.

The last is not to be confused with the 'long drop' in which an eagle dives towards its perch from high elevation with the wings furled back, rather than being held horizontally, and the legs thrust out, at least towards the end of the drop, rather than being tucked into the undertail coverts as is the case in the display. The long drop can, at times, be reminiscent of a display but it appears to have no such purpose and is simply a bird dropping to land.

The sky dance is commonly perceived as being the most demonstrative and definitive of territorial displays but it is by no means as simple as that: it is probably the most misinterpreted piece of golden eagle behaviour. It is neither solely nor usually performed for territorial purposes.

Firstly, the numerical majority of sky dances are part of the pair-bonding process, performed by the pair together or by one member of a pair to its partner. This can be said because the majority of performances take place below the ridge top elevation within the box confines of the nesting glen and mostly occur during the nestling period. In fact, it is not unusual for golden eagles to sky dance to the nest while carrying prey or nest material and sky dance off the nest after nest relief (Walker 1991). These display flights cannot possibly be territorial or for the benefit of other eagles.

In the same way, when the sky dance is performed at high elevation by a single bird inside its own territory, it is most usually an attraction display for the bird's mate, and one that is most commonly performed by the female during the male's wandering period. The same can also sometimes be seen during the nestling period when the male is approaching with prey from a distance; it is as if the female is demanding its mate's return.

Secondly, golden eagles not only sky dance inside their own territories but will do so inside the territory of other pairs; they will sky dance without animosity when they are flying with eagles other than their own mate; unpaired and non-territorial eagles will sky dance; and eagles will sky dance when they are not inside any known territory and in locations that are highly unlikely to become territories. In other words, it cannot be reliably assumed that two golden eagles sky dancing together are either a pair or resident in that location.

Thirdly, as most sky dancing occurs above and within the core area, rather than around the territory fringe, it is not being used to define the territory. Although this has been suggested (Watson 2010) the frequency with which the sky dance is performed in locations that are known not to be territory boundaries argues against such simple relationships, especially as these performances might be made by eagles that are not associated with the territory.

It can be seen that while sky dancing is typically assumed to be of a territorial nature, most performances are not for that reason. When the sky dance is performed for the benefit of other eagles it is much more intense in appearance than usual, the flights usually begin more purposefully and the dips appear to be more forceful; it is not simply about performing an undulating flight. Walker (2009) describes a resident pair responding to the presence of other eagles outside the breeding season by making a swinging dip display in which the birds' undulations had a pendulum motion, which saw them reversing the direction at the top of each climb to describe a shallow 'V'-shaped pattern in the air in a high-intensity performance.

Encounters between residents and neighbours generally do not result in this type of flight (presumably because of familiarity within the local population) and an intense performance is probably reserved for genuine intruders. Even so, and contrary to the previous example, on another occasion an intruder inside the same nesting valley elicited only a brief performance of the basic sky dance during the incubation period. It is possible that the breeding season bird was known to the residents while the earlier ones were not.

Although the sky dance is not usually associated with human disturbance, a situation in which it was undeniably the result of the observer's presence has been described (Walker 2009). In this, the adult eagles found the observer where they had last seen the recently-fledged juvenile and responded with sky dancing in tandem before the male flew to the relocated juvenile and the female repeatedly sky danced until the observer had greatly increased the distance between himself and the juvenile.

It can be seen that while the sky dance is obviously a flight display, correctly interpreting or determining its purpose is not as straightforward as may be assumed and requires more evidence than seeing a performance. The traditional interpretations and expectations are not fully reliable and this can be seen with other aspects of display performances.

TIMING OF DISPLAYS

One of the ideas about which there is most certainty in golden eagle ecology is the incidence of flight displays, but this also best illustrates how the casual nature of the available evidence is so widely and commonly ignored. There is broad, almost total, agreement that, while it is possible to see them at any time of year, soaring and sky dancing displays are mostly performed during the late winter period, the pre-laying season. In fact, all the major sources of information, including Gordon (1955), Brown (1976), Newton (1979), Cramp and Simmons (1979), Hardey *et al* (2009) and Watson (1997 and 2010) agree on this and other sources enhance the idea's reliability with its unquestioned repetition. Furthermore, most fieldworkers accept and believe that this is when most flight displays are performed. However, none of these acts as or provides evidence to support the belief.

Figure 6, drawn from Table 31 in Watson (2010), shows the expected pattern of occurrence with displays recorded in most months but with their incidence peaking in the late winter and falling away to the late summer before beginning to increase again. However, it can also be seen that the recorded observer effort (the number of contacts) closely matches the pattern of occurrence. This shows that the expected incidence of displays is an artefact of effort: the greater the number of observations, the more likely is the observer to see a display flight.

The generally unrecognised influence of observer bias can be illustrated in other ways from the same figure. The peaks in effort coincide with the timing of checks for occupancy, incubation, hatching, fledging and juvenile survival. It can also be used to illustrate breeding performance: there are more pairs than pairs which lay eggs, than pairs which hatch eggs, than pairs which fledge young. There are fewer site visits as the breeding season progresses because failed sites tend not to be revisited with any regularity. On top of this, it could be said that observers are looking for birds in flight during the first quarter of the year but that their attention is more focused on the nest during the nesting period, and the further into the breeding season the observations are made, the less likely are observers simply to be looking for eagles in flight, because they want to know if eggs have hatched and how many chicks survive. Figure 6 also shows that effort changes at the times when a change in activity is expected to take place.

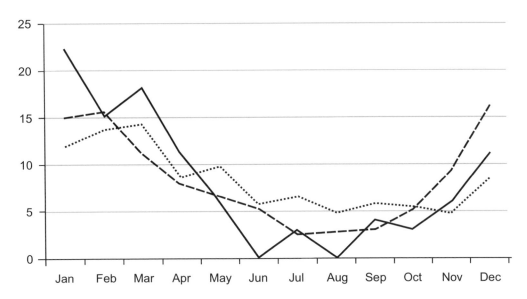

Figure 6: The monthly incidence (% of annual total) of sky dancing (solid line) and soaring (dashed) displays, plus observer effort (dotted); from Watson (2010)

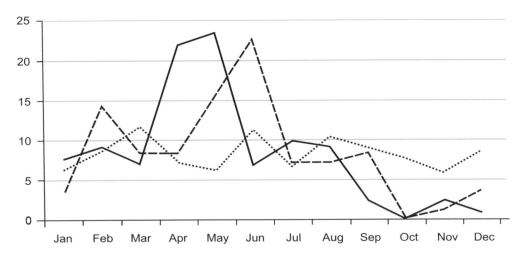

Figure 7: The monthly incidence (% of annual total) of sky dancing (solid line) and soaring (dashed) displays, plus observer effort (dotted). Ten years of data from an Argyll territory (NRP)

The standard belief about the Figure 6 pattern is that it makes sense for golden eagles to demonstrate occupancy, dominance of a location and, perhaps, their intentions prior to the onset of breeding, because only one bird is available to perform the territorial duties once incubation has begun. The incidence then falls away in individual territories as the season progresses, either as a result of breeding failure or because of the extra effort needed to sustain a successful breeding attempt.

However, as patrolling the site is a typical piece of activity during the nestling period and commonly involves the female holding station above the nest site, there should be, at the very least, a peak of soaring in May or June rather than the recorded continued decline in visible activity shown in Figure 6.

The results presented in Figure 7 are clearly very different from those in Figure 6. There is very little correlation between the incidence of displays and observer effort and this is probably because fieldwork in this project was specifically about the recording of flight activity, and the eagles' breeding performance had no relevance to observer effort. In this study, data were collected during watches of equal length on the same number of occasions per three-month period and with the same observation posts used in each year. Figure 7 presents the results of a systematic study while Figure 6 is the result of casual observation.

In Figure 7, the incidence of both flight displays have clear peaks occuring at about or shortly after the hatching time and it seems more logical for eagles to demonstrate their presence and dominance at this time than at any other. The greater territory area immediately becomes more important because it might from then on have to sustain three or possibly four eagles. Contrary to what is seen in Figure 6, sky dancing becomes incredibly obvious around the hatching time and a successful pair will often hold station above the nest area during June, especially when the female is awaiting the male.

Put simply, the territory does not have to be defended or overtly advertised before the expected laying date of a breeding attempt that might not happen or that might fail before there is a demand for additional food. However, at the time of the hatch, the entire territory will have to be used and in a successful breeding attempt it will probably have to support an additional number of resident eagles until at least October. Even with a breeding failure, the resident birds probably need to protect the greater territory area after April more than they do prior to incubation to secure their future security and to ensure that area is not lost to adjacent pairs foraging further afield for their own nestlings.

Interestingly, Figure 7 shows the incidence of recorded displays descending to zero from September to October, coinciding with the time at which juveniles typically enter their independence phase. It has already been noted that adults typically look to avoid their own young at this time of year and overtly displaying their presence would defeat that objective.

The acceptance that the incidence of flight displays is as presented in Figure 6 is one of the best examples of how the received wisdom about golden eagles is the unseen result of casual observation that lacks supporting evidence. Although all the major sources of information present the pattern as being reliable and accurate, there appears to be no study that has produced those results; it is only assumed to be correct and reliable because it illustrates what is expected to happen.

Data from the Argyll study can be used to illustrate further how observer bias probably influences this type of recording. Rather than considering the total number of recorded flight displays during watches which produced contacts with eagles, as in Figures 6 and 7, Figure 8 considers the number of watches during which at least one flight display was recorded as a percentage of the annual total number of all observation sessions, including those without eagle contacts. It can be seen that the two resultant patterns resemble one another closely enough to be linked: the greater the number of observation sessions, the greater the number during which flight displays were seen.

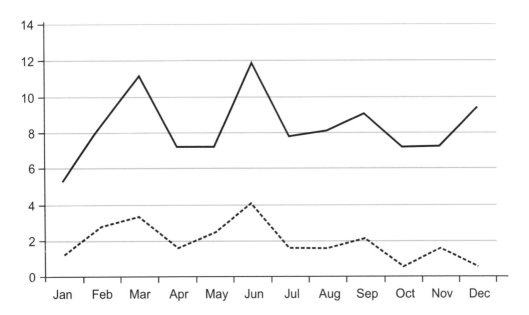

Figure 8: Observation sessions (solid line) as a percentage of the annual total with the percentage of sessions during which flight displays were recorded (dashed) during the Argyll study

PURSUIT FLIGHTS, FLIGHT ROLLS AND TALON GRAPPLING

The other most obvious flight display is probably also the least recorded and the one that is most likely to be seriously misidentified. It has rarely been recognised or described as a display and instead the pair-bonding pursuit flight is usually recorded as, or mistaken for, aggressive territorial defence.

In a typical example, an eagle would leave the nest and eggs unattended to meet or confront an incoming bird. The latter swerves away and is pursued in a rapid twisting and weaving flight quite close to the ridge until the distance between them is narrowed and one or both flight-rolls to present, touch or flash talons before one continues away, the speed reduces and the other turns back to the nest. In every detail this looks like successful aggressive nest area defence behaviour against an intruder which is chased to a safe distance, and this is how such flights have been interpreted (Watson 2010) but, in all of the examples witnessed in several different locations during this study, the activity always involved the members of the pair. It is pair bonding, not aggression.

That is not to say that aggressive defence does not sometimes involve these actions, and pursuits and talon grappling between opponents are not at all unusual, but they seem usually to take place in open air rather than close to the ground. As with prey, it must be easier to evade an opponent when there are more possible directions of escape than when a crash landing is likely. When aggression does result in physical combat, a grounding or both birds going to ground with interlocked talons, it is also usually a much slower occurrence, with the contact involving a stalled flight to present talons and grapple rather than high-speed precision manoeuvres.

Talon grappling, flashing and touching between the members of a pair is also more common than many believe, as is grappling between the adults (especially the female) and their juveniles close to the independence date. While the latter cannot be called a display (it is a form of stylised begging that the adults try to avoid) the former is at least part of a display. Flight rolls, talon grappling, flashing and touching between the members of a pair often just occurs during ordinary flights where there appears to be no reason for it, and it often goes without a response. The display probably has its origins in the aerial food pass which in turn probably originates with the aerial capture of prey. Juvenile eagles will even flash (present talons) at sheep and deer but this is not an indication of desperation for food: the eagles are practising their skills and can be seen also flashing at rocks and trees, in a way that is similar to the way in which flying eagles snap off branches for use as nest material.

Talon flashing is the most common variant to be seen, with the bird or birds simply stretching out their legs as if to show their talons without touching or rolling through even 90°. This happens with surprising frequency and can appear as little more than a bird flicking one wing out of beat while the pair is flying together.

Talon touching is less commonly recorded but it is also not particularly unusual, as it takes little more than the birds being closer together when they flash or roll. It is often of very short duration and does not always involve the eagles clutching one another, although it is often difficult to determine if the talons are intertwined. Flashing and touching as part of the display appear to be interchangeable and whether one or the other takes place is probably no more than a matter of positioning or motivation.

Talon grappling is always given greater importance by observers but it is usually little more than a successful presentation, or a flash or touch made at the correct distance. It does not appear to have greater significance than flashing or touching in that it does not appear to result in any different behaviour or a stronger bond within the pair. The birds most usually simply join talons for a few seconds, one above the other, and then release, but it is during grappling that most rolling is seen. In this the birds join talons and then perform one or more 360° rolls. These are usually performed quite rapidly, with the wings less than fully open but not fully closed, and while usually performed in the horizontal plain some near-vertical (head up) rolls have also been seen.

Cartwheeling, in which two eagles remain with talons locked while rolling and descending with spread wings (more commonly associated with species such as the white-tailed eagle) has only rarely been reported in the golden eagle (Watson 2010) and would seem most likely to occur between a resident and an intruder, with each trying to hold the other as far away as possible. In this study, two golden eagles watched cartwheeling in this way near Oban involved a resident and an intruder which locked talons and tumbled to the ground where they fought for about ten minutes before separating and flying off in different directions.

OTHER DISPLAYS

What constitutes a display is very open to interpretation. The dropping of prey items and nest material from one member of the pair to the other is usually called a game rather than a display but it could easily be a form of pair bonding. However, it also usually appears to be accidental rather than deliberate. There have been many occasions on which an eagle has been seen to drop food or material without the mate being present or with the mate on the nest and out of sight of the partner. It is by no means unusual for the eagle dropping the item to immediately twist-dive and catch it before it reaches the ground and also not unusual for the item to reach the ground and be retrieved or for the eagle to watch it fall and then leave it where it lands. Its suggestion as a display probably results from the infrequency with which it is seen. Such actions are similar to those seen between adult and juvenile, when the former drops food to the ground ahead of the advancing juvenile, and by the juvenile itself as it develops its flying ability. The dropping and catching or ignoring the item can be a feature of the juvenile's development and is commonly performed when no other eagles are present.

Walker (2004) describes a number of postures and positions taken on perches which may constitute display activities. Talon grappling on the ground is described with one perched member of a pair jumping up and over backwards to present talons and grapple its mate as the latter arrived to land; the two then stood side by side. That the same actions are described for one of the same adults defending a carrion carcass against its own juvenile illustrates not only how these same actions might be used in different situations, but also how the interpretation of events is not at all straightforward unless the relationship of the eagles is known.

Walker (2004) also lists a number of different perched positions assumed by golden eagles prior to copulation. The full mating sequence is that, when perched together, the birds bow towards the ground with their beaks closer than their tails, the female remains in that position and the male mounts, dismounts, bows and both stand upright. There may or may not be calling and other matings might see any element of the performance excluded, with some simply involving the male arriving directly from flight and leaving immediately afterwards.

The same eagles at which these postures were recorded were also, on one occasion, seen to stand upright on stretched legs with wings raised and partly open (in the classic heraldic pose) when one arrived at a carcass from which the other was feeding. Both held this apparent show of strength for several seconds before the first (the male) relented and gave way to its mate.

OTHER ACTIVITY

Given that discussions are typically centred on specific aspects of eagle activity, it might be suspected that most of an eagle's life is engaged in foraging, displaying and breeding. In reality, these occupy little of an eagle's time and most of most days is spent in a casual fashion. Most golden eagle flights appear not to be foraging or display but simply moving from one place to another and many seem to be little more than one member of the pair, usually the female, looking for the other. A pair does not always appear stimulated to take action in response to any situation, even if another eagle is sighted, and what occurs appears, more often than not, to be little more than a token effort.

Drifting patrolling flights may encompass the entire territory and slide beyond the boundaries but even these appear to have little real purpose. They are not specifically territorial, about enlarging the territory by usurping adjoining areas; they usually do not involve active foraging and commonly end after a casual encounter with other eagles that amounts to nothing more than some brief circling. Again, as the pairs within a population are likely to be able to recognize one another and accept their position based on dominance, there needs to be little or no real conflict for a conclusion to be reached.

The question of whether or not a pair acts as a pair in most situations also needs to be considered because of the regularity with which two eagles are reported as a pair when that has not been confirmed. It can be seen that during a successful breeding attempt there is a period of about 25 weeks during which even an observer in a nesting glen may seldom see both members of a pair in flight at the same time. That does not mean, though, that they will usually be together during the remaining 27 weeks of the year or when there is not a breeding attempt. With the female more closely linked to the nesting area, the birds are most likely to be seen as a pair while in the core area, but that does not preclude them from being seen together elsewhere, and especially outside the breeding season and when weather conditions place limitations on foraging activity.

However, it can be inferred that there is a high possibility that two birds seen together in the outer reaches of a territory during the nesting season are not a pair. It is possible that they are, but it cannot be assumed to be the case. As suggested throughout this work, the correct interpretation of the observed behaviour is not straightforward and may be inconclusive. As noted, even two birds showing no animosity inside a nest glen do not have to be a pair or a resident pair, so the status of birds seen together away from the nest glen has to be given more careful consideration in the field. It should not be concluded that any two golden eagles are members of the same pair until it has been conclusively proved by means other than a simple sighting.

It is important to accept these points and most especially the idea that golden eagles are not always actively or intensively engaged in a specific action. The correct and reliable interpretation of behaviour can be difficult to achieve because there is commonly insufficient evidence on which to reach a reliable conclusion, but believing that the golden eagle is an easily-understood species encourages the reaching of simplistic conclusions. Observers tend to see what they expect to see, interpret what they see in a way that supports what they expect and generally fail to consider possible ambiguities or alternative explanations and situations. The limitations of the available evidence are seemingly seldom given full and proper consideration simply because the golden eagle is believed to be a well-known species. The correct interpretation of events essentially relies on the observer knowing the status of the observed birds, knowing their relationship to the location and seeing the beginning, ending and stimulus for the observed activity.

OTHER SPECIES

It is worth giving some consideration to the other animals found in golden eagle territories, if only because the idea of the eagle as a simple predator encourages observers only to see other species in terms of their presumed value as food. As a result, many species have been undervalued, their usefulness overlooked and their influence ignored. It is probably safe to say that most eagle workers take little interest in the animals they see unless they are predators, thought to be valuable or are unusual in that location. This is a great pity because it means that much useful information has been missed over the years and, for example, changes in circumstances that may have been evident at an early stage are not recognised until it is too late for them to be addressed.

One of the curiosities that best highlights this problem is that even the supposedly most important species, such as red grouse, have been only very rarely systematically counted or had their numbers quantified per territory over a period of years as part of an eagle study, even though many sources freely discuss the value of red grouse to golden eagles. In addition, few observers count deer and sheep, and species such as the hooded crow are typically ignored altogether.

The other species present at a site also have more relevance than their value as food. While it is often considered to be the top predator, the golden eagle is still in almost constant competition with other species in most territories. Although only the white-tailed eagle is considered by many to be a major competitor (Whitfield *et al* 2008) the golden eagle directly competes with, at the very least, fox, hen harrier, common buzzard, peregrine, raven and hooded crow. The number of species and individuals may vary from site to site but all six are present at many sites, can be present throughout the year and can help to deplete the food available in a territory. For example, in some years at the Argyll study site, more than 60 foxes were controlled without apparently reducing their overall presence; there were usually two pairs of hen harriers using the site, seven or eight pairs of buzzards, one or two pairs of peregrines, three pairs of ravens (with single counts or up to 30 birds) and an average daily count of about twelve hooded crows, with single counts of more than 100 being recorded. All of these utilised and depleted the food sources available to the eagles. Elsewhere, Walker (2009) describes how a raven flock prevented eagles from feeding and even forced them out of the nesting valley, so the influence of other species should not be ignored or its importance underplayed.

This is important because giving due consideration to other species alters the way in which territories need to be evaluated, not least because observers and studies typically reach conclusions and explain breeding performance in terms of, but without measuring, food supply: Haworth and Fielding (2013) do this when concluding that low productivity is most likely to result from low live prey availability. The presence or absence of certain species does not guarantee the presence or absence of golden eagles and neither does it make a location suitable or unsuitable for successful breeding attempts.

The general importance, value or usability of the other species present in a territory or location should also not be overlooked. While small mammals and small birds may be of little determining value (an eagle territory will not be formed or breeding success determined by voles and pipits), they, along with the other largely ignored species, still form the community which creates the situation that allows the eagle's presence and its productivity.

The seasonal community must also not be overlooked; by concentrating field effort during the breeding season, it is easy to record a surplus food supply, but in many cases that will include species, sources and numbers that are only available for four or five months of the year. If, as is believed (Newton 1979), pre-laying food supply ultimately determines breeding performance – and the laying of infertile eggs is a pre-laying rather than an incubation period failure – then there is little value in any conclusion reached about breeding performance on the basis of the species recorded as food during the nestling period.

The other species can also be of great value to eagle watchers, not least in their ability to reveal the presence of an eagle. Alarm calls and sudden movements in an otherwise peaceful scene can reveal an eagle's location even when it is perched. Corvids are the most useful species for watchers as they are common, have distinctive contact and alarm calls, different flight patterns under different circumstances and mob eagles in flight and on the ground. In fact, the first sign of an eagle's presence is often a corvid's alarm call and its anxious behaviour above a skyline when the eagle is still out of sight to the observer. It is even possible to follow an eagle's unseen progress behind a ridge by watching corvids, provided that the eagle does eventually fly into view to confirm its presence after an unbroken passage of activity. On such occasions the eagle landing while out of sight might even be inferred from the way in which the corvids move; at such times they too will often land and then make almost vertical swooping sorties in the same place against the eagle. In fact, a seemingly unusual gathering of corvids, even of small numbers, can reveal an eagle that might otherwise have been missed because, provided the corvids can keep the eagle in sight, they will perch and even feed while an eagle is close by.

Because of these things it is difficult to say at what elevation eagles will or will not cause a reaction. While corvids will commonly perch close to eagles, presumably relying on their escape speed to keep them safe, those low down in the bottom of a glen might react in alarm to an eagle passing overhead at great altitude. There may, of course, be two sets of corvids in the same area, those that utilise the upland areas and those which more or less limit their movements to the low ground.

An eagle's presence does not always initiate panicked alarm calling because there are situations in which its presence will be continuously known to the other species, such as when they are in the nesting glen. Mobbing and defensive behaviour do not take place for 24 hours a day in these situations, the eagle is largely ignored and its presence only noted and made known by the other species when it changes position. Even at these times, the calling may not be extensive or continuous but just enough to indicate that a change has occurred. It is not uncommon, in fact, to see corvids behaving as if oblivious to an eagle's close presence.

While observers usually do remember to look around when they hear a crow or raven, mammal calls would seem to be less appreciated, even though red deer can be particularly useful. Many people might think only in terms of stags roaring during the rut, but the various snorts and grunts that can be heard at any time of year can be very illuminating. Unlike sheep, which might flinch but then carry on, red deer will often snort and then stand and stare at a passing or perched eagle in a way that shows them to be alert. As the opportunity to count deer should always be taken if no eagles are in view, knowing where they are and observing changes in their behaviour or location can help to locate an eagle that has not been found by the usual methods.

Not knowing for certain if 'no eagles in view' is the same as 'no eagles present' is one of the greatest frustrations felt by eagle workers, and believing that they have the same meaning is a conclusion that is too often and too easily reached. Eagles are not always obviously in view; they can perch in obscure locations and the observer might not know the location of all the roosts or favourite perches. There will usually still be at least one animal that is aware of the eagle's position (even if that is nothing more than a mobbing chaffinch visible only through a telescope) and that will reveal the eagle to the observer if it can be found.

The one other species in need of specific consideration is, of course, the human. Raptor workers can be very suspicious of other humans, both because of persecution and the thoughtless, if often innocent, behaviour of visitors and birdwatchers. Suspicion, though, can mean that a real impact is missed. Unless they are close to a nest, the presence of hill walkers, farmers and foresters usually goes unrecorded and unconsidered, but their presence can disrupt foraging in any part of a territory at any time of year and thereby influence what is seen by the watcher. The watcher, too, of course, can also influence what is seen.

There can also be a time lag , with a disturbed eagle not resuming foraging in a location as soon as the human has departed and, depending on the time of day, possibly not returning at all during an observation session. If, of course, the human intrusion is not seen by the observer, such a lack of activity or use may be taken to indicate a lack of value to the eagles. Such a conclusion could be entirely wrong but, as with considering the reasons for breeding failure, the absence of information is commonly explained without actually explaining why the absence occurred. It must also be remembered that an eagle is likely to see a watcher before the watcher sees the eagle and so will already be reacting to the human before they are even aware of the eagle's presence. Even the most conscientious of observers, using carefully chosen observation posts, can have an impact on what is seen.

Unfortunately, in general terms, little regard seems to be given to these considerations, not least because most effort is directed towards the nest and that does not move. Because the received wisdom is held in such high esteem, there are strong preconceived ideas about the impact and value of other species to be encountered, with the result that their true value is seldom seen or appreciated. Worst of all, many watchers and studies simply do not associate the eagle with other species unless they are believed to be important as prey. The fact that most studies fail to accept that sheep and red deer are available as live prey as well as carrion is a simple example both of this and the overall failing properly to consider the other species present in a territory.

When considering any aspect of golden eagle ecology, when producing guidance and advice for species management or even if the goal is simply to have interesting encounters with golden eagles, the importance of all the other species in a location should neither be overlooked nor undervalued. It is not possible to reach fully reliable conclusions about golden eagles without understanding their relationship to the other species present in the location.

A GOLDEN EAGLE ALMANAC

The annual cycle of golden eagle activity is not easily summarised but the idea that it is straightforward underlies many of the problems arising in fieldwork, especially those of over-confidence and the quality of the available evidence. The goal can be achieved to some extent in terms of events, such as with the chapter headings, but when activity levels are considered the task becomes much more complicated. This is because all the age groups and the status of all individuals have to be taken into account when considering a species; it cannot be assumed that all eagles have the same activity patterns or are equally active at the same time, and it should also not be assumed that the activities of those breeding successfully represent the species as a whole.

Most data collection revolves around these successful breeders, but because the national surveys have shown that the majority of pairs do not in fact fledge young in any given year, it can be argued that those which breed successfully are behaving atypically and are not representative of the majority of the population. It is important to remember this point because the requirements of the majority (single, failed and non-breeding eagles) are largely ignored or dismissed as unimportant without any recognition that they are simply different.

Activity levels vary across the year for all categories of golden eagle; they are not active at a constant level or, indeed, in a way that might be expected. While pairs breeding successfully might be thought of as being more active than those which fail or make no breeding attempt, it does not mean that they are always more active than other eagles and, in fact, there are times of year when successful pairs can be less active than the others. It is easy to see how this would apply to the incubation period but it might be less expected during the nestling and post-fledging periods when extra food is required for the nestling or when there may be four free-flying eagles at the site. There is also the member of a pair to be taken into consideration; it cannot be assumed that males and females have the same activity levels or, as already suggested, use the territory in the same way.

Walker (1991) attempted to illustrate activity levels during the different phases of a successful breeding year. The results provided were reliable for the selected days and if they could be combined and still maintain an acceptable level of reliability, they would show an interesting comparison of gender-related activity levels. Not surprisingly, they would demonstrate that the female spends the greater amount of time on the nest – c.84% of the daylight period during the incubation period and c.68% during the early nestling period – but also how little time was spent in flight in the nesting area (the male c.7.9% and the female only c.3.9% of the daylight period).

The results also reveal a number of potentially surprising points, perhaps not least of which the amount of time spent on the roost during the daylight period, time that predominantly resulted from the bird lingering in the morning rather than taking an early roost: the male c.21.9% and the female c.13.2% of the annual totals. During the late nestling period these became c.35% for the male and c.12% for the female. In fact, at this time of year, the figures indicate that the male might spend as much as c.87% of the daylight period on a perch. If nothing else it can be seen from this why even resident eagles are not always easily seen, why checking for site occupancy is not always straightforward and why the golden eagle's image as a species renowned for soaring majestically above its territory is not very helpful. At this stage in the annual cycle there is, of course, little for breeding pairs to do except wait for the nestling to fledge.

The figures in Walker (1991) do not best illustrate the conclusion that female eagles are more closely associated with the nesting area than their mate. Prime among a number of reasons for this is the role played by the individual eagles during the post-fledging confinement period; when the male was present, the female was absent for up to c.52% of the time. However, during the later post-fledging period, and just as there were incubation and nestling period days on which neither adult left the nest area, there were days when the male was absent and the female present for 100% of the time. The incubation period figures show the male being absent for c.68% of the daylight period compared to the female's c.13% and for c.26% of the early nestling period compared to the female's c.15%. Males can be noticeably absent from the nesting area unless they are replenishing the nest, or loafing after having done so during the nestling period, while females remain close by for most of their time.

However, what these figures imply is that a small sample size is unlikely to be truly representative of a situation and that without the type of detailed involvement underlying Walker (1991) observers are either unlikely to be present on or able to recognise a typical day at the site under examination.

This is because there are so many other factors to be taken into proper consideration. The size and openness of the nesting area can be of great importance, as can the available food sources. At the above site the valley was large and open, with sheep carrion being of great importance, while, for example, the Argyll study nesting valley was small and enclosed and offered little more than crows. Eagles at the former site commonly foraged inside the nesting area while those at the latter site were usually out of the nesting area when they foraged. Observations in other areas show similar variations in patterns of behaviour and involvement and also suggest that more time may be spent foraging where live prey dominates the diet.

Discussing individual activity levels may not seem to be a valuable exercise but it should help to raise awareness of the variable ecology that can be seen and should help to question the use of generalisations in species management; no two sites are the same and no two birds use their areas in the same way, and only by recognising this can management be fit for its purpose.

This is perhaps most apparent when considering changes of land use: if the timing of data collection for impact assessments coincides with a period of low activity or if the records collected during that time are only seen to be part of an annual total, the results can be misleading. This subject has already been raised under various headings but the main point bears simple repetition here: a location that produces comparatively few records is not necessarily of low value because when it is used it may have high value; value is not always easily determined by the frequency of use, especially as only one member of the pair may be active. It has to be determined by the intensity and reasons for use.

Because the status of all eagles has to be considered, the monthly and seasonal summaries presented here are to provide an insight into how activity changes across the year. As always, the most difficult birds to discuss with a high degree of certainty are the immature-plumaged eagles that have not entered the paired population because little of the relevant information results from confirmed and defined observations. That said, patterns of activity can be identified and can be presented in a way that provides some insight into the interpretation of their involvement, variations in the seasonal value of territory areas and the likelihood of recognising indicative behaviour.

The suggestion presented in Figure 8 may well be subjective and simplistic but it illustrates the level of activity that might be expected at occupied sites during fieldwork at any time of year: there is a generally low level of activity (a score of 1) which involves basic foraging and existence. All territory-holding eagles have increasing activity levels through February and into March as they refurbish nests, regardless of whether or not a breeding attempt will be made, or even if they have a mate. Activity then drops away during the incubation period and when eggs have not been laid. It rises sharply in late April but falls quickly for those which do not hatch eggs. These birds then enter the pattern followed by non-breeders, which is a near-continuous low level of activity. The activity of birds which lose small young also drops to this level soon after the failure.

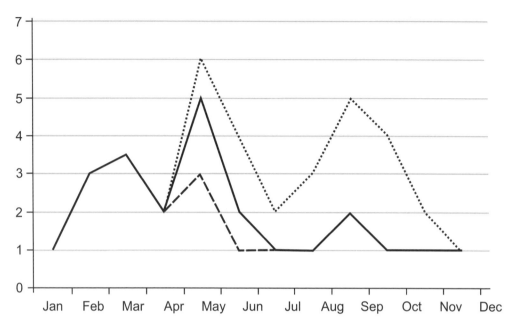

Figure 9: A simplified indication of basic activity levels for golden eagles: a pair breeding successfully (dotted line), a pair failing on eggs (dashed) and a pair failing with young (solid)

Pairs with surviving young do not maintain a high level of activity and it falls away as the nestlings grow during June and drops even further as the adults wait for the young to fledge in July. Activity increases again as the juvenile develops and reaches another peak in September when the juvenile becomes a truly free-flying eagle and the adults, especially the male, respond to its activity. Adult activity levels then drop in October as the juvenile approaches independence and fall further away in November before reaching the basic level again in December.

This is a very broad summary, of course, that can be influenced by numerous factors (including the length of time the juvenile spends in the natal territory) but it is a fair representation of what can be expected and helps to illustrate how data collection can be affected by time of year. Within the three categories considered, there can still be bursts of activity at any time with, for example, birds from all three building and refurbishing nests during the late summer period. Some pairs also do not exert a great deal of energy during the pre-laying period and some have a consistently higher year-round level of activity.

However, it can be seen that a successful breeding attempt does not mean that there will be a lengthy continuous period with a high level of activity and it may be surprising to see that the adults' activity actually decreases when there is a nestling and even a fledged juvenile. It may even be suggested that activity levels drop lower than shown (as indicated by the time spent perched) and it has only been presented as shown to allow for the possibility of there being three or four free-flying birds at the site.

The problem of expectation might also be inferred from Figure 9. An observer expecting to confirm occupancy or a breeding attempt on the basis of observed behaviour may see very little activity and with most eagles not involved in successful breeding attempts, there is generally little reliable indicative activity to be seen, and often too little to support any conclusion that might be reached.

When considering Figure 9 and activity levels in general, it must also be recognised that this is not really about bouts of activity, such as the collection of nest material, it is about general activity. Flight displays, nest building or adornment, mating and foraging can all happen at any time (all have been recorded in every month of the year) but they are usually quite brief moments within a longer period. General activity is really about how visible the eagles are to an observer and what that can mean for the interpretation of events.

WINTER: DECEMBER–FEBRUARY

It can be quite easy to get the impression that the winter is little more than a time of near-dormancy for golden eagles, a period that is of little interest or relevance. That would be a gross miscalculation, not least because the breeding season begins in winter and breeding performance might be determined by events at this time. It is also the most variable of seasons, both in terms of the likely weather conditions and in the way in which activity is influenced by external factors.

Weather conditions play an important role at this time but possibly not in exactly the way that might be expected. While severe conditions can and will limit eagle activity, fair conditions do not necessarily guarantee increased activity levels. In fact, as at any time of year, an eagle is more likely to be perched than in flight. While the search for food during the darkest part of winter may seem to be an unenviable chore, the fact is that most golden eagles do not struggle to find food.

Foraging can be affected by the prevailing conditions but the evidence suggests that survival is not difficult for territory-holding pairs. While it has already been suggested that changes of partner are probably missed more often than is thought, the fact that there is no very obvious reduction in numbers over the winter suggests that established birds generally survive and probably die at other times. What happens with unpaired birds is less well known and their winter mortality may well be quite high.

Snow and freezing temperatures can be a regular problem and a limiting factor in the high mountainous areas but they might be little more than a vague possibility in some other areas. A coastal pair may only rarely see snow on their nests while the nests of a not-too-distant inland pair might be snowbound for two or three months. Equally, of course, the coastal site may suffer more greatly from gale and storm force winds than might an inland pair. In this way it can already be seen that it is difficult to produce a summary that is equally applicable to the population as a whole and also how local circumstances will influence what is seen.

Food source availability, distribution and accessibility are probably of overriding importance, both within and outside territories, at this time of year. Birds with easy access to reliable food sources can appear to be more active than those with more scattered food sources, even if birds in both situations are actually active for roughly the same amount of time. While it may seem likely that the birds using larger areas should be more active, it has already been noted that foraging does not involve continuous flying.

It might be thought that there would be more carrion and less live prey available at this time than at any other but there is often very little carrion to be found during the early part of the winter unless there has been a severe weather event; the resident live prey species are not only still present, but are also present in higher numbers than in the spring and probably have higher availability than in the summer. Winter-coated mountain hare and ptarmigan can be very visible if there is little snow cover, while the red grouse can be very visible when there is snow cover.

A note must also be made in respect of observer effort. Little real effort has been made to obtain records during harsh weather or during the early part of the winter and this can give a misleading impression of events. The popular image of eagles soaring above their nesting areas on fine winter days is the result of fair-weather birdwatching, it does happen, but the behaviour is not typical of this time of year.

DECEMBER

The first major snow storms of the winter usually come in December as does the first lengthy period of sub-zero temperatures, but there can also be periods of fine, if not warm, weather. The daylight period is also effectively at its shortest.

Resident pairs

The members of most pairs are usually to be seen together and they will roost, perch, forage and travel side by side or in close proximity. That said, and because foraging is usually not difficult, established pairs can be very inactive and may seldom wander far from the core area unless there is extensive snow cover. When this does happen, the birds are easily missed as they often only use the core area for roosting and commonly depart early and return late in the day.

While flight displays are recorded, they are not frequent and even high-level transitional flights are not that common in most locations, with the birds often only appearing at height when above the nesting area. There appears to be little territorial activity at this time, probably as a result of the continued avoidance of juveniles, both those born at the site and those born elsewhere. Year-round records suggest that there are few intrusions into occupied territories by older birds at this time of year and those which do occur are most likely in outlying parts of the territory and likely to be missed by the residents. It seems to be the case that most resident eagles really are resident at this time, even those which did not breed successfully.

December is probably the month in which there is the least nest building and refurbishment. When adjustments do occur they usually involve an established nest rather than a new one, even if new nests have been started in earlier months, and the sessions are usually brief, involving maybe only one member of the pair and with only a small number of items collected. There are also few casual nest visits at this time of year and while those seen might be thought to be an indication of nest selection for the following season, there are cases in which the nest seen to be visited was not that used the next year. Although it has been recorded, nests are not usually used as roosts and the sheltered main winter roost will be in almost daily use now, even if the members of a pair have separate favoured locations.

When a juvenile has not gained independence in the autumn, the behaviour of the adults is very similar to that seen during the usual post-fledging period, with the male accompanying the bird and the female seeming to avoid contact with it by spending even more time in the nesting area and usually foraging alone. The greater territory area is used more than in years without young, the foraging areas are targeted and other areas produce more frequent contacts. With the female generally not being a part of this activity, there is the possibility of the male/juvenile combination being mistaken for a pair of eagles at this time.

This seems to contradict the idea that adult eagles try to avoid juveniles at this point in the year and it can probably only be explained by suggesting that, because juveniles are not driven away by the adults, the male's instinct to accompany the juvenile must, in fact, be determined by the juvenile's continuous presence.

Juveniles
In spite of some satellite tagging results, it still seems likely that most juvenile golden eagles will have gained full independence by December. What then happens is largely unknown but most travel quite widely and might be found in unlikely locations. The development process has not been completed and they not unusually behave as dependent juveniles, spending time on the ground and making mock attacks on various animals and items. That said, they also perform very high flights and can gain great elevation before turning to travel to the next location. There are no certain records of juveniles performing flight displays at this time.

Juveniles tend not to settle in any one place for lengthy periods unless it provides good foraging during poor weather. However, because these birds are easily overtaken by weather events and even by nightfall, the presence of a juvenile should not be taken as an indication of a location's suitability for golden eagles. Most of the locations visited by juveniles have little more than a momentary attraction.

Many juveniles probably return to the natal territory at times during their first winter but most of the juveniles seen at this time are probably unrelated to the location. Unless the bird has been individually and recognisably marked, there is no easy way of knowing its relationship to an occupied territory and even the single flight of a juvenile could easily see the bird visiting four or five, if not more, territories on the same day, with all the relevant sets of adults behaving towards it in the same way.

That some juveniles are now known to stay on or in the vicinity of the natal territory throughout their first winter only complicates the problem. The juvenile can, at times, be accompanied by the male as if in the post-fledging period but it can also operate independently, both foraging and roosting alone. There is very little evidence of real aggression being shown by adults to any juvenile at this time of year, so any suspected aggression probably involves an older immature.

Immature-plumaged eagles

It can be seen that very little is known about juvenile eagles after they have left the natal territory and the same can be said of all eagles that are outside the paired population. In fact, although this group is of tremendous importance to the future of the species, virtually no time has been deliberately devoted to studying their ecology; it is just assumed that they cope with life.

There can be great variation in the activity of these birds, not least because of their varying ages. Some will have joined the paired population and behave as adults, while others behave more like juveniles. In broad terms, with their greater experience, they are generally more sedentary than juveniles and can be quite difficult to see in December. Some will still be passing from safe haven to safe haven but quietly occupying a reliable food source is the best strategy and the one that seems to be most often followed.

These birds, therefore, are not particularly active in December although, because their areas overlap, congregations of three or four immature-plumaged eagles can be seen. Flight play takes place, with the birds swooping together and chasing one another, but they still seem to arrive, forage and depart independently, and it is not known if they roost together. There is no evidence to suggest that pairs are formed at such times although associations can develop, especially when in safe havens, and these may stay together if a suitable location is available.

Single adults

The behaviour of these eagles is slightly different from that of paired birds, regardless of whether they have lost a mate or never found one. These birds are typically even less active than pairs, some seldom venture far beyond the nesting area and most will quickly return after feeding elsewhere. They appear to have quite small activity areas, seem to spend little time in flight and will often gain their roost some time before darkness falls; nest visits and display flights are unusual.

It is often only the presence of another eagle that produces any real activity at this time and on these occasions flights can be prolonged and continue after the other bird has left the area. It is easy to suggest that such encounters may be the prelude to pairing but this has not been proven and, as most encounters will be with young immatures or established adults, pair formation is probably unlikely at this time of year.

JANUARY

January is usually the coldest month and typically has the most frequent and severe storms, with harsh weather systems often lasting for several days at a time. Snow cover often persists throughout the month on the higher ground and may even lie at lower levels for several weeks.

Food sources can be very scarce in practical terms, as prolonged snow cover and freezing temperatures can make carrion unavailable or inedible. During severe weather conditions there can be little food available on the higher ground but it can result in concentrations on the lower slopes, in valley bottoms and along any forest edge fence line.

Resident pairs

The between-month differences in activity levels can be slight at first, as activity will be linked to daylight time rather than calendar dates. There is a gradual expansion of activity as the month progresses but this still need not expand far beyond the core area or be particularly obvious. Activity is very dependent on food source distribution, however, and eagles sometimes spend little more than roosting time in the core area, even if there is not persistent snow cover. It is by no means unusual to see golden eagles over enclosed farmland and, where circumstances demanded, resident birds have been seen foraging over fields more than nine kilometres from their nests.

Persistent snow cover can lead to some resident eagles vacating their core area for other parts of the territory and becoming resident in outlying parts for several weeks. In such cases, the birds behave as if in the core area and develop regular perches and roosts that might not be used at any other time of year or under different conditions. A territory can appear to have been vacated under such circumstances if observer effort is targeted at the nest group and it could also mean that the birds involved might be mistaken for a different or new pair that later disappears.

Resident pairs gradually spend more time in the air as the month progresses and perform more seemingly casual drifting flights. These are not always at great elevation and often simply involve the pair apparently aimlessly sailing along ridge sides or over moorland. The birds often follow the ridge edge and contour around their sites rather than flying out across a valley or over moorland. High level, open flights do occur but mostly when other eagles have been spotted or when inside the nesting valley.

The frequency of flight displays increases but they are still not a major feature of activity, with sky dancing usually being little more apparent than in the autumn. The displays that are seen tend to be of low intensity and usually inside the nesting valley or core area. An eagle displaying outside the known nesting area is as likely to be a visitor as a resident and two eagles displaying together may or may not be a pair. Territorial activity can be more in evidence as the number of intrusions by other birds begins to increase but this often involves little more than high circling.

The members of a pair are still generally to be seen together; they typically arrive at and leave the roost at about the same time, foraging is still a typically co-operative affair (probably because it is easier for two birds to find food at this time) and matings become more common. Matings do not always occur inside the core area and can be seen almost anywhere within the territory.

Although nest material can be collected and delivered at any time of year some, perhaps many, pairs begin nest refurbishment in late January. This is usually a low-key affair with few items being collected in each session, sessions not occurring every day and material often being taken to more than one nest. The first nest to be adorned is not always that used for the breeding attempt and material might also be carried to other locations. As for those birds wintering elsewhere in their territory, not even visiting the core at this time, it is not unknown for them to start new nests on the wintering grounds.

While this may generally imply that the birds must be spending more time in the nesting area, they are not unusually to be seen simply flying in, adding some material and then leaving again. It is also common for only one member of the pair to be actively engaged in refurbishment. As female golden eagles appear to have fairly stable laying dates, and with pre-laying judged to last about seven weeks, whether or not there is nest refurbishment in January may well be influenced by the female's usual laying date.

Single adults

The behaviour and activity of single birds is broadly similar to that of paired adults and this can make it difficult to separate the two or confirm the presence of a pair in January, a problem exacerbated by the amount of time any eagle might spend perched. These birds seem to display less than paired adults and seem not to collect as much nest material. Single birds of both genders have been observed and seen to behave similarly.

Juveniles and other unpaired immature-plumaged eagles

There is virtually no good-quality information available about these eagles, with most records being of birds visiting occupied territories or casual observations where the relationship with the location is unknown. It can only be surmised that most of these birds will be fairly settled and utilising the resources they have identified. When they do travel, they typically gain some elevation before moving on as if moving from spot to spot rather than travelling and searching simultaneously; it often appears as if they have a destination in mind.

That this group does travel is evidenced by the increased number of intrusions into the cores of established territories. However, this might be as a result of limited food supplies forcing them further afield rather than it being a particular trait. These intrusions can be lengthy and commonly involve the bird slowly drifting across the countryside at fairly high elevation, often as if teasing any residents. How these birds are dealt with by resident birds appears to be dependent on their age, with the youngest generally tolerated.

Those birds with access to a suitable food supply also wander but seem to remain, more or less, on station and are generally very inactive. Juveniles that have not left the natal territory or its immediate vicinity continue to interact with the adults, may roost in the nesting area and generally behave as if they were residents.

The immature associations that can have the appearance of territory-holding pairs also behave as established birds and are usually to be seen together, hunting co-operatively, and they may even begin to build nests. These birds perform more flight displays and are often to be seen chasing, performing flight rolls and talon grappling in apparently random locations. As the majority of immature-plumaged eagles are mostly operating inside areas occupied by other eagles, their presence cannot be taken to be indicative of residency.

FEBRUARY

Even though closer to the spring than the winter equinox, February often feels like the dullest month, as the slightly higher temperatures result in more clinging mists and grey days with drizzly rain or snow. There can be both heavy snow and rainfall and there can be continuous snow cover throughout the month or a sequence of thaws and falls, leaving only the higher ground with a patchy covering.

Food availability becomes more complex at this time, as while carrion amounts can be increasing, this can be dependent on the number and distribution of sheep as red deer mortality remains low and not all core areas hold sheep during the winter. The more traditional live prey species can also be little in evidence as their numbers begin to fall more noticeably and at some sites ptarmigan may be the only numerous source available. As with all potential prey species whose numbers are low, any greater than usual reliance placed on them as a result of conditions could affect future events. The presence or absence of ptarmigan and their numerical availability can also influence area use by eagles, as those without ptarmigan spend little time foraging the high tops or the upper slopes of mountains.

Resident pairs

Food source availability is still the most influential factor at this point in the year so the amount of time spent in and around the nesting area can be largely dependent on what sources are available. Pairs with good local foraging tend not to venture further afield with any frequency and it is not unusual for them to remain about the nesting valley for the entire day. Pairs with less good core area winter foraging and all those with snow-bound nesting areas spend extensive periods away and will roost away should conditions deteriorate or dictate that it is better to stay close to an available food source. The presence of an immature-plumaged bird in a pair does not appear to produce any differences in activity from that seen when two adults are present.

As the typical pre-laying period starts at the beginning of February, nest building, repairs and adornment becomes an increasing feature of eagle activity. All pairs and probably almost all single territory-holding birds repair nests at this time, so the activity is still not indicative of what might happen next: a pair repairing a nest does not have to lay eggs. Also, for example, pairs have been seen collecting nest material inside the core area of a territory that was not actually occupied; while this might be interpreted as evidence of territory occupancy or amalgamation, it is insufficient evidence on which to reach either conclusion.

As well as being more frequent, nest refurbishment becomes a more active pursuit and pairs can spend several hours collecting and adding material on one day, often with the female remaining on the nest and arranging material delivered by the male, although both members of the pair will collect and arrange material and do so without the mate's involvement. The longer sessions do not simply become more frequent as time passes and pairs may add little or nothing on some days, but then add an obvious layer on another. There is variation and while some nests might be almost completed in mid-February, others might only have a handful of items added to them. More than one nest might also be under repair and entirely new nests have been built in February. The importance of the established nesting area becomes apparent now, as even those birds effectively wintering away make return visits to repair their nests. It is also not at all unusual for eagles to build on top of a deep layer of snow covering an existing nest.

In simple terms this activity means that a greater amount of time is spent in flight now and repair bouts are commonly followed by the pair gaining height and then leaving the area, even if they have already eaten. More time is spent in general flights; pairs often perch-hop their way around the territory and also make drifting, what might be called soaring, flights that encompass large parts of the territory. The number of true flight displays also increases but, remembering that soaring is not always a display, these are mostly seen within the box-confines of the nesting valley, with the sky dance often performed to and from the nest and when carrying nest material. Displays are usually taken to be indicative behaviour but even two eagles performing together do not have to be a pair or resident in that location. That all said, displays do not take long and eagles can still spend an inordinate amount of time perched if there is no stimulus for activity.

There are more matings and, even if the pair spends time away, there is a general sense that they are now more associated than before with the nest group. This can be seen in the level of nest area defence against corvids, especially ravens, which can have the appearance of looking to disperse rather than chasing to catch. As the number of intrusions by other eagles is still increasing, encounters with intruders become more frequent and are mostly concentrated in the nesting area. Residents tend not to pursue intruders over long distances although a flight may be prolonged by the near presence of another eagle.

Single adults

Single territory-holding adults almost always repair nests at this time and their lack of a mate does not prevent at least some from constructing entirely new nests. Because of this, their activities are very similar to paired birds and their nest refurbishment efforts are no less intensive than is seen with pairs. Single birds seem not to start new nests away from the usual group. As with pairs, an intensive bout of building is often followed by the bird settling on a perch and waiting there until roosting time, several hours later.

That said, single adults do travel (although an absence from the nest area does not mean that the eagle is any distance away) and probably do spend some time in other territories in a way that might be expected, searching for a mate or a vacancy. There is, however, no evidence of eagles bringing a new mate to a site. This is the smallest eagle category: the 1992 survey found only 32 single territory-holding adult eagles (Green 1996) and while these birds probably account for most adult intrusions, it is also why most intrusions involve immature-plumaged birds.

Foraging is, again, largely determined by availability and singletons will feed from carrion or kill as circumstances allow or demand. This group of eagles should have little difficulty in finding sufficient food so foraging can take up very little of their time, even if they have to leave the nesting area to forage successfully. These birds can be very inactive when carrion is available.

Although rapidly approaching incubation time, there is nothing to suggest that single eagles make any concerted effort to attract a mate at this time. Single eagles perform flight displays in the same way as paired birds, and have been seen to sky dance to and from the nest when there were clearly no other eagles present or in sight. Their general sailing (or soaring) flights might be taken to be an attraction display but it is difficult to separate attraction from deterrent behaviour and single birds do perform territorial defence activity. That the gender and status of any intruder will usually be unknown to the observer makes separating these behaviours even more difficult.

Immature-plumaged eagles

Again, there is little good information available other than for sightings made inside occupied territories. These birds are seen in their safe havens and, as already noted, while they may cover areas larger than a typical territory, they behave as if they are in a territory, exploiting the various food sources when necessary and using established roosts and perches. The youngest birds probably range over the largest areas and have the fewest ties, either to locations or to other eagles, and are probably those which spend the most time in flight and intruding into occupied territories.

The older immatures are not unusually in associations that could be mistaken for pairs at this time, not least because nests might be constructed or at least started. They perform flight displays above their home bases but the same birds can be seen doing so in a number of locations rather than only in one. Some of these birds have a stronger tie to one location than others and this can give the impression that a new territory is being established.

The movements of all the birds in this group are probably heavily influenced by food source availability because they will not be occupying the best areas and availability is reducing at this time. This sees the number of intrusions into occupied territories increasing because the birds are looking for food. Rather than deliberately looking for vacancies in the population, young eagles probably find them in this way: occupying safe havens with larger roaming areas and fairly regular habits allows them to encounter vacancies without extra effort.

The stay-at-home juveniles have been better observed than others in this group and their generally behaving as resident birds becomes an irritant to the adults. Such birds have been seen to roost on nest crags and one was seen on the nest with the adults adding material around it. This immediately preceded some aggression, both with the juvenile on the ground and in flight, which intensified as time passed and was the adults attempting to drive their youngster from the site. It is not known for how long adults recognise their own young but there is clearly a point at which they are no longer tolerated.

SPRING: MARCH–MAY

The nesting period immediately increases the amount of interest in golden eagles and field effort is concentrated in this season. Observer attention is focused on the nesting area and little time is spent in other parts of territories. Spring sees the onset of breeding, the entire incubation period and the beginning of the nestling period. That said, the number of pairs deemed to be active rapidly drops as some fail to make a breeding attempt, pairs can fail at any point during incubation and others fail after having hatched an egg or two. By the end of the season only a minority part of the population is engaged in a breeding attempt.

The weather has generally ameliorated and brought higher temperatures, although it can still have an influence and severe weather events can happen at any time. While the weather is highly unlikely to be a direct cause of non-breeding, breeding failures have been caused by weather events in each month and snow storms probably cause more breeding failures (and mistaken reports of non-breeding) than is generally realised. Rainfall can cause failures after the hatch and lengthy periods of continuous rain can possibly also cause desertions during incubation.

Food is potentially more important in spring than in any other season but foraging activity can be limited by the weather, especially where carrion is important, although it can also help to increase carrion amounts. Red deer mortality is still typically low in March but increases as the season progresses. Sheep mortality is high in March and continues to increase where flocks are allowed to lamb on the hill. Large herbivore mortality in March may determine whether or not some pairs produce fertile eggs or even make breeding attempts.

As the season progresses, live prey availability also increases where more species become available but can remain low where there are few hill waders or a small number of resident species. It is still relatively low prior to egg laying with the resident species almost reduced to their breeding populations, although this is not a great problem in grouse management areas. The practical availability of the main live prey species continues to fall once they begin breeding and even species such as the hooded crow and raven can become less obvious as their winter flocks begin to separate into their individual pairs and territories. In April, the hills of western Scotland can seem to be particularly devoid of food sources.

MARCH

There are more likely to be severe weather events than lengthy periods of severe weather in March but the weather can still be damaging. With some pairs beginning incubation during the first half and almost all breeding attempts beginning at some point in the month, they are particularly prone to heavy snowfall, perhaps most especially where this is coupled to strong driving winds that cause snow to drift. It can, however, be surprising just what conditions do not result in a failure.

Food availability is probably of greatest importance in March, as the eagles have to attain breeding condition at this time. Although this might actually be a longer process, it would appear that there is a greater chance of producing fertile eggs where amounts increase towards the laying date. While this may make it more difficult for pairs where there are few sheep, it does not preclude the production of fertile eggs as other species, often those largely ignored by studies, can enhance availability.

Resident pairs

Because the change from non-breeding to breeding happens over a spread of dates rather than at one time, the way in which pairs behave during March is largely determined by when, and if, they lay eggs. The non-breeding part of the month may last for one week or all four, which also means that neighbouring pairs may be behaving very differently and that, at some point, the pairs in a local population will include non-, early, late and failed breeders.

In spite of its general importance, food source distribution becomes less relevant to eagle activity during March, even though sources can be even more concentrated at this time. The importance of the nesting area takes precedence so foraging trips to more distant sources can be more direct; less time is spent searching for foraging opportunities. The members of a pair might forage co-operatively prior to egg-laying, especially under limiting weather conditions, but the increasing evidence of pre-laying supplementary provisioning of the female sees the male dominating the foraging effort and therefore using more of the territory area than does its mate. Foraging can still be problematical, of course, and the pair might still be away from the nesting area for much of the day, and only present around the roosting times.

However, more time is clearly spent in the core area but this not a guarantee of increased activity and established pairs often spend lengthy periods perched as if uninterested. This might suggest pre-laying lethargy but it is more likely to be a part of territory defence behaviour. As the pair becomes more closely associated with the nest, less time is spent both in flight and in outlying parts of the territory. At this time, and even before the eggs are laid, nest-site security appears to be of overriding importance and it is best achieved by remaining in the nest vicinity.

There is an increase in the use of flight displays and these are principally performed inside the core area, if not the nesting valley. The members of a pair may sail above the nesting area but they often spend little time in open flight and casual drifting flights are mostly seen at the later breeding pairs; even intruding eagles may not be pursued far beyond the immediate area.

The pair continues to titivate the chosen nest but this is commonly a low-key activity as less work is required as egg-laying approaches; the nest lining and cup is usually added some days before the first egg is laid. The pair might not even visit the nest on some days but may be seen on more than one nest on others. At other times, one or both birds will spend time simply standing on the chosen nest and looking out over the view. There appears to be no easy means of determining when the first egg is to be laid, although a series of brief nest visits has been seen to immediately precede the onset of incubation on more than one occasion.

Breeding pairs
The onset of breeding sees a huge reduction in general activity. With one bird effectively on the nest at all times, there is only one to undertake all other duties. As the off-duty bird has to be ready to relieve its mate, it spends a great deal of time perched nearby and engaged in nest area defence, often mostly against corvids. The number of flight displays, drifting casual flights and, perhaps more surprisingly, general territorial activity decreases. The pair is generally about the nesting area for most of every day and it is only when foraging takes place further afield that lengthy absences are seen. The outer parts of some territories can see very little use at this time. Nest material continues to be added during incubation and some pairs also take food to the nest. The amount of foraging is largely dependent on the available sources and carrion is readily used when available.

Failed breeders
An early breeding failure can give the impression that breeding has not yet been attempted, with the pair often actively refurbishing and spending time perched on nests. This activity

soon passes and many failed pairs then desert the nesting area for other parts of the territory where nest building may be resumed and roosting seen in previously unknown locations. This can look like preparation for a re-lay, but second clutches are so rare that this type of nest building is probably no more than a form of displacement behaviour. These birds are often to be seen above the new location and sometimes perform flight displays and so can also be mistaken for a different pair of birds.

Non-breeding

Confirming non-breeding is more difficult than confirming breeding or failure. Pairs which fail to make breeding attempts typically go through all the motions of those which do breed; they build, repair and line nests, perform flight displays, defend the nest area and limit their movements in the same way. Because of this, non-breeding cannot be confirmed at any site until all possibility of breeding or an early failure has been absolutely dismissed. Non-breeding is usually marked by the gradual cessation of nest refurbishment, rather than a sudden stop, and these birds generally spend more time in the nesting area than pairs which have failed in their breeding attempt.

Single adults

Given that this behavior has been recorded in a number of different locations, it is likely that all single adults behave as if they were in pairs; they build, repair and line nests, perform flight displays, defend the nest area and spend a great deal of time perched inside the nesting valley and core area. Although they generally limit their movements to their own territory, the fact that recognisable single adults have been seen in other occupied core areas suggests that they will travel further afield in a way that suggests searching for a vacancy or a new mate. Whether or not this goal is actually achieved has never been proven and records of birds changing territory, or pair, lack certainty.

Immature-plumaged birds

Excluding those in pairs or occupying existing territories, there is very little known about this group of eagles. It can be said that they do become more active and roam over larger areas at this time and are responsible for most of the increased number of intrusions into occupied territories. This may still be mostly because of the difficulty of finding food and intrusions into core areas are probably simply an artefact of this behaviour. Although some vacancies might be filled in this way, it still seems likely that most deep intrusions into occupied territories involve the youngest birds that are probably most desperate to find a food source and that are not looking to join a pair. Immature-plumaged birds often travel at high elevation between locations and their encounters with adults can be prolonged by their lack of motivation; the presence of an adult pair does not easily deter them.

Juveniles that have wintered in the natal territory may still be on site in March and still occupying the territory as if a resident, but the adults now treat them more as an intruder than their own young. The adults' response can even be stronger to their own young than to strangers at such times and active defence can be seen to be time-consuming, although it is still mostly performed in the core area if not being limited to the nesting valley. These encounters can be extreme, with both adults chasing, stooping and flight-rolling at the juvenile. The increased intensity probably results from the juvenile having knowledge of the site and being able to use it in a more disruptive manner than visiting outsiders.

APRIL

The worst of the weather has now passed but that does not mean that it cannot be influential, and breeding attempts have failed because of snowfall in every week of the month. Although persistent rain can limit foraging efficiency, this does not appear to be a major problem and is unlikely to cause failures. The ambient temperature also means that any fresh snow and frosts are seldom long-lived on the lower slopes where most of the food will be found.

Depending on the types of sources present in a territory, the practical availability of food can be very low in April at some sites. While the amount of red deer carrion will be increasing during the month, the amount of sheep carrion, where sheep are present on the hill, can level off and even decrease. Where sheep are returning to the hills there can be very little carrion and even that which is present is often not found in the usual places. The smaller live prey species, such as red grouse and ptarmigan, become less obvious as their breeding attempts begin, with birds behaving more surreptitiously and becoming more alert as individuals. Corvids can also be largely absent from many areas. The summer visitors are appearing on the hills and it is not unusual to find quite sizeable flocks, as many as several hundreds, of golden plovers on ground where they are not known to breed. (Such flocks sometimes occur in late March and have also been seen in January).

Breeding pairs

As only a small number of pairs hatch eggs before the last week of the month, April can, for ease, be thought of as being composed entirely of the incubation period: the behaviour of those which do hatch eggs in April is no different from those which hatch in May.

The incubation period continues to be a period of low activity levels, the eagles' routine is well set and the off-duty birds can spend very little time in flight. There can be days when little more than the comings and goings around the nest might be seen. The number of changeovers on the nest varies considerably from day to day and there can seem to be no reason for many of the changes of duty. Nest material continues to be collected and delivered, both at changeovers and on nest visits, and material has been seen to be delivered to nests other than the one in use. As the female seems almost invariably to incubate overnight, only the male needs to find a roost and the one chosen on most nights is usually the favoured year-round roost; males do not change their habits to roost closer to the nest because it is in use.

It is not unusual for both members of a pair to be off the nest at the same time, for them to circle together on such occasions or for them to perch together. Although these actions seldom persist for more than a few minutes, absences of about 20 minutes are not uncommon. A pair with eggs might also be seen mating and some pairs regularly take food to the nest well before the eggs are due to hatch. It can be seen how an observer's over-confidence in their ability to reach conclusions can make it very easy to reach the wrong conclusion at this time of year.

The incidence of flight display is low, with most sky dancing performed to and from the active nest. Soaring or high circling as a display is difficult to confirm but is usually little in evidence at this time, with nest area defence taking priority over territory defence or advertising. There are generally few drifting or wide-scale patrolling flights and where it is necessary for the birds to forage over a wider area, such flights are usually fairly direct and determined. That said, a female breeding in the Lake District was known to make regular incubation period flights to a food source, a grouse moor, eight to ten kilometres from the nest and be away for two to four hours. By contrast, that female's replacement rarely, if ever, made such flights. This shows how a good food source can be utilised regardless of its location in relation to the active nest and how different birds will behave and utilise resources differently under virtually identical conditions.

Failed breeders

Failure can happen at any time during the month and the response is the same as that seen with March failures, with the birds' nest area activity gradually decreasing after bouts of nest building. There is, however, in both months, the problem that the eagles do not desert the nest at the point of failure. With many of the so-called incubation period failures actually being pre-laying failures (the failure to lay fertile eggs), incubation period failures can be very difficult to confirm, because failure is commonly not noted until after the eggs were expected to hatch and it is usually not known if the deserted eggs were fertile. Because of that, in reality, most of the pairs that will fail behave in exactly the same way as the pairs that will hatch their eggs and the two cannot be separated during this period.

When the nest has been deserted (without the eggs being removed) the birds usually linger in the nest area, are usually seen together, will perform bouts of nest refurbishment (sometimes burying the eggs) and may add to or build other nests. They will stand on nests as if judging their security but they do not appear to perform many flight displays. These activities can be pronounced but the birds typically begin to lose interest, perhaps after about a fortnight, and can then become very inconspicuous. They often abandon the nesting area and can be found perching for lengthy periods almost anywhere in the territory. When eggs have been removed or scavenged the bouts of activity are usually shorter and the nest area can be more immediately abandoned.

As with other aspects of eagle activity, what actually happens in any given location depends heavily on topography and the distribution of food sources but these activities have been recorded in a variety of locations with different circumstances.

Non-breeding pairs

Eagles in this group can continue to behave as if expecting to make a breeding attempt, although the intensity of their efforts decreases with time. The pair is usually to be seen together, nest material will be collected and flight displays are not uncommon but the time spent perched increases, as does the time spent away from the nest area. A successful foraging trip can see the pair remain in outlying parts of the territory almost until roosting time; roosting is usually within the nesting area and the birds sometimes go to roost well in advance of darkness.

Single adults

These birds seem to continue the pre-laying activity but at a lower intensity than is seen with pairs. They can still be seen repairing nests and performing flight displays but these are generally not time-consuming. No difference has been seen between the behaviour and activity of single males and single females apart from their usual gender-related differences.

These birds are not always present at the site and it seems likely that they are responsible for some of the intrusions into other territories (something that reaches its peak in April), although they can be very difficult to find in spite of generally using a relatively small home base. The wanderings of these birds at this time can increase the confusion over what is seen in almost any location and are probably responsible for many records of pairs that do not actually exist.

Immature-plumaged eagles

Yet again, most of the available information about these eagles is the result of sightings during the monitoring of territories that are known to be occupied. Elsewhere, those in pairs behave as paired adults and singles holding territories behave as do single adults. The wandering birds are constantly intruding into occupied territories and interacting with the residents. These intrusions can be prolonged if a resident reacts but can also involve little more than the birds circling and flying together in a fairly casual manner. These birds appear to be little affected by the territorial response they produce and seem to move on at a whim rather than because of anything an adult might do. Even an aggressive encounter does not always result in the youngster immediately retreating, although an over-wintering juvenile born at a site the previous year has been seen to flee its aggressive parents.

Most of these birds are probably still wandering in search of feeding opportunities and, after feeding, have little impetus to be active in any specific way. They can cover large areas during the course of a day, or move very little at other times, probably select roosts on the basis of where they are and probably commonly roost inside occupied territories.

MAY

The weather conditions have greatly improved by now but there can still be severe events and prolonged periods of precipitation that can result in breeding failures. Rainfall around the time of hatching can prevent food for the chicks from being delivered to the nest and, as unlikely as it may seem, this is strongly believed to have been a cause of failure.

Food availability is more obviously increasing now; deer start calving during May and there is more red deer carrion than before, if there are hill sheep these will be lambing, the summer visitors to the hills such as curlews, golden plover and common gull will be on the breeding grounds along with others and the resident species will be more active. It is this flush of availability coincidental with the hatching time that probably explains why eagles breed when they do.

Breeding pairs

For convenience here, the nestling period can be said to start on 1 May. As eagle clutches hatch asynchronously and only one egg of two might hatch, there can be very little difference in behaviour from the incubation period at this time, as the birds are often simultaneously incubating an egg and brooding a chick. As small chicks need as much protection as eggs, this means that the pattern of nest relief can at first be no different from that seen during full incubation. Changeovers can be slower once an egg has hatched, with the incoming bird standing for longer, but can still appear as if the incomer is simply turning the eggs before sitting. As small chicks also need little food, while there may be more standing and sitting as if the adult is uncomfortable, the on-duty bird may sit continuously for several hours and not stand until relieved. This basic nesting activity can continue into the second half of the month as the female in particular will brood chicks until it can no longer do so comfortably. Once it is no longer brooding continuously the female will spend much time perched nearby, only flying when absolutely necessary.

The male performs most of the foraging at this time and, while the early food might be collected from close to the nest, most males expand their foraging range as the month progresses and demand increases; males more obviously begin to range over a larger area than before. Females also forage to provision the nest as the chicks grow but they seldom leave the nest area, even when the male is on site; they obtain much of their food intake from what is delivered by the male and will carry food from the nest to feed on a perch. While the male will often perch after delivering food, it is also likely to then leave the area and forage for its own needs outside the immediate nest area.

The number of flight displays now dramatically increases, with the incidence of sky dancing reaching its peak. Many of these flights are performed by the male carrying food to the nest and then displaying on leaving and so are below the ridge tops. High level displays are also flown and pairs can be very conspicuous at this time as they demonstrate their status in order to protect their food sources. Females display less frequently than males but often become quite vocal around food deliveries. Soaring flights are not that common unless an intruding eagle has been seen and the birds do not habitually sail above their sites.

Failed breeders

Pairs which fail because of the death of chicks lose interest in the used nest but often almost immediately show some interest in one of their other ones, adding material and standing on it for several minutes at a time. This activity usually passes more quickly than when the same behaviour follows the loss of eggs and, as with pairs failing earlier in the season, the birds often soon abandon the nesting area for other parts of the territory. These birds can be very inconspicuous and are often to be found perched for lengthy periods in unexceptional parts of their land, and so not always in prominent locations or within obvious foraging areas. Their roosting habits are very variable and while they will still use the main nest area roosts, their first flights of the day often immediately take them away from the area. Perhaps unexpectedly, these birds perform flight displays and will sky dance above the nesting area, implying that it is the time of year that determines display rather than it being linked to an event in the breeding cycle.

Non-breeders

Eagles that have made no breeding attempt often become more obvious at this time and can usually be found within the nesting area, even if they are only perched. As they are only foraging for themselves, and with food availability increasing, these birds often have little need to forage over a wide area. Perhaps as a result of innate habit, males still wander more widely and spend less time in the nest area than do females. Non-breeders also perform flight displays and, in spite of having no active nest, also perform them more frequently than at other times. They do not appear to show much interest in nests although there is always the possibility of material being added on any given day.

Single eagles

It is possible that these birds display even more frequently and intensively than do pairs with chicks, and single eagles of both genders have been seen to sky dance at high elevation for extended periods. These performances regularly involve upwards of one hundred dips; the eagle may then high circle for a while and then perform again, and birds have been watched doing this for more than three hours until they were eventually lost from view. A common alternative ending is for the bird to then make a spiraling, descending long-drop to a perch on which it then spends several hours. However, single eagles can still be very inconspicuous at this time because much of this flight activity is performed at extreme elevation (where it will not be casually observed) and they show little interest in their nests.

Unpaired immature plumaged eagles

Even less is known about these birds at this time and it can only be assumed that they continue to behave in a way that allows them to survive. There are fewer intrusions into the hearts of territories with active breeding attempts, although they will continue to visit occupied sites and at times pass by relatively closely to the active nest. These birds are often to be seen lingering in unoccupied areas and often make high circling flights before travelling to a new location; they can clearly cover large areas over the course of a day and, when encountered, often seem to be wandering rather aimlessly. Their foraging appears to be mostly opportunistic and most of their flights appear to have little to do with foraging.

SUMMER: JUNE–AUGUST

While there are obviously gaps in our knowledge of golden eagle ecology, it is possibly during the summer that these are least recognised, given that this is when fieldworkers are most active and so most confident. Unfortunately, concentrating on successful breeding attempts not only means that the greater part of the population is largely ignored: it means that active nests become even more of a focus of attention, with ringing commonly being an end to observer effort. The actual fledging of any young (ringed or not) is commonly never proven and there is virtually no interest in what happens after this point. It can be seen that observer interest has always waned just as eagle activity begins to increase and become more interesting.

Although a time of fine weather, with there being little likelihood of severe events, conditions can still be influential as golden eagles in the UK do not seem to cope well with heat and can appear quite distressed if there are lengthy hot and dry periods. It is likely that some chicks die because of heat in most years. As the season progresses, weather conditions might even influence the time of fledging as overheating nestlings seek whatever shelter they can find on or close to the nest and do not appear keen to expose themselves to the open elements.

Food can also be a problem for successful pairs at this time, as demand rapidly increases from little more than what is needed by the adults to, in some cases, what is needed by four adult-sized eagles. This must not only stretch resources at many sites, but must also put a strain on the adults. The nestlings/juveniles might fledge at a time of high food abundance but they have to reach that point via periods of low availability. There is typically little carrion available at this time, the young of the large herbivores are generally healthy and able to protect themselves or have already died, the other live prey species begin the summer very inconspicuously and species such as the red grouse only become fully available in late summer. Over the same period, sources such as the hill waders and gulls can have a flush of abundance and then a noticeable drop in availability; resident species, such as the corvids, might become more obvious and there might also be wildfowl available. In other words, there might be the greatest variety of food sources at this time but they all have very variable availability. In a practical sense, it is not simply a case of more food being available at this time.

JUNE

There is little likelihood of the weather being especially disruptive or damaging in June and the greater daylight period means that most eagles have more than enough time in which to complete their daily tasks.

After noticeably increasing during May, food availability in June can be surprisingly low away from grouse management areas. While the number of individuals of most species may well be increasing, they can be very difficult to locate as most of the increase is in the form of immature animals that are smaller than adults and which can easily hide in the now lush undergrowth. This practical side of availability is generally overlooked. In a similar way, while many red deer calves are born in June, they are quickly active and soon running with the herd.

Breeding pairs

Eagles with young in the nest are not necessarily more active than those without young. Rather than increasing as the month progresses, adult activity at the nest (the number, frequency and duration of visits) decreases. This is mainly because of the pestering to which they are subjected by the young. That said, food and nest material are still collected and delivered, the breeding female will feed the nestling beak to beak at times and will also shelter it from rain or strong sunlight.

Females continue to spend most of their time in the nest area but will now perch further away and in locations from which they can view the nest and its approaches without drawing the nestling's attention. Females also generally now collect more food than before and do not rely on the male to provision the nest. Males might spend lengthy periods perched after delivering food, often alongside the female, but they are mostly out of the area and foraging over the entire territory. It is at this time when active nests may hold little stored food and when breeding eagles may be seen foraging and carrying food well beyond the core area; 'unusual' prey items are also commonly recorded at this time.

Females effectively stay close to the nest to protect and defend it and while they may spend a great amount of time perched in order to achieve this goal, they also sail above the site, probably simultaneously visually searching for the male and, possibly as a by-product, demonstrating the active occupancy of the site. As a result the incidence of what can be called soaring display flights increases and peaks in June. Eagles do sky dance in June, especially the male flying to and from the nest, but its incidence now decreases, probably because males are more actively engaged in foraging as they are still also providing a large proportion of what the female eats.

It is usually at this time that the main winter roost is vacated in favour of more open or alternative locations. The female will still roost on the nest from time to time but will often roost on its favourite day perch, with the male not even roosting inside the nesting valley on some nights. In most territories, the roosts used at this time are often at a much higher elevation than those used during the winter and spring.

Failed and non-breeding pairs

Pairs with breeding attempts that have already failed behave no differently from those which made no attempt. They can be very inconspicuous as they have no attachment to the nesting area and only have to forage for themselves; few display flights are flown and little or no material will be taken to any nest. An inference as to the division of labour can still be drawn, as females still spend more time than males in the nesting area. However, as the male is not foraging to provision the nest, and females forage for their own needs, the pair might be seen together or individually some distance from the nests. As a result, time is spent in outlying parts of the territory and the pair might make broad casual drifting flights that take them into other territories.

Pairs with breeding attempts which fail during June usually abandon the nest and the nesting area very quickly and not unusually spend very little time in the core area. These birds can be very difficult to find as many seldom roost in the core area and seldom spend much time in flight. It is by no means unusual to find these birds settled on an out-of-the-way perch in a valley or location that might not even be thought to be a part, or at least an important part, of their area.

With most of the paired population now falling into this category, even large areas that are known to hold golden eagles can seem to be devoid of the species.

Single territory-holding adults

These birds can be as inactive as the failed pairs but their displaying is still usually more obvious than it is with pairs, at least during the early part of the month. They will perform high flights above their nesting area but are often to be found simply perched and waiting. Some gender variation has been noted with, again, females not only generally remaining about the core area but also seldom leaving the territory and males not unusually being absent from the core and travelling further afield. If their behaviour is similar, which it probably is, this may be when near-adult birds without an established territory begin to find vacancies within the population.

Unpaired immature-plumaged eagles

Although little is known about this group, these birds do appear to become more obvious now, but this is probably because most are wandering quite widely and are likely to be found in locations with which they have no real association. Given the general food availability, this wandering is probably still mostly linked to food and, because of this, it might be suggested that these birds are unlikely to join a pair or even settle in a location at this time.

Those that are already occupying or using safe havens do so as if they were on territories and it is not unusual for these to attract several immature-plumaged eagles at this time. Associations might be formed but as these locations are not prime sites the number of birds present or using the site can vary greatly from day to day. Flight displays appear to be unusual, especially the sky dance, and most high flights are usually a precursor to travelling rather than a demonstration of occupancy or status.

JULY

While there can be rain and mists that make foraging more difficult and limit flight activity, the main concern is now heat. Golden eagles do not appear well equipped to deal with high temperatures and while observers might like to be active on fine summer days, eagles are often to be found perched in the shade or at high elevation as they attempt to avoid the worst of the heat.

General food availability is now increasing as the young of the grouse and hare species grow in size and become more active; family parties mingle and sizeable packs can be found by the end of the month. This is not so obvious away from the grouse management areas or where there are only small numbers of hares or ptarmigan; little more than family parties might be found in these places. Corvids become more obvious in some areas and the availability of other medium-sized species probably also peaks now. There is usually little carrion to be found and the carcasses that do occur are mostly found in fairly random locations.

Successful breeders

Eagles with nestlings can be surprisingly inactive and as the month progresses there is the suspicion that the pair is simply waiting for the nestling to fledge. As a result the pair will spend a great deal of time perched, often some distance from and not unusually out of sight of the nest. It is also not unusual for the members of a pair to be active together several kilometres from the nest. A successful pair can be neither active nor obvious in the nest area. The nestling still requires food so the adults do visit the nest, and might sky dance away from it, but there are often days on which neither adult visits the nest but simply floats by as if checking the site before going to a perch or leaving the area.

The male still dominates the foraging effort but it is no longer providing food that will always be eaten by the female as well. As the nestling is now capable of plucking and tearing food, and its needs meet the requirements of a full-grown eagle, the female increases its foraging activity and forages for both the nestling and its own needs more frequently than before. This is necessitated by the demanding nestling usually preventing the female from feeding on the nest by mantling over any food that is delivered.

There is also little flight display now, especially away from nest visits, unless an intruder is encountered but intrusions seem to be fairly uncommon at this time. The adults, especially the female, might still wait on above the site in a way that might appear to be a display and either member of a pair may make a high-level checking visit, coming in to sail above the site for a few minutes before turning away and returning to the foraging grounds. The female usually roosts within sight or earshot of the active nest but the male may again roost away.

Most eaglets fledge in July but the event is seldom, if ever, marked by any great change in adult activity levels. There is surprisingly little flight display associated with fledging, certainly when compared to events at the hatching time, and it is not unusual for the adults to miss the moment of fledging.

Other territorial pairs

Failed and non-breeding eagles can become even less obvious than they were in earlier months. With long daylight periods of usually fine weather and an abundance of food that is not being reduced by nestlings, these birds spend even longer on perches and lingering on roosts. These birds will readily utilise whatever carrion is available and many probably also fail to feed on some days as they are under no pressure to survive.

These pairs are often to be found and may be resident in secondary parts of the territory, operating around alternative or new nests as if in a core area. There does not appear to be a great deal of nest building or refurbishment at this time (although it can happen at any time) but it is not unusual to see what might be called prospecting flights in which the birds (usually one at a time and usually the male) visit a variety of ledges to stand and look out; they also make slow passing flights close to these potential nest sites.

As with pairs of all status and at other times of year, the male is more likely to be operating further afield than the female, but it is also likely to be largely inactive at these times, spending time perched or casually sailing in outlying areas. The birds do sometimes operate as a pair and on these occasions might drift into the outer parts of adjoining territories.

That said, females are less likely to leave the core area and might do little more than make a few short perch-to-perch flights during the course of a day. It is as if the nest area still needs to be protected. These eagles can be seen sailing above their sites and might indulge in prolonged but fairly casual and distant confrontations with their neighbours but these are not common and, for most of the time, their flights are seemingly without much purpose.

Single adult and non-territorial immature-plumaged eagles

As always, little is really known about these birds at this time, with single territory-holding adults apparently being very inactive, usually paying little attention to the nests and performing few flight displays. Those studied are not known to have travelled far beyond their usual territories although single males do seem to be more adventurous than single females.

As there appear to be few intrusions into occupied core areas at this time, and non-paired and non-territorial birds have few responsibilities, it might be surmised that all these birds are fairly inactive at a time of abundant food availability. However, that does not appear to be the case and those in immature plumage are commonly found around

the fringes and over ground that is just outside occupied territories. They can be much
more active than territorial birds, often travelling quite long distances via circuitous
routes and at high elevation, actively foraging in suitable areas but also lingering where
there seem to be few opportunities. Their safe havens appear to hold less of an attraction
for them, presumably because of improved conditions, and where they roost is largely
unknown. At least some are suspected of using conifer plantations but, given good
weather conditions, most are likely to roost wherever is most convenient at the time.

If more than one such eagle is present there can be lengthy interactions with tremendous
elevations being reached and chasing in a way that could be interpreted as pair formation.
Whether or not new pairs are formed now is not known but there must be a great amount
of contact between unpaired birds at this time and some associations must be made.

AUGUST

There are now more free-flying eagles than at any other time of year but that does not
mean that there is an extensive record to access or consult, and the young leaving the
nest does not mean that there is an immediate increase in flight activity.

Although there might be rain and low cloud that reduces foraging efficiency, the main
problem is again heat and even successful territories can seem to be devoid of eagles
during the hottest weather. Although bathing can be seen at almost any time of the year,
more records have been collected during hot spells in August than at any other and birds
have been seen to soak their bodies in wet moss as well as bathing fully in streams.

Food is usually not a great problem in August even though the diversity of sources
may be reducing as summer visitors leave the hill ground. The resident species are still
numerous and corvid flocks can become more apparent; where there are rookeries in
adjacent areas, flocks of more than one thousand birds can be seen and these provide easy
targets for adult eagles. Carrion is usually in low supply with carcasses widely scattered
and if there are no sheep on the hills there might be no fresh carcasses at all during the
month. Once red deer stalking is in full progress, there can be gralloch and sometimes
carcasses left overnight that are readily used by golden eagles.

Successful pairs

Most nestlings probably fledge in late July but some are still on the nest in early August
because of the varying laying dates and the varying lengths of the nestling period. The
act of fledging does not greatly increase adult activity; the male continues to provide
most, if not all, of the juvenile's food and forages and rests as it does during the late
nestling period; the female remains on guard in the nest area but now has much less
involvement with the youngster.

The separate adult roles become more apparent as the month progresses and the
juvenile becomes more active. The available evidence shows that the male will try to
provide the juvenile with freshly-killed prey, will forage over the entire territory and

beyond if necessary and may target outlying sources to obtain this food and its own. These birds can be seen many kilometres from the nest and can be seen carrying prey over quite long distances (at least 12 kilometres has been recorded in Argyll), and in a way that might suggest the bird to be linked to a different location. The female stands guard over the juvenile's location but commonly leaves the area almost as soon as the male returns. Females then forage for their own needs over quite wide areas and, even if they have fed there, can spend lengthy periods away from the nest area. This separation of roles has been seen in different locations and even when two young have been fledged.

Both adults typically roost in the nest area throughout the month, and they not unusually roost close to the juvenile. Nest visits are occasionally made but August is the month in which the least nest material is collected by this category of eagle.

There is little flight display performed and even high sailing above the site becomes less apparent and is mostly performed by the female as it gains height prior to leaving the area. High sailing can be seen in outlying parts of the territory but this usually involves the bird preparing to travel rather than it being easily confirmed as a display. As there are very few intrusions at this time of year, it helps raise the point of whether display flights are used to deter intrusions or are the result of intrusions.

Newly-fledged juveniles can be very difficult to locate at first and they are often only located as a result of their calling. They become increasingly active during the month and their flying ability improves over time but the available evidence shows that they are still typically to be found within the nest area, if not the nest valley. Juveniles at some sites might not even move more than a few hundred metres from the nest during August.

For convenience it can be suggested that a juvenile's confinement period finishes at the end of August. There is some variation in the length and actual timing of this period, of course, with some juveniles becoming adventurous in mid-August and some not until early September, but most are usually to be found close at hand throughout August.

Other pairs

The failed and non-breeding pairs continue in an inconspicuous vein. They can be about the nesting area for most of any day or entirely absent from it, depending on their foraging success. Although males will continue to roam further afield, the pair might be seen together in any part of the territory and might perch together for several hours in any location.

Foraging and feeding at this time may involve little more than finding a usable carcass or simply killing an easy target and there are probably days on which eagles do not feed to any great extent, although several small items might be consumed. However, these birds are generally inactive, perform few flight displays and show little if any interest in their nests. During periods of hot weather they may do no more than find a shady perch on which to spend the day before going to roost. As a result, these eagles can be difficult to find and, because they do not always use their favourite perches, their territories can appear to be deserted.

Single and immature-plumaged eagles

The available information on this group of eagles is extremely slight and is mostly the result of casual sightings where the bird's status might not be accurately known.

Where single territory-holding adults have been watched, their behaviour is similar to that seen with paired birds; males spend less time in the nesting area than do females, but both may spend lengthy periods there or in other parts of the territory. Their daily routine is dominated by the need to find food so they can be very inactive. They show little interest in their nests and perform very few display flights.

Although they have no real ties and are under little pressure to survive, and although they are responsible for most of the intrusions, non-territorial eagles are seldom seen deep inside occupied sites during August. The general activity of successful pairs seems to be sufficient to deter regular intrusions but there have also been few intrusions noted where lengthy and detailed observations have been made at failed and non-breeding pairs. Although these birds clearly wander quite widely, at times they seem also to concentrate their activity around the outside or on the fringe of occupied sites. They will travel at low elevation but generally move from place to place at high elevation.

As foraging is not difficult, these birds have little to hold their attention and their movements seem to be fairly random choices; if there is a stimulus it is not easily recognised. They can spend quite lengthy periods behaving almost as newly-fledged juveniles, searching, scrambling and making low-level flights. When there is more than one bird present they often closely interact with one another, with chases and stooping when one is perched, but they still generally behave as individuals. When one leaves it is not always followed; similarly, if more than one high circle together, the birds do not always then travel in the same direction. As the ages of these birds are not known and are likely to vary, and because they generally cannot be recognised as individuals, it cannot be said how, and if, any of this behaviour might be linked to pair formation.

The immature-plumaged eagles holding safe havens seem to behave as if on territory and appear to spend much time perched and flying at low elevation. These birds probably do roam further afield but there are too few records to be certain of how they behave.

AUTUMN: SEPTEMBER–NOVEMBER

The autumn is probably more a time of change than any other season. While the winter sees the build-up towards breeding, spring is mostly concerned with the nest and summer is focused on the needs of the young, the autumn sees a fundamental change in the behaviour of successful pairs and the need to survive plays a greater role with all eagles. It is also a time that has proved to be of little interest to eagle watchers, principally because the nest is no longer in use but also because it is generally perceived as being an unproductive time to be making observations, largely because of mistaken ideas about the post-fledging period. And, of course, there has never been any great interest in pairs that have not produced young or in the lifestyles of the immature and unpaired part of the population.

The weather begins to be more influential again and while the season can begin with moderate conditions, by the end of autumn there can be snow storms, gales and torrential rain that can limit activity and make foraging and survival much more difficult. Such conditions must influence how young eagles behave and survive but they also influence established territory- holding adults.

The food supply also changes during the autumn as live prey availability begins to decline and carrion availability increases. While the numbers of game birds and hares may still be high, they are also fully grown and mobile and their practical availability can be quite low; the same is true where they are not present in large numbers. The summer visitors have left the hills and there can be a stark contrast in the apparent richness of a territory, even between mid-August and mid-September, once they have left. Carrion amounts increase during the season (though often beginning at almost zero) as more sheep begin to die and the red deer rut can result in stag carcasses that can be a boon to golden eagles.

SEPTEMBER

While their numbers may now be slightly reduced and their visibility still not great, the odds of seeing a golden eagle, especially in unexpected locations, are increased as juveniles begin to roam further from home.

Weather conditions are usually amenable and while the first frosts of autumn used to accompany what were often quite lengthy dry spells in the past, more recent Septembers seem to have been milder and wetter, which have a general overall effect on the development of young eagles. Limiting weather events are still unusual and with lengthy daylight periods there is usually sufficient time at any point during the month for eagles to accomplish their tasks with ease.

The available food supply can appear to be more limited than is actually the case because medium-sized live prey species are generally not very demonstrative at this time. As they mostly feed on the ground at a time of high invertebrate and vegetative availability, the grouse and hare species might also be easily sated and largely inactive as a result. Carrion amounts can also be disguised by carcasses being widely scattered over a large area rather than being easily found by an observer. These elements of practical availability also affect eagles as they appear to rely on movement (even the movement of corvids at carcasses) to locate much of their food.

Successful pairs
A great deal of a pair's activity is still largely determined by the presence of their young. The male continues to be closely associated with the juvenile but will now be following

it as it begins to explore a larger area. The male's activity might still not involve much more than flying between perches and watching over the youngster but it will offer active protection and defence if that is needed. As the juvenile wanders over the greater territory area and adjoining, often low-lying, ground, a territorial male eagle might not only be seen in apparently little-used parts of its own territory, but can be led into and through adjacent ones. This can result not only in males roosting away from their preferred places but also, potentially, roosting inside other territories. However, as this juvenile habit becomes more frequent, the male becomes less inclined to follow the juvenile and has usually returned to roost in the nest area by the end of the month.

The female now has even less involvement with the juvenile and although the two may be seen together (and the juvenile may still beg for food when perched) almost all such interactions are initiated by the juvenile or are chance encounters. Females typically linger about the nesting area while the others are away and might spend little time in flight. They still continue to make their own foraging excursions but can be much less obvious than the male in everything they do. Females almost always roost in the nesting area at this time.

The eagles perform very few flight displays and even generalised high-circling seems to be fairly unusual, although male and juvenile may be seen circling almost anywhere within the territory, not unusually outside of the territory and sometimes with other eagles in adjoining locations.

By contrast with adults, and becoming more adventurous as the month progresses, juveniles are increasingly less likely to be seen in the nesting area from which they originated. Their wanderings appear to be random and, as they are led by neither adult, their foraging and their finding of suitable foraging areas is self-taught and perhaps a matter of luck; they often 'give up' and move on very quickly if food is not easily located. These eagles make very few kills because of their inexperience.

Juvenile flights are often close to the ground, be that at high, medium or low altitude, are often very circuitous and the birds will even cross valleys at low elevation, towards the mouth and where there is more human activity. Their inexperience and exploratory behaviour can make separating juveniles from older immature-plumaged eagles fairly straightforward at times.

Juveniles can also roost in seemingly random locations and their not returning to the nest area is not always the result of the distance travelled. Distance becomes more of a factor as the month progresses and most juveniles are probably roosting away on a regular basis by the end of September. This, along with the increased number of intrusions into neighbouring territories (and those even further afield), can give the impression of a territory being successful when it was not and even of a territory being occupied when it is not. These birds seldom remain in a location for any length of time, often seem to move on a whim and seem to show no explainable pattern of exploration; their movements are not determined by the distribution of food sources.

The juvenile activity and adult roles when two chicks have been successfully reared appear to be little different from when there is only a single juvenile. A juvenile that eventually remains on territory throughout its first winter can appear to be no less adventurous than one which will leave and it might make excursions and even spend multiple nights away from the site. As there is so much variation in the development of individual eagles, such things are often only recognised during retrospective analysis and direct observations can be misleading.

Failed and non-breeders

Those paired adults that did not produce young can become more apparent at this time and they seem to be more generally active than earlier. They still perform few flight displays but general high sailing above the nest and foraging areas is not unusual and may extend for quite lengthy periods. They also operate as a pair more often than successful birds and commonly cover their greater territory area on a succession of days. They will still roost away from nest area but this habit is already declining and even the favourite winter roost may be in regular use by now.

Most of their activity does not appear to be linked to foraging opportunity and this might suggest that it is the result of juvenile intruders, being territorial behaviour in the face of what can be regular intrusions. The juveniles are a nuisance rather than any real threat to resident eagles, which may simply approach and watch without combat or much interference. That said, some very obvious territorial displays and defence flights have been noted from non-breeding pairs in September when intruding adults have been sighted.

Single and immature-plumaged eagles

The activity of eagles in this group is so under-recorded as to make almost any suggestion of typicality have dubious value. Only single adult-plumaged birds have been observed in any detail and these seem to have the same behaviour patterns as paired birds of their own gender. Males cover larger areas than females and probably travel beyond their usual area as if accompanying a juvenile, with females spending more time closer to the nests but making foraging and roaming excursions within and about the territory.

The immature-plumaged birds that are not juveniles may well extend their ranging activities and may behave as their gender dictates but, as the age of the individuals involved will not be known, the observed behaviour may be entirely typical or not. It has long been suspected that these birds still wander between locations but they are probably also still likely to spend longer in each safe haven than is a younger bird or than they may at other times of year. Their activity is probably also determined, or at least greatly influenced, by the ease of foraging and the presence or absence of eagles of a similar age.

These birds' interactions within their age group may well see the formation of new pairings and associations that might be best described as trial pairings. In these they may settle, albeit temporarily, in unused locations and abandoned or vacated territories.

OCTOBER

The weather conditions more noticeably deteriorate now; gales and heavy rain become more frequent and snowfall can coat the hills, albeit usually temporarily away from the high tops. As well as directly affecting general eagle activity levels, this also makes foraging more difficult and so increases the value of stable food sources. While the birds may have been free almost to forage at will since April, the weather can now restrict the amount of opportunistic foraging that takes place as the minor food sources become scarcer.

Food availability is changing, again especially away from the grouse management areas. Where there is little or no such management, grouse may remain in their family parties, rather than forming larger packs, and can be very inconspicuous in their preferred habitat, the more so given that unmanaged red grouse are usually found at lower density and have lower productivity. The same might be said of other species such as mountain hare and ptarmigan; where the habitat is not ideal, the numbers will be low and individuals scattered.

Carrion amounts, while usually still relatively small in most places, increase more noticeably now, with weakened sheep and red deer more likely to succumb to conditions. With the red deer rut in full swing there can be fatalities or injuries that will later prove to be fatal and the same can be said about accidental deaths and injuries as a result of icy, precipitous paths; the young of any species are prone to accidental death as a result of changing conditions.

Successful pairs

The behaviour of these pairs is still influenced by their young to some extent, even where the latter become fully independent and leave the natal territory on a more or less permanent basis. The male may still show an interest in the juvenile if it remains in the vicinity and during the early part of the month may be absent from the nesting area for entire days, still occasionally roosting away from there.

There can then be a rapid or sudden change in behaviour after that, with the male abandoning the juvenile to spend almost all of its time with the female and the pair sometimes not leaving the core area during the course of a day. The pair mostly moves around together now and will commonly feed from the same source and spend lengthy periods perched together. This gives the impression that they are avoiding the juvenile, which is likely to be nearby and probably still visiting outlying parts of the territory.

Possibly as a part of this avoidance behaviour, there are very few flight displays during October. The sky dance is very unusual at this time and even soaring flights are less apparent. The pair will still gain height to move between locations but their flights are often at lower elevation and the circling is of short duration. If the juvenile returns to the core area the adults try to avoid it by landing (although the male may stay in flight to watch) and when its presence initiates flight rolls, the adult usually breaks away, showing that this is not aggression designed to evict the juvenile.

Where juveniles are known to have remained on site throughout the winter, the adult's behaviour can be very varied, especially that of the male, which can seem to be confused. As freshly-killed prey has been seen to be delivered to juveniles in late October, the male may actually, probably unintentionally, be encouraging the youngster to remain on site.

There is often some resurgence in nest building at this time with material being delivered to established nests and to new locations. It is not unusual for material to be taken to four or five places at this time, although this often amounts to little more than a few sticks per site. Few of the new sites seem to develop into full-sized nests although small amounts of material, usually sticks, may be added in more than one year. Some such locations have been used as roosts while others have not.

Other pairs
The activity of failed and non-breeding pairs can be very similar to that of successful pairs, with the birds usually being seen together, some nest building or repairs and few flight displays being flown. Presumably as a result of there being no juvenile, these pairs do seem to cover more of their territories and on a more regular basis than the others and may also intrude further into adjoining territories. They are still inactive for long periods of time and may be so outside the core area as they do not simply linger close to the nests. They are most likely to be using the main roosts but they might not access these until very late in the day. This group is also prone to having days on which very little happens. Although the ease of foraging has reduced, it is still relatively easy for all territorial eagles, and while most of this group will probably make regular kills it is not unusual for them to exist almost entirely on carrion at this time.

Single and unpaired immature-plumaged eagles
While territory-holding birds behave as their gender determines, the others seem to be increasingly active now, wandering further afield and more easily seen intruding into occupied territories. They make mock attacks on sheep and deer and what can seem to be a determined pursuit of potential prey often turns out to be no more than a play-chase. They are often seen in twos and threes and will indulge in flight play with rolls and sweeping chases that, contrary to what may be imagined, have no relevance to the location and are not indicative of residency. Their movements between locations can be very direct but can also show that they are not stimulated by any requirement by making long, drifting flights without apparent purpose.

As they begin to mix with juveniles of the year, determining the status of any immature-plumaged eagle at this time is fraught with difficulties and the movements of all can make it difficult to determine if the same or different birds are being seen in the location, even at different times on the same day. However, juveniles tend to be more vocal than older immatures (they may call when no other eagle is visible) and can have strikingly varying activity levels, often changing from seemingly frantic activity to a lack of interest in a very short space of time. By contrast, older immatures have adult-like activity levels and seldom dash from place to place without reason or spend as much time on the ground as opposed to perches.

Very little is known about the roosting habits of this group and most probably have few regular roosts. As the older birds may be mostly limiting their movements to within the safe haven, with longer excursions, their repeat-use roosts are likely to be widely spread throughout the area.

It is probably most likely to be at this time of year that most vacancies are filled within the populations as encounters with territory-holding older birds may well be more attractive than earlier in the year. Even if this only involves the first tentative steps, with the new bird uncertain of its position, it will be encouraged by the presence of secure foraging areas.

NOVEMBER

The weather conditions are now noticeably deteriorating, with storms being a common feature of the month. There can be lengthy periods of heavy continuous rain and snowfall becomes an increasing problem. Often wet and heavy at this time, the snow falling in November may easily lie until the following May and at times may coat the entire hill ground. The snowline is already dropping lower down the hillsides and the high ground might be made almost inaccessible and unusable by clinging cloud. Many eagles now typically almost limit their activities to the lower elevations within their territories.

Food availability is in steady decline in most territories and the weather conditions can reduce food's practical availability. Weather conditions, though, can assist foraging as, while species such as the ptarmigan may linger at high altitudes, snow cover and heavy rain can force the large herbivores down to the lower slopes and so make carrion more easily available. The number of carrion carcasses usually shows a slight increase at this time but carrion amounts are often determined by the number of accidental deaths rather than by weakness or ill health. As this probably mostly involves the youngest and smallest animals, actual amounts might be quite small, especially where there are few red deer.

Live prey numbers are more obviously reduced in many territories in November as all of the summer visitors will have left the hills and sites may, in effect, be left with only their grouse and lagomorphs. Those sites with a diverse resident fauna may show little change from the earlier months but, while the resident medium-sized prey species may still seem to be relatively numerous, their availability is decreasing. Corvid numbers can increase again on low-lying land, especially where this fringes with woodland, but even these common species can be largely absent from an eagle territory once the conditions change for the worse.

Successful pairs

The recognition and correct interpretation of activity patterns become even more complicated in November because of the different development regimes of different juveniles and the difficulty of knowing into which of these categories the observed birds belong. A successful pair responds differently to their own young than they do to young arriving from elsewhere and behave differently towards their own young that have dispersed or remained on site, or those that are still in the process of determining this situation: a juvenile fledged in mid-July will reach full independence (roughly 90 days after leaving the nest) in mid-October while one that has not fledged until the first week of August will not reach this moment until early November. The observer must be aware of whichever situation applies before any conclusions can be reached about activity patterns.

That said, and in a general sense, if the juvenile is still on site the adult's activity will be as it is during the latter part of any post-fledging period, with the male more likely to be away from the nesting area than the female. Successful pairs with fully independent juveniles now behave as does any other territorial pair of eagles and will usually roost in close proximity on their favourite sites within the core area.

The members of a pair are often to be found together and commonly cover large parts of their territory each day, spending extended periods away from the nesting area as if reasserting their dominance or simply reacquainting themselves after the limitations imposed by the juvenile. They are often perched unobtrusively at such times but also perform seemingly casual drifting flights about the area which are often also at low elevation over the high ground and often along the drop-off point of a ridge.

Few flight displays are performed (again probably to avoid attracting juveniles) and, probably because of the number of intrusions resulting from wandering juveniles before food sources are severely limited, territorial defence activity seems to be suppressed. Open, high elevation flights mostly seem to be made when needing to cross barriers but will be made within the core area and at the furthest point to which the eagle has travelled; in both cases the circling to gain height is usually made over open ground rather than above a ridge. Depending on food source type and distribution, and the influence of weather conditions, there are often very few open flights to be seen during November.

Roosts are often not accessed until after sunset and, while the morning departure may be delayed by weather conditions, the birds are often away before sunrise the next day. The collection of nest material and nest visits are fairly common at sites from which the juvenile has departed but are less common where it has remained. These activities can take place at any time of day but seem mostly to occur after feeding. Foraging itself continues to be a fairly low-intensity activity in most locations and the use of carrion is common and often greatly reduces the amount of flight activity.

Other pairs

While the level and intensity of activity can vary tremendously between sites and from day to day at any one site, especially when it is compared to that at successful sites, the basic patterns are now the same for all pairs. The members of the pair are usually seen together, especially when within the core area, and will travel, forage, perch and roost together, even if they arrive at the roost separately as a result of their not feeding simultaneously.

Few flight displays are made, there is little nest building activity and because food is unlikely to be at a premium at most sites (and foraging is relatively straightforward) these pairs can be very inactive and inconspicuous. Although these birds probably have more time and opportunity than any others and so do wander further afield at times, they seem mostly to remain on their own site, even if they are not about the core area. While successful pairs appear to avoid juveniles during October and November, these pairs probably encounter juveniles much more frequently and have more active confrontations with them. Even so, there seems to be little real territorial activity involved and the encounters often appear confused; there may be chases and flight rolls but these seldom appear to be aggressive and the juveniles usually lose interest and continue on their travels.

Single adults

The members of this small group of eagles appear to behave as their gender determines, whether they have lost a mate or have never had one, although there may be less variation between the genders at this time. These birds also tend to behave as do the members of unsuccessful pairs and they can be very inactive or little in evidence. Their long absences from the core area and their late arrival at the roost may or may not be the result of wandering more widely but the need to maintain occupancy or dominance of a usable location is probably more important than searching for a mate or vacancy.

Non-territory holding immature eagles

There is virtually no information available about these birds apart from casual observations, usually made when the observer in is an occupied territory. Those birds using the safe havens probably behave as if on a territory but there is such a wide range of ages within this group (as well as two genders) that it can be expected that behaviour and activity patterns will vary considerably between birds and even between birds using the same location at the same time.

Their most likely main requirements are food and safe roosting and as these are both usually quite easily obtained at this time, these birds may have an enormous amount of spare time, even if the night-time period is quite lengthy by the end of the month. This may mean that they wander in a similar way to juveniles but, being older and more experienced, they are probably more likely to find and remain in a safe area with good foraging than put themselves at risk by wandering more widely.

As the independent juveniles will still be learning how to survive, and most have probably not had to struggle greatly to survive until now, November may well be the time when juvenile mortality begins to increase. These birds have been seen flying at low elevation in what would be called unusual situations and not unusually roost in dangerous situations. It is no surprise that most juveniles probably revisit the natal territory at this time and that some have used their visits to feed voraciously as if they had not eaten for some time. What happens next to any individual is largely unknown.

It can be seen that our knowledge of the various aspects of golden eagle ecology is not always complete and that habitat, food availability and various other pressure points vary between territories to such an extent as to make even some broad comments of questionable merit. Our knowledge can be improved, but only if it is accepted that it is not already extensive and reliable.

IN CONCLUSION

In this work I have tried to show that what is seen in the field does not necessarily match what is thought to be known about golden eagles and that what is thought to be known is not necessarily supported by robust or detailed evidence.

The simple reasons for this are that most observations are of a casual nature and most research is targeted and selective; the limitations of the available evidence are seldom given proper consideration and so there is a broad agreement on all aspects of golden eagle ornithology without there being sufficient information available to guarantee reliability.

It may be that some of the contradictory information presented here is difficult to accept because of the certainty that exists, and it might be argued that some of the alternative evidence and interpretations come from too small a sample. They are, at least, the result of detailed long-term and year-round examination rather than sampling or casual observation.

It may have been noticed that, broadly speaking, the more recent the publication date of a reference cited, the more likely it was that its reliability would be questioned in this work. This is because of the contrived generic nature of most modern research, the need for professional conservation to produce generalised guidance that can be applied by non-specialists and the failure of the consultation process. Unfortunately this results in non-specialists producing inappropriate guidance that may not be criticised.

It is accepted that management has had to change in line with modern concerns and it might be argued that the use of modern technology results from a recognition of the poor quality of most of the available evidence. That, though, does not make a theoretical assessment unquestionably better than good quality evidence and the use of the former should not be at the expense of the latter. Unfortunately, the belief that professional evidence is always better than field evidence and can replace it is far too widely believed.

What is often forgotten is that with a large, long-lived, site-faithful, truly resident and often individualistic generalist species every aspect of management has to be considered on a site-by-site basis and that any variation from this is likely to be detrimental on a larger scale. What is relevant in one location may apply in general to others but it will not apply in fact.

With the golden eagle, the problem of uncertainty is unavoidable because most people believe that there is none. It is a fact that while few people would speak authoritatively on an equally rare species without having some form of involvement, few think twice about speaking of the golden eagle when they have no active involvement whatsoever. This situation is, in fact, worsening because of the professional control of information, involvement and management. In a similar way, information often does not fail to be accepted because it is wrong: it fails to be accepted because it does not agree with what is thought to be known.

Until it is accepted that not everything is known and that not everything can be correctly explained and understood at first glance, with few data or by statistical analysis, golden eagle study and management will continue to be a retrospective consideration, with positive adjustments being largely cosmetic and only coming after negative impacts have had their effect.

While we need not be desperately concerned about the golden eagle's future at the present time, there is no room for complacency as it is a species that could crash with great rapidity. If that is to be prevented, reliable information has to be collected in a reliable fashion and on a greater scale, and that can only be achieved by dedicated fieldworkers working without preconceived ideas and using guidance based on a broad understanding of the species. It cannot be achieved by people who see only what they expect to see.

REFERENCES

Brown, L. 1976 *British Birds of Prey*, Collins, London

Brown, L.H. & Watson, A. 1964 The Golden Eagle in relation to its food supply. *Ibis*, 106: 78–100

Cramp, S. & Simmons, K.E.L. (eds) 1979 *The Birds of the Western Palearctic, Vol. II*, Oxford University Press, Oxford

Crane, K. & Nellist, K. 1999 *Island Eagles: 20 years of observing eagles on the Isle of Skye*, Cartwheeling Press, Skye

Deane, C.D. 1962 Irish Golden Eagles and a link with Scotland. *British Birds*, 55: 272–274

Dennis, R.H., Ellis, P.M., Broad, R.A.B. & Langslow, D.R. 1984 The status of the Golden Eagle in Britain. *British Birds*, 77: 592–607

Eaton, M.A., Dillon, I.A., Stirling-Aird, P. & Whitfield, D. P. 2007 Status of the Golden Eagle *Aquila chrysaetos* in Britain in 2003. *Bird Study*, 54: 212–220

Everett, M. J. 1971 The Golden Eagle survey in Scotland 1964–1969. *British Birds*, 64: 49–56

Everett, M. J. 1981 Role male Golden Eagle during incubation. *British Birds*, 74: 309–310

Evans, R. J., O'Toole, L. & Whitfield, D. P. 2012 The history of Eagles in Britain and Ireland: an ecological review and documentary evidence of place names from the last 1500 years. *Bird Study*, DETAILS?

Fielding, A. H. & Haworth, P. F. 2014 *Golden Eagle in the south of Scotland: an overview*. Scottish Natural Heritage Commissioned Report No 626

Fraser Darling, F. 1947 *Natural History in the Highlands and Islands*, Collins, London

Gerrard, J. M. And Bortolotti, G. R. 1988 *The Bald Eagle, Haunts and Habits of a Wilderness Monarch*, Smithsonian Institute Press, Washington

Gordon, S. 1927 *Days with the Golden Eagle*, Williams and Norgate, London

Gordon, S. 1955 *The Golden Eagle: King of Birds*, Collins, London

Green, R.E. 1996a The status of the Golden Eagle in 1992. *Bird Study*, 43: 20–27

Green, R. E. 1996b The status of the Golden Eagle in 1992. *Bird Study*, 43: 253–254

Gregory, M. 2010 Wind farms and Golden Eagles, the Argyll experience – an update. *Scottish Birds* 30(2): 129–130

Gregory, M. J. P., Gordon, A. G. & Moss, R. 2003 Impact of nest trapping and radiotagging on breeding golden eagles *Aquila chrysaetos* in Argyll, Scotland. *Ibis*, 145:113–119

Hardey, J., Crick, H., Wernham, C., Riley, H., Etheridge, B. & Thompson, D. 2009 *Raptors: a field guide for surveys and monitoring*, The Stationery Office, Edinburgh

Haworth, P. and Fielding, A. 2013 *Expanding woodlands in Special Protection Areas for Golden Eagles.* Forestry Commission Scotland Practice Note 2013, FCS, Edinburgh

Haworth, P. F., Fielding, A. H., Whitfield, D. P. & Reid, R. 2009 *Diet and breeding success in Golden eagles: implications for land use.* Unpublished report to Scottish Natural Heritage

Haworth, P. F., McGrady, M. J., Whitfield, D. P., Fielding, A. H. & McLeod, D. R. A 2006 Ranging distance of adult Golden Eagles *Aquila chrysaetos* in western Scotland according to season and breeding status. *Bird Study*, 53:265–273

Holloway, S. 1996 The *Historical Atlas of Breeding Birds in Britain and Ireland, 1875–1900*, T. & A.D. Poyser, London

Housten and Holden 2009

Lockie, J.D. & Ratcliffe, D.A. 1964 Insecticides and Scottish Golden Eagles. *British Birds*, 57: 89–102

Lockie, J.D. & Stephen, D. 1959 Eagles, lambs and land management on Lewis. *Journal of Animal Ecology*, 28: 43–50

Love, J.A. 1983 *The Return of the Sea Eagle*, University Press, Cambridge

MacPherson, H. B. 1909 *The Home Life of a Golden Eagle*, Witherby, London

McGrady, M.J., McLeod, D.M., Petty, S.M., Grant, J.R. & Bainbridge, I.P. 1997 *Eagles and Forestry*. Forestry Commission Research Information Note No. 292, HMSO, London

McLeod, D.R.A., Whitfield, D.P., Fielding, A.H. Haworth, P & McGrady, M.J. 2003 Predicting home range use by Golden Eagles *Aquila chrysaetos* in western Scotland. *Avian Science*, 2:183–198

MacNally, L. 1977 *The Ways of an Eagle*, Collins and Harvill, London

Marquiss, M., Ratcliffe, D.A. & Roxburgh, R. 1985 The numbers, breeding success and diet of Golden Eagles in southern Scotland in relation to changes in land use. *Biological Conservation*, 33: 1–17

Nicholson, E.M. 1957 The Golden Eagle *Aquila chrysaetos*, *British Birds*, 50-131–135

Orton, D. A. 1974 Talon Grappling by Golden Eagles. *Bird Study*, 21:210–211

O'Toole, L., Fielding, A.H. & Haworth, P.F. 2002 Re-introduction of the Golden Eagle into the Republic of Ireland. *Biological Conservation*, 103:303–312

Sharrock, J.T.R. 1976 *The Atlas of Breeding Birds in Britain and Ireland*, T. & A.D. Poyser, Carlton

Walker, D. 1988 Unusual call of the golden eagle. *Scottish Bird News*, 9:8.

Walker, D. 2009 *Call of the Eagle*, Whittles Publishing, Dunbeath

Walker, D. G. 1991 *The Lakeland Eagles*, 1st Edition, Penrith

Walker, D. G. 2004 *The Lakeland Eagles*, 2nd Edition, Penrith

Walker, D. G. 1987 Observations on the post-fledging period of the Golden Eagle *Aquila chrysaetos* in England. *Ibis*, 129: 92–96

Walker, D. G. 1988 The behaviour and movements of a juvenile Golden Eagle *Aquila chrysaetos* in England in 1986. *Ibis*, 130:564–565

Walker, D. G. DATE *The Golden Eagle: Guidance note for Fieldworkers*. Unpublished report to Natural Research (Projects)

Walker, D. G., McGrady, M. J., McCluskie, A., Madders, M. & McLeod, D.R.A. 2005 Resident Golden Eagle ranging behaviour before and after construction of a windfarm in Argyll. *Scottish Birds*, 25: 24–40

Walker, D., Sheridan, S., Burrows, B. & Cameron, D. 2014 Do Expectations about Golden Eagle Ecology Produce Reliable Guidance for Species managers? Proceedings of *Eagles of Palearctic: Study and Conservation* Elabuga, Russia 2013

Watson, A. 1957 The breeding success of golden eagles in the north-east Highlands. *Scottish Naturalist*, 69: 153–169

Watson, J. 1997 *The Golden Eagle* 1st Edition, T. & A.D. Poyser, London

Watson, J. 2010 *The Golden Eagle* 2nd Edition, T. & A.D. Poyser, London

Watson, J. & Dennis, R. H. 1992 Nest site selection by Golden Eagles *Aquikla chrysaetos* in Scotland. *British Birds*, 85: 469–481

Watson, J., Leitch, A.F. & Rae, S.R. 1993 The diet of Golden eagles *Aquila chrysaetos* in Scotland. *Ibis*, 135: 387–393

Watson, J., Rae, S.R. & Stillman 1992 Nesting Density and Breeding Success of Golden Eagles *Aquila chrysaetos* in relation to food supply In Scotland. *Journal of Animal Ecology*, 61:543–550

Watson, J., Fielding, A.H., Whitfield, D.P., Broad, R.A., Haworth, P.F., Nellist, K. Crane, K. & MacDonald, E.J. 2003 'Golden Eagle (*Aquila chrysaetos*) breeding performance in relation to climate in Western Scotland during the period 1981–2000'. In: *Birds in a Changing Environment* (Eds, D.B.A. Thompson, S.M. Redpath, A.H. Fielding, M. Marquiss & C.A. Galbraith), The Stationery Office, Edinburgh

Whitfield, D. P., McLeod, D. R. A., Fielding, A. H., Broad, R. A. B., Evans, R. J. And Haworth, P. F. 2001The effects of forestry on golden eagles on the island of Mull, western Scotland. *Journal of Applied Ecology*, 38: 1208–1220

Whitfield, D. P., Fielding A. H., McLeod, D. R. A. & Haworth, P. F 2008 *A conservation framework for the Golden Eagle in Scotland*, PUBLISHER/PUBLICATION

Vasey-Fitzgerald, B. 1953 *British Game*, Collins, London

INDEX

£18.99   978-184995-029-9

Kestrels for Company

GORDON RIDDLE

...this fascinating and absorbing book written by a dedicated expert. Over
40 years the author has assembled a wealth of information... ...is easily read
and contains large numbers of excellent photographs... **Scottish Birds**

...an appealing portrait of this beautiful bird... **Daily Mail**

An appealing book that rightfully raises the profile of the kestrel. It provides an
extensive picture of this delightful falcon. ...through this personal and well-informed
account the reader gains access to the world of the kestrel. **NHBS**

www.whittlespublishing.com

£22.99   978-184995-130-2

...I love this book... The inclusion of tables and figures, with data from the 1950s through the 2000s, is a much-appreciated bonus. ... is truly an inspirational successor to Colin Tubb's The Buzzard, published as long ago as 1974. **British Birds**

...a joy to read in the best traditions of natural history writing. The author's knowledge and passion for the subject comes through without detracting from the detail of work. **ECOS**

...a readable and informative account of the Buzzard's year with extensive sections on food, demography and population. Anyone...with an interest in birds of prey will enjoy this book... I found it a fascinating read. **Scottish Birds**

www.whittlespublishing.com

Growing
Barn Owls
in my
Garden

PAUL HACKNEY

£16.99   978-184995-027-5

...a well written story of how Paul Hackney became committed to doing something about the plight of the barn owl. ... This book will serve as an inspiration to those who may be called to help preserve one of our most beautiful owls in the future. **Peregrine**

An enjoyable book, written in an enthusiastic, light, easy style and crammed full of anecdotes that bring life to the subject. A good read. **Scottish Birds**

This is a fascinating book... ...it leaves you with a genuine sense of the richness of the many points of contact we have with birds... **Scottish Birds**

...Each chapter begins with a personal anecdote, set around Smith's own encounters with birds, places, and peoples... I can only recommend Malcolm Smith's Life with Birds as a vivid tour ... and as a valuable introduction to our wider cultural interrelationships with the birds. **IBIS**

...a thorough and all-embracing examination of our interdependence with birds: our exploitation of them and their exploitation of us. ... Malcolm Smith's intriguing narrative is both informative and constantly engaging. **Birding World**

Life with Birds
A Story of Mutual Exploitation

MALCOLM SMITH

£18.99   978-184995-028-2

a life of ospreys

£19.99   978-1904445-26-5

roy dennis

...a remarkable book. It is also an inspirational book... The sheer weight of acutely-observed detail amassed in this account is testimony to the knowledge of its author, and the clarity with which it is organised and presented establishes the book in the front rank of Scottish wildlife monographs. **Scots Magazine**

...one of the most arresting nature books this year. ...the story of the return of this great fish-hawk to Britain, by a man involved in it almost from the start. ... His book has excellent photographs and also information on where to see osprey eyries. **The Times**

...He writes with first-hand knowledge gained from a lifetime's experience of working with ospreys in the wild, punctuating the text with excerpts from his diaries, giving the book an added dimension. ... Everything one could ever wish to know about these birds seems to be covered in this book. **John Muir Trust Journal**

www.whittlespublishing.com